cathedrals of the flesh

cathedrals of the flesh
my search for the perfect bath

alexia brue

BLOOMSBURY

Published by Bloomsbury, New York and London
Distributed to the trade by Holtzbrinck Publishers

ISBN 1-58234-360-8

First published by Bloomsbury in hardcover in 2003
This paperback edition published in 2004

1 3 5 7 9 10 8 6 4 2

Typeset by Hewer Text Ltd, Edinburgh
Printed in the United States of America
by RR Donnelley & Sons, Harrisonburg

To Suzanne and Nord

contents

the initiation

By night we danced in Les Bains Douches, a steamy Parisian nightclub in a converted Turkish bath where Marina, complaining of the heat, would strip to her camisole. All around me clothes flew off and the energy of the club pulsed with orgy potential. Violet spotlights cut through the cigarette haze and the sweat evaporating off the half-naked bodies. Fishnetted legs and bangled arms vibrated to MC Solaar's 'Gangster Moderne.' Three girls and a boy in a cowboy hat jiggled on a marble octagonal platform. It was deliriously hot, but my camisole was more Lands' End than La Perla, so I sweated through the night, trying to imagine this space crowded with bathers instead of dancers.

After exhausting ourselves in hamams remodeled as chic nightclubs, we craved still-functioning baths. Everyone has a special Paris agenda, whether it be a complete tour of the Louvre or eating every napoleon they meet. Marina and I were in Paris simply to bathe. It was a genuine cultural mission – to visit Paris's hamams, elaborate and ornate Turkish steam baths, delicious havens from the modern world. We dreamed of all the fairy-tale ingredients of a Turkish bath experience: marble rooms filled with steam (not cigarette smoke), nude bodies luxuriating on couches, zaftig Arab women scrubbing our bodies, and endless cups of mint tea. All the delights that Les Bains Douches would have offered before Philippe Starck transfigured it into a legendary nightclub over twenty years ago.

Marina, who knows where to find all sorts of things that might not be termed 'necessities,' knew exactly where to find hamams that still served up real steam. This trait impressed me when we met as freshmen (our camaraderie instantly established by our being the only two girls on our midwestern campus to wear heels). In Marina's dorm room, the gray institutional furniture had somehow been swapped for an off-white, near spotless secondhand sofa. On the walls, instead of the typical college posters, was her already growing collection of *suzanis*, thick embroidered tribal wall hangings used in the *yurts* of her native Central Asia.

I should mention that Marina is a Kazakhstani princess, or would have been if her grandfather hadn't helped Lenin overthrow the family monarchy in 1918, a regrettable fact in Marina's mind. Her deposed princess status explains a few of her eccentricities: the regal bearing that at first makes her seem aloof, the unself-conscious way she held a handbag and attached fox fur collars to her coats at eighteen, and her packing philosophy (tiny bag, five pairs of shoes). Yet through her self-parodied materialism shines a finely honed sense of the absurd and the sweetest, most loyal soul.

Once I asked Marina where she was going for spring break. 'Somewhere where native boys will serve me coconut drinks on the beach,' she replied, only half joking. Marina gives hedonism a good name because she's not riddled with the American compunction of justifying physical indulgences. To her more European sensibility, there is nothing profane or undeserved about pleasure. As her friend, I would tag along without the guilt of having hatched the decadent plan myself. Pleasure was an end in itself worth pursuing. Shocking. Especially to my strict New England code of punishment and reward. But as an innocent bystander I reveled in her decadence, and during that January trip to Paris, I followed her, a libertine in the making, through days spent in functioning hamams and nights spent in hamams reincarnated as nightclubs.

France might not seem the obvious destination to discover the pleasures of the Turkish bath. But I soon learned otherwise. France's four million Muslims from Tunisia, Morocco, Algeria, and Turkey have made sure that the hamam, aka Turkish bath in the West, tradition continues in their adopted country. Hamams – their architecture as well as the social life and services that surrounded them – were, and in some areas still are, a way of life in Muslim countries. But like so many native customs, hamams flourish on foreign soil where maintaining native institutions takes on greater urgency for uprooted Arabs. Hamams also satisfy the Muslim code of hygiene detailed in the Koran: mandatory baths after sex and before prayer, deeper ablutions periodically.

Marina, with the true soul of a collector, said we must try two hamams: the French version, a decadent pleasure dome with no allegiance to Allah; and a traditional hamam catering to expatriate Arabs. For the first, we made our way down rue des Blancs Manteaux, one of the more ignored streets in the fashionable Marais, past centuries-old Jewish bakeries and freshly painted art galleries and costume jewelry boutiques. The minute you walk into Les Bains du Marais, you feel you've arrived at a point in history that never happened – it's what a hamam would have looked like in a French-conquered Turkey. Les Bains du Marais is a glimpse back to the Ottoman Empire with a softer, slightly more delicate French touch. The honey-colored walls, the Middle Eastern café in the rear where red-faced patrons in robes nibble on baklava, the spiral staircase leading down to the baths – all fit for a sultan vacationing in Paris.

Marina and I signed the guest book (noticing that Bruce Willis had signed in the day before) and headed for the changing room. It was mixed bathing day, men and women luxuriating together in the steam and reliving the sybaritic glories of pagan Rome. Bathing in the ancient world was, depending on the emperor's tolerance and personal predilections, a coed affair. Then the killjoy church fathers, hardly ardent bathers themselves (Saint Anthony, who never so much as washed his feet, was held up as a paradigm of good hygiene), entered the picture and made mixed bathing a confession-worthy activity. Muslims never wavered on the issue of coed bathing. Given that many Muslims consider it risqué for a woman to parade around without a veil, it follows that mixed bathing falls into the same category as Salman Rushdie.

But we were far from fatwas in the passageways of this underground bath. Now changed into complimentary white, fluffy robes and bath sandals, we walked past Euro-chic men sitting underneath potted palms in the hallway's wicker chairs. They looked up and nodded hello in a nonleering, genuinely friendly manner. Marina winked at me.

I couldn't see through the steamed-up glass door, but I expected a typical American steamroom: a small, white-tiled box with evanescent steam that gusted up and then fell quickly to the ground, only to gust up again with an abrasive sound like a 747 taking off. Once I stepped inside, however, a delicate steam washed over me. The central room wasn't as enormous as the room we'd danced in the previous night, but it had all the same features. I recognized the raised octagonal platform in the middle, which Marina called the 'bellystone,' glistening with humidity. Lanterns on the walls illuminated the room in shadows, giving it a grandeur beyond its dimensions. Anxiously, I looked at Marina. For a first-timer there is confusion. What are all these people doing? Where do I sit? How do I sit? For how long? Marina smiled back at me. She was radiant. She was positively in her element, like the sultan's favorite in the harem.

I reminded myself, There is nothing to feel uncomfortable about. This was no different from a country club without clothes. It was just like a spa, only instead of partitioning people in different cubicles to await the individual attention of a doctorly aesthetician, everyone was together, slathering stuff onto their bodies. Cleansing had been turned into a ritual, a shared social activity.

All around us people were sitting on benches cropping out from the wall: a couple in matching silver metallic bathing suits looking very St Tropez, two Mediterranean men with cultivated stubble, three women discussing an upcoming wedding, a lone older woman looking intoxicated with the heat, her eyes closed and her head bent back and resting on the wall. While I was having déjà vus from Fellini's *Satyricon,* Marina had already walked over to one of the recessed shower stalls and, with her body arched into a crescent, washed her hair. I followed. I learned rule one of bath etiquette: Always shower before the bathing commences. The bath's steam opens the body's pores, and if the skin is dirty or clogged with gloopy products, the sweating and detoxifying process is inhibited.

After drying off and enjoying my new lavender smell, I followed Marina over to the bellystone, the town square of a hamam. I mimicked her every move. In a strange way, this felt like an initiation. And I could tell already that it was the start of a serious habit. I was reveling in the sensation of doing something so private in such a public place and having no one act as though it were the least bit out of the ordinary.

We removed our towels and stretched out on the warm tiled platform so that the crowns of our heads touched. The bellystone was raised several feet off the ground. In the old days, a furnace directly underneath would have kept the marble warm.

'Marina,' I whispered, 'are you sure this is what we're supposed to do?'

'Yes, you lie on your back to loosen up your shoulders until they call us.'

'Call us for what?'

'Be patient,' she said with a smile.

We lay silently on the bellystone and inhaled the damp vapor in the room. I felt my chest expanding with each inhalation. I closed my eyes, raindrops forming on my eyelashes. I listened to the sound of running water, someone taking a shower in the distance. A tall woman holding a thin black hose emerged from a nook and seemed to motion to us.

'Marina, does she mean us?'

'Yes. Are you ready for your gommage?'

'Gommage, that means eraser, like pencil eraser, in French, doesn't it?'

'Exactly.'

'What is she going to erase?'

'Your sins.'

'Have you brought me to a church?'

'Yes, a cathedral of the flesh.'

We followed the priestess of the baths into a small ancillary room with two foam-covered massage tables. Steam still surrounded us. Everything looked gauzy, reality bettered by heat and low light. The tall Moroccan attendant wore a one-piece bathing suit. I envied her; instead of worrying about running out of stockings for work, she has to worry about making sure she has a dry bathing suit. She turned us over to two women also clad in bathing suits.

One, a statuesque, slender North African, was stunning, while the other, at least twenty years older, was shorter and wider. We discarded our towels and bathing suits and lay naked on the matted tables. We looked across the room at each other and burst out laughing. We were so far away, so far removed from where we'd met, from what our everyday lives were now. Enjoying the pleasure of sharing pleasure. An across-the-room wink, a nudge, a telling smile. A memory in the making. No matter how bad our jobs, no matter how capricious our boyfriends, we have times like these, when we're just girlfriends erasing our sins at the bath.

The regal North African woman began scrubbing me with a horsehair mitt, or at least that's what Marina insisted it was. She worked in small, swift, up-and-down motions. It felt like a sand-paper massage, reminding me of the way walls get smoothed and primed before painting. After a couple of minutes, she tapped me on the shoulders. *'Regardez votre peau,'* she said. (Look at your skin.) The rough mitt had scraped away the dingy top layer of skin, creating brown polka dots across the entire landscape of my body. She hosed me off, the polka dots disappearing down the drain.

The glove now off, she came at me with a sudsy washcloth and proceeded to soap and scrub every corner of my body, including areas generally addressed, at least in France, by a bidet. I was a huge soapy monster; the suds seemed to swell and expand as I was overwhelmed by a volcanic flow of foam. Then she massaged my shoulder blades, my feet, and my calves. The smell of lavender from the mountains of soap was permeating my chafed skin, and she again took the hose and, with the force bumped up a notch, hosed me off. I heard a combination of a screech and a laugh from Marina and assumed she was at the same point in her gommage. We sat up, as told, and they hosed the front of us, then washed around our breasts. Not in conscious memory had anyone ever washed me so thoroughly. The pleasure of having someone else take care of a basic need and elevate it to an art was a strange and reassuring sensation, like being spoon-fed chocolate ice cream as an adult, a delicious momentary regression to childhood.

We bade the gommage ladies good-bye, and Marina pulled me back into the hamam. A glass door on the far side of the hamam led into another room that was steamier and hotter. In a genuine hamam, this room would be called the *sıcaklık*. The room for serious detoxification. Inside this fiercely hot and eucalyptus-scented room, there was a lot of conversation about the climate. In a mélange of French, Italian, and English, bathers compared theories on how much heat is a good thing. A guy from Sienna suggested staying in as long as you can stand it. Marina lectured me on rule two of bathing: 'Don't sit or you'll get dizzy. Lie down so your entire body is exposed to the same level of heat, allowing you to tolerate the climate for the maximum amount of time.' We stayed until our pores had soaked up as much moisture as they seemed to demand. Then we needed to recover from the heat.

We entered the *salle de repose,* or relaxation room. Divans the color of dried mint surrounded the room, and light coming from hanging fabric lanterns cast a soft glow. The ubiquitous bath priestess popped her head in to offer us mint tea. It came Turkish style, intensely sweet and in tall glasses with tiny saucers. We dimmed the lights and sipped our tea.

'Imagine if this was our life.' I sighed.

'It could be,' Marina said.

'Yeah, like either of us could be ladies who lunch.' I took another sip. 'Well, maybe you could.'

She shook her head. 'I'm serious,' she said. 'Our lives could really be like this.'

'How's that?'

'We could open a hamam.'

'And whose trust fund should we use, yours or mine?' I said.

'I'm not kidding. We could write the perfect business plan, raise the capital, I'll move to New York. Stranger things have happened. A Turkish bath in Manhattan. Just imagine how popular it would be.'

'Marina, far be it from me to play the skeptic, but I think a public bath would be a tough sell. Americans might be a bit squeamish about bathing en masse. Yeah, spas are popular, but people book spa appointments almost like they book doctors' appointments. I mean, the person who signs up for an oxygenating facial or a seaweed cellulite removal isn't going to while away the afternoon in a steam room, no matter how beautiful.'

Marina, perched on the adjacent couch, regarded me like the young child who must be told she can't live exclusively on macaroni and cheese. 'Think of the public baths in Roman times – the Romans visited the baths for all the same reasons we visit spas. The baths had masseuses, hair removers, perfumers, even doctors.'

I leaned my head back on the cushion and looked at the ceiling. 'So,' I said, thinking out loud, 'public baths are the original spas.'

'Exactly, and not only would our bath be a place to sweat and exfoliate the old fashioned way, our hamam would also offer a refuge from this century. Imagine – an oasis of Ottoman elegance, where steam makes marble glisten and mint tea flows from silver spouts . . .'

Thus Marina's speech crescendoed, and I expected music, perhaps a dramatic chord of Bach, as an exclamation point. Instead, exhausted by her prophetic outpouring, Marina took another sip of mint tea and sank back into the divan. She was convincing, but nothing was as convincing as how rejuvenated, relaxed, and at peace I felt after an afternoon at Les Bains du Marais. This was a seductive lifestyle.

We indulged again the very next day (hey, we could have been stuffing our faces with napoleons). On the periphery of the Latin Quarter is the generically named Arab Mosque, built by the French government in 1926 as a thank-you gesture to the North Africans for their service in World War I. In addition to a tea salon and full restaurant, the Arab Mosque offers a hamam, alternating between days for men and women. At this hamam, pandemonium greeted us rather than the tranquil, choreographed calm of Les Bains du Marais. This time we heard Arabic and Turkish and other hard-consonant languages. There were only a smattering of interlopers like ourselves, French women who had acquired the taste, and Lonely Planet tourists who had read about the place.

We stepped right up to command central – a huge counter elevated above the rest of the room. A young woman with olive skin and widely spaced green eyes was in her multitasking glory. She poured tea from a huge silver urn and passed it to reposing bathers lying on divans surrounding the huge reception room. She collected valuables from incoming bathers and sold bath, gommage, and massage tickets. She laughed with regular customers and disciplined a masseuse who seemed to be complaining about the onslaught of massage seekers. Ladies were lined up five deep for every table. The bath was hopping.

She handed us a little white plastic cup, filled with brown sludge and topped off with a blue chip. Marina, who had been here before, explained, 'You wash with the brown stuff before the gommage. Then you give the token to the massage lady to prove you've paid.'

To get to the cramped dressing room, we had to walk through this buzzing central room, which mushroomed up into a domed cupola on the second floor. It was a colonnaded room with a fountain in the middle, which the massage ladies used to clean their hands between customers. Behind the elaborately adorned columns, the bathers reclined on worn blue cushions. The busy, overladen room seemed to incorporate every element of Arabic design – every geometric pattern, every color sequence – in order not to offend anyone's culture by omission. The women on the massage tables in the center of the room glistened with oil. I thought with a smile of the United States, where in a private room the masseuse delicately makes sure you are not showing any skin. Here everything was on display. A few women wore underwear, but most people were nude, just sitting on towels. From the looks of things, the massages included upper thigh, breasts, and abdomen as much as they did shoulders and back. Walking by the massage tables fully dressed in a parka and clutching a backpack was an odd sensation. It felt as if we should enter the dressing room via tunnel so as not to disturb the pure naked abandon these women were enjoying. So we hurried by, Marina feeling just as ill at ease as I did.

We quickly shed our belongings and headed into the hamam, holding our little white cups filled with briny sledge. Unlike yesterday's hamam, this one was huge, labyrinthine, and lined with gray, white-veined marble.

'This is the real deal,' said Marina. 'This is halfway to Istanbul.'

Only halfway? After showering (rule one applies everywhere), we entered a steamroom much bigger than yesterday's little Les Bains du Marais. Never had I felt so skinny. I loved the whole cast of characters, but I remained fixated on one woman. She had hips that took over the room, and she moved with the grace of a belly dancer. She wore lacy lilac underwear, and her stomach could have been sculpted by Rodin. Taking turns, she and her friend scrubbed each other. The other women, women I could tell were regulars, also gommaged each other. We neophytes, without mitts and wash-cloths of our own, had to seek out our gommage from the one gommage lady. It was not the luxurious experience of yesterday. She scrubbed with distracted ennui, using a ratty mitt. She wore a tattered cotton flower dress and smelled strongly of perspiration. I tried to be French about it and remind myself how natural pher-omones are. It was about seven in the evening, and I wondered how many hours she'd been scrubbing women today.

After the gommage, Marina and I found an empty patch of the bellystone to recline on. We compared the redness of our pallor. My Scandinavian coloring meant I bore the marks of a fierce scrubbing, whereas Marina's Asiatic complexion masked the hamam chafing. Les Bains du Marais was what the French would call *raffiné,* refined, polished; the Arab Mosque was coarse and visceral, soulful and mysterious. The difference between the two experiences was as marked as the chasm between a fancy, nouveau French feast and a rustic, peasant repast where you scrape up the contents of your plate with a piece of crusty bread. Both experiences are deliciously satisfying, but they transport you to different places.

Watching the groups of women in the *halvets* (small private bathing areas surrounding the central bellystone), chatting good-naturedly, happy and serene, Marina and I began to hatch a plan. We would open our own hamam, which we would call simply the Hamam. We would create an oasis as exotic as an Eastern spice bazaar, where people could shed their make-it-happen mentality for a couple of hours and just chill out, so to speak, in the heat.

How much money would we need? How big would it be? What kinds of treatments would we offer? And how could I open a hamam having seen only two re-creations in France? If this was only 'halfway to Istanbul,' I still had a lot to learn.

'Marina, this would require research. Visiting hamams in Turkey, taking measurements, seeing what kind of marble they use, how the rooms are laid out. We need some actual facts.'

'You have unused vacation time,' Marina said. 'Why not go to Istanbul for a couple of weeks? In two weeks, you'll get the flavor of the hamams. You can map out all the different floor plans, talk to some of the owners, get a sense of what's involved. If I can get away, I'll meet you for a long weekend.'

'Istanbul, Constantinople, Byzantium.'

'I'd forgotten you were a classics major.'

'Me too.' I laughed. 'So I go to Istanbul for a couple of weeks. You come and visit, and then we write a business plan for world hamam domination. Is that the plan?'

'Exactly.'

I lay back on the warm marble, breathing in the steam. I thought of Emperor Justinian's vast, underground cistern in Old Stamboul. Did the fifth-century cistern still feed the hamams? How many hamams would Istanbul have? Hundreds? Thousands? So it was resolved. I would take a working vacation to Istanbul. For the first time in my life I felt driven by a personal project; for the first time I wasn't doing someone else's bidding. The Hamam. Maybe nothing would come of it, but I needed to take this leap of faith. I'd come home with sketched-out blueprints and travel notes on how the hamams operate, and Marina and I would set about creating a business plan. Who knows, with the stars aligned we might even be able to open our hamam within two years.

turkey:
taking the measurements

As you set out for Ithaka
hope the voyage is a long one,
full of adventure, full of discovery.
— Constantine Cavafy, 'Ithaka'

When I first arrived in Istanbul, my plan seemed simple. Over the course of two weeks, I would have a *kese* scrub at every bath in Istanbul; I would meet the regulars, who would show me how to henna my hair and share their personal baklava recipes; I would smoke narghile and drink mint tea with hamam owners who would divulge their business secrets — 'It's all about the size of your bellystone'; I would discover local beauty products — pistachio face masks, Black Sea loofahs, and Cappadocia salt scrubs — and I would import these elixirs to New York. I would, as Marina and I termed it, 'take the measurements.' And with my measurements carefully documented, I would go home.

Once back in New York, Marina and I would set about writing the most tantalizing business plan ever to cross Ian Schrager's desk.

As a life-altering plan, it was both practical and inspired. Never mind that I didn't speak Turkish and didn't have a place to stay. That I knew little about Turkey and hadn't even seen *Midnight Express*. I was heading to Istanbul prepared to be lucky and efficient, eager for a crash course in hamams. I showed up with one contact name – Baksim Kocer. Baksim, an Istanbul native, had attended college in the States with a good friend of mine, and to me he was a familiar name without a corresponding face. As I planned the trip from New York, Baksim and I exchanged introductory e-mails in which he offered his help and hospitality. His advice on where to stay boiled down to an uninspiring 'Don't worry, I'll take care of everything.'

Though I certainly never expected it, Baksim took me under his wing from the first night. He had reserved a room for me in a hotel owned by his uncle. In Turkey everyone has an uncle who can help you out. At 8:00 P.M. I met Baksim in the hotel's bar for a night out with his childhood friend, Mehmet. Turkish hospitality not only dictated that Baksim take me out for that introductory dinner that friends of friends are internationally obliged to cater, but also stretched to helping me find an apartment (two weeks in a hotel felt too cold and would have cost too much). To Baksim's Middle Eastern sensibility, it would have been rude and potentially danger-ous to leave me, especially as a woman traveling alone, to find my own lodgings in the male-dominated streets of Istanbul. As a strictly practical matter, I was only too happy to submit to Baksim's paternalism and to end my previous two weeks of e-mail brokering with a Turkish real estate agent who insisted that Istanbul rents were on par with Manhattan's.

I woke up the first morning following my arrival in Baksim's guest room, my head throbbing after a dramatic collision of jet lag and too much rakı, the national drink of anise-flavored liquor. We had eaten dinner – an endless stream of meze, small plates of succulent eggplant concoctions, dolma and sarma (stuffed peppers and grape leaves), and calamari – at an apparently famous restaurant that served food from the Black Sea coast. The rakı left more of an impression than the food, and my head ached as the clanking of dishes echoed from the kitchen. Mehmet had also spent the night in the other guest room, as he often did when his wife was out of town. I made myself presentable and joined them for a breakfast of Nescafé and cigarettes.

'Today we go to Tuzla. You'll love it,' Baksim announced when he saw me.

'Where's Tuzla? It sounds far away,' I said, rubbing my head and pulling my mess of hair back into a ponytail.

'It's where Mehmet and I practically grew up. It's a little seaside town on the Asian side, about an hour from here, where our parents have places. There's tennis and swimming and sailing. Oh, Mehmet, maybe Kemal will be sailing today.'

'Are there any hamams there?' I asked, eager to start visiting the first of the city's hundred or so remaining hamams.

'No, but you'll meet people who can tell you all about hamams. My uncle will be there. He knows everyone and everything about Istanbul. Now let's get dressed.' He stubbed out his cigarette in the ashtray as if to bolster the finality of the decision. At a mere twenty-seven, a slight five feet six, and with an eyebrow as dark and thick as Humphrey Bogart's, Baksim possessed the authority of a Turkish godfather figure. He didn't make plans or propose outings, he simply announced them.

We drove an hour east in Baksim's red Fiat, traversing a two-mile-long suspension bridge that connects Europe to Asia. The *geconkondu* (random groupings of houses built out of scrap parts – rugs, wheels, corrugated cardboard – where recent rural immigrants to Istanbul would first make their homes) and planned housing developments flew by. Soon we outdistanced the long-fingered sprawl of Istanbul and veered onto a road that led to a small settlement of houses. Tiny, tranquil Tuzla, hidden scarcely an hour outside of Istanbul, had impressive houses on quiet, shaded streets where children could learn to ride bikes. Front yards were adorned with carefully planned gardens, a telltale sign of affluence, which in Turkey stood out like a Fabergé egg in a mudslide.

The moment I saw the waterfront I was glad I'd been bullied into coming. Tulza is one of those unobtrusively beautiful places, where the longer you let it work on you, the more mesmerizing it becomes, like a plain face with perfect bone structure. Set in a little nook on the Sea of Marmara, Tuzla gazes placidly toward Istanbul to the northwest. Despite the cranes of a nearby shipyard, I could make out the clustered domes of the *külliyes* across Istanbul's skyline. *Külliyes* are groupings of domed structures that contain all the buildings essential to Ottoman life – a mosque, a library, a school, a hospital, and, invariably, a hamam.

Walking around Tulza is similar, I imagine, to stumbling into an uncataloged museum spanning the fourth century onward. Remnants of antiquity are scattered like a Caesar's garage sale. At the clubhouse, marble bases of Corinthian columns served as coffee tables. A coffin–size tablet decorated with Greek script was used to hold glasses of cold rakı and that morning's issue of *Hürriyet* (translation *Freedom*, though the Turkish government still throws the odd journalist in jail). The pool, which was badly damaged last year by the Islamic fundamentalist Fazilet political party (they oppose all kinds of immodesty, including swimming in Victorian swimming costumes), was surrounded by a crumbling colonnade of withering Doric columns. Baksim and Mehmet had a proud, offhanded attitude about the antiquities, as if to say 'Look what our ancestors built! Their tablets are our coffee tables.'

After lunch Baksim announced, 'Now we will visit Kemal.' His name had come up several times with no supporting biographical data and only enigmatic asides. We traipsed through a gate and down a dusty road, only to end up at another gate, this one with a mangy dog and her pup barking to greet us. Baksim shouted, *'Allo, allo, Kemal?'* and after a minute of silence we let ourselves in. Once past the yapping Cerberuses, I could see a huge, lush, and elegantly unkempt garden stretched out before us. The garden was framed by a vine-covered trellis and a semicircle of little cottages. Had we just walked into an artists' colony, or did all these dwellings belong to one person? Could I live *here?* I wondered. My commute to the hamams of downtown Istanbul would be rather difficult, but who could complain about commuting from paradise?

The garden was patterned with a dried-up marble fountain, scattered stumps of byzantine columns, a pagoda, and, dominating the landscape, six antique wooden sailboat hulls sitting on the lawn like carcasses waiting to be skinned. It took a minute to process the pandemonium of the scene. My eye traveled to the edge of the thickly reeded Marmara shores. Only then did I realize that a garden party was in progress. From our relative distance, it felt as if we were spying on a Renoir painting of a languid late-afternoon gathering. I counted six people reclining on wooden furniture, sipping tea, and chatting with the air of old friends while sun danced across the water and their faces.

I glanced at Baksim, expecting us to retreat from their intimate gathering before anyone saw us, but instead we barged right in. One of the men folded the newspaper on his lap, stood up, and put on a smile the way you might unroll a dirty sock. 'Baksim,' he said with what little enthusiasm he could muster. The arrival of guests meant the making of more tea, the fetching of cups and saucers and sugar cubes, the offering of food, all the tiring elements of Turkish hospitality.

Baksim introduced me to Kemal as a 'guest from New York,' and Mehmet apparently needed no introduction, since the dogs were nuzzling him with excessive familiarity. Kemal was so tall that he stooped apologetically from his six-foot-three-inch height. He appeared deliberately disheveled in a wrinkled striped dress shirt and paint-splattered khakis. His angular jaw was covered in grayish stubble; his thick salt-and-pepper hair was brushed back off his ruddy face. If I could have pushed back his shoulders and made him stand up straight, he would have cut a dashing figure. As it was, he still cut a dashing figure, though he appeared slightly raffish and discombobulated, like a paper doll put together at off-kilter angles.

A round of introductions followed. All my social awkwardness, which at home is so often paralyzing, was gone. I felt calm, relaxed, supremely confident. I wasn't expected to know the etiquette of Turkish society, whether or not it was rude to arrive unannounced. That was Baksim and Mehmet's problem.

Kemal left to fetch tea, and I wondered if he needed help. He seemed like the kind of person who might get overwhelmed by life's little details. Baksim and Mehmet discussed the wood-hulled boats on the lawn. A new one had been added, and Kemal was in the middle of restoring five already.

'Why did he buy another one?' Mehmet wondered.

'He wants a fleet of nineteenth-century dinghies,' replied Baksim.

Kemal arrived with the tea and offered me a cup. As I took the saucer, I felt all thumbs. I looked around for a place to settle my glass teacup, and the only options were the base of an Ionic capital or a large tablet with Greek writing. 'Where did you find these?' I asked.

'Over there,' he said distractedly, and he pointed about fifty feet away. Soon everyone had their tea and the appropriate number of sugar cubes, and the group got deep into a discussion about the latest Galatasaray-Leeds soccer game, which had ended in the deaths of two English fans who had been burning a Turkish flag. The verdict: 'The Brits deserved it.'

Kemal, apparently not a soccer fan, scanned the garden. He looked like someone who liked to putter around, and I could tell he was sizing up summer improvement projects. Then, as if remembering that he was the host of this little tea party, he turned to me and said: 'So tell me, what brings you to Istanbul?'

'I'm here to study Turkish baths.'

'Whatever for?' he asked in thickly accented but perfect English.

'Well, it's a long story, really, but I'll give you the short version.

My friend Marina and I want to open a hamam in Manhattan. I'm in Istanbul to learn how its properly done.'

He nodded. 'It's a fascinating area of study, but Turks don't go anymore, you know. Very unhygienic business. You must be careful.' He said the last part softly, as if divulging a secret that he wanted me to take to heart.

Kemal didn't know it, but he couldn't have said anything crueler to me. I'd come halfway around the world to indulge in what I imagined was a distinctly Turkish pastime, and now I was being told that most Turks wouldn't set foot in a hamam.

'What do you mean, Turks don't go anymore?'

'Oh, you look sad. Let me explain. Modern Turks, like me or Baksim, consider hamams an old-fashioned habit, the kind of thing our grandparents' generation did. Turkey has modernized because of Atatürk's marvelous leadership.' This was my first induction into the cult of Atatürk, the first prime minister of modern Turkey and a beloved secular hero, a combination of Superman and Winston Churchill. 'Indoor plumbing became common, and people stopped needing to go to the public baths. Though some people still enjoy the ritual and the camaraderie. I think Mehmet and Baksim go to the hamam at the Hilton hotel from time to time. But it's more of a lark. Of course, I could be completely wrong,' he said in an attempt to comfort me. I shouldn't have been so surprised by what Kemal was saying. I had been in Istanbul just over twenty-four hours and every single Turkish person I had canvased about hamams always used the word *unhygienic* in their response, along with 'Be careful.'

Kemal continued, 'Maybe there still is bathing culture in Istanbul. I just don't know about it.' He paused and scratched his scruffy chin. 'You seem genuinely interested in baths. I think I have something that might interest you very much.' He grinned, displaying sharp incisors but twinkling eyes that seemed to offset the malevolence of his teeth. I wondered if he was married, though he seemed more the confirmed bachelor type. He was probably in his late thirties, and no one here seemed to be his wife or girlfriend.

I raised an eyebrow, playing along.

'I am *just now* excavating a Turkish bath in this *very* garden.' Kemal spoke slowly and clearly, emphasizing all the adverbial words like a posh Englishman. I made a mental note to ask if he'd spent his formative years at Eton.

'Last month I started to dig over there,' he said, pointing to a large rectangular hole in the ground covered by a bamboo roof about fifty yards away. 'I wanted to make a pottery studio using the walls that had been my sister's house, but I needed to dig deeper in the ground so it would be cool like a cellar in the summertime. After a day of digging, one of my workmen hit a floor about six feet under this ground level we see today. I had no idea what it was, so we kept digging a broader swath to see just how big this floor might be. Then we hit what I'm sure must be drainpipes.' He paused so I could register the import of this discovery. 'A most incredible thing. The drainpipes crisscross the floor. Surely it must be some kind of very old Turkish bath. What else could account for the presence of all of these drainpipes?'

'Well, that sounds entirely plausible,' I said, assuming the mantle of distinguished archaeology professor. 'Can I have a look?' Seven years ago, I'd taken a semester of Roman art and archaeology. Though I'd napped through most of the interminable slide shows, I'd perked up during the Roman bath section. And in my hazy recollection, drainpipes did not a bath make.

'Yes, yes, of course. So, now, really, what an incredible coincidence to meet. Have you read *The Celestine Prophecy*? A most amazing book. Meeting you is something straight out of that book.' I apologized for not having read *The Celestine Prophecy* but agreed that it was a huge coincidence our interests should so overlap.

'Come. Let's have a look at the thing.' He jumped up, and the rest of the tea party, still discussing the soccer deaths, looked over at us.

Kemal, with what I'd later see as a charming social ineptitude, wasn't going to explain our field trip to his guests, but sensing the question marks on everyone's faces, I said, 'Kemal and I are going on an archaeological excursion.'

I followed his long, sandaled legs to the last of the houses on the semicircle.

'Are all these houses yours?' I asked.

'For the time being, yes,' he responded with the indifference of someone either too rich or too eccentric to care.

We reached the 'dig area.' To the untrained eye, it was a gaping pile of rubble covered by a lean-to bamboo roof. To my untrained but optimistic eye, it looked like the contours of a modest bath built sometime during the reign of Justinian, circa fifth century A.D. This made sense, because Tuzla's first settlers were fifth-century Byzantine monks, according to Mehmet. Kemal waved to the two workers and greeted them: *'Selâm. Ne var ne yok?'* One guy, in dirt-covered jeans and a T-shirt, removed a wheelbarrow full of debris from the pit. The other guy swung a pickax at random parts of the floor in what looked more like an anger management exercise than a careful attempt to unearth buried booty.

'Meet my archaeologists,' Kemal declared proudly. Call me conservative, but their methods seemed crude, more exorcism than excavation. There were no field notebooks normally kept by archaeologists, no division of the area into trenches and buckets.

Kemal jumped down into the pit and offered me his hand. This was the fast-paced, intuitive world of archaeology I had dreamed of since *Raiders of the Lost Ark*. Here on the shores of the Marmara there were no permits to file and no authorities to meddle. Hey, Kemal and I *were* the authorities. We stood side by side, six feet below modern ground level, in a twelve-foot-by-twelve-foot moldy pit strewn with debris, discussing things we knew nothing about, comparing ill-founded theories, and planning how to proceed.

Kemal touched a pile of terra-cotta tablets stacked one on top of the other.

'Now what would these be? If this is the floor that we're standing on, why would rows of little pillars line the floor?'

'Well,' I said, trying not to sound too pleased with myself, 'these piles of terra-cotta tablets were called *pilae*. The Romans invented *pilae* to support the floor over the hypocaust system – that's the underground heating system. So here in this hypocaust area, the heat from the furnace would float around and heat the floor laid on top of the *pilae*. Ancient radiant heat. Pretty ingenious, eh?' I was surprised that all this was waterlogged in my brain. Why didn't I remember more important things like my bank balance or the birthdays of friends?

Kemal marveled at my intelligence or something on the floor. 'So you agree this really is an ancient bath?'

'Yes. But what else was in the area during ancient times? Why would the Byzantines have built a bath in this particular location?' I asked.

'This area is called Monaster, because of the fifth-century monastery that was here. Actually, my stone house was the last building used as a monastery. Just think – from monks to me.' He winked at me. 'Oh yes, and this area used to have productive salt mines. Tuzla actually means "with salt." '

Kemal and I invented an elaborate theory that this was once the bath for the workers of the Tuzla salt mines. After a long day of collecting salt under dark and claustrophobic conditions, Greek-speaking workers found warmth, light, heat, and rest in this little jewel of a bathhouse under the watchful eyes of the celibate monks. The bath's location near the salt mine explained why the design was small and functional as opposed to the more grandiose marble-paved hamams in central Istanbul.

'Do you think there is any way I could get the bath up and running again?' Kemal asked. 'How much do you think it would cost?'

'I really have no idea. I suppose it depends if you want to restore it with the original heating system or if you want to refurbish it as a more modern hamam. You could reline the walls with marble, the same marble you've redone the house in, and then put in some sort of furnace. It could be really lovely with just a very simple restoration. Or you could mount a dome on top and maybe install some windows in the side to look out onto the Marmara.' A daydream took shape in my head as I suggested these alternatives to Kemal. Maybe Marina and I could do a practice run restoring Kemal's ancient bath. With all these empty houses, living on-site certainly wouldn't be a problem.

Suddenly Kemal's excitement turned to paranoia. 'You're not going to tell anyone about this?' he asked. I was demoted from co-developer to potential informer.

'Kemal, what do I look like, the archaeological police?' He narrowed his light blue eyes. Was it, I wondered, the trench coat? 'If you let me help you excavate the bath, I promise I won't tell the authorities,' I teased, charmed by Kemal's suspicion.

We returned to the tea party; Baksim reminded Kemal, to my complete surprise, that I might be interested in renting his city house in Ortaköy.

'I will give Baksim the key so you can go have a look tomorrow,' Kemal said to me.

We had emptied our teacups, and the sun lowered across the water. It was time to make haste back to Istanbul.

Kemal waved good-bye and said, 'I hope you'll like my house.' Baksim, Mehmet, and I lingered for a few minutes, playing with dogs. A moment later Kemal intercepted us at the gate, his face even more drawn and serious than before. 'Don't tell anyone what you saw here, OK?' Baksim and Mehmet tried not to laugh; apparently Kemal was prone to these mini–anxiety attacks. I kissed him on both cheeks and promised not to turn him in. He blushed and said something about 'necessary precautions.'

On my second day in Istanbul, I'd met a charmingly neurotic man with an ancient bath in his backyard who was going to rent me his 'city' house. In the process of meeting all these new people, we had discussed personal situations – I knew all about Mehmet's wife and Baksim's prospects, and I'd gleaned that Kemal was unattached. Not once had I mentioned that I had a serious boyfriend whom I lived with back in New York City. I just put off mentioning Charles, again and again, until it crept up on me as something I was hiding. But the omission was easy enough to justify. Being in Istanbul was a delicious adventure, and I wanted to put a protective white sheet over anything that reminded me of home.

Just when I thought the day could not be any more perfect or serendipitous, Baksim said, 'Let's just say a very quick hello to my aunt and uncle before heading back into Istanbul.'

We ventured from Kemal's bohemian fantasy world to the manicured, refined world of Mehmet's uncle and aunt, where tea appeared magically, sugar cubes and all, and drawing room conversation followed the predictable lines of weather, traffic, and tennis. His aunt and uncle were the Turkish equivalent of Connecticut WASPs or English landed gentry. They were tidy, genteel people in their late fifties, the kind of people who wake up early, play tennis, and have card games with the neighbors. Baksim's uncle and I quickly fell into a conversation about hamams. One thing I immediately noticed about Turks was their highly extroverted interest in other people. Turkish people hold up much more than their end of the conversation. It was effortless and completely delightful to socialize in this country.

'I wonder very much what is left of hamam culture,' Baksim's uncle said wistfully. 'Well, there's someone I know with whom you should definitely speak. Her name is Tülay Tascioglu, and she wrote a gorgeous book called *The Turkish Bath* several years ago. It explains the origins of hamams and hamam culture and has some magnificent drawings and photographs. She's a very accomplished woman, and

I'm sure she'd love to meet someone with similar interests. Hold on just a moment and I'll find her telephone number for you.' Baksim smiled at me from across the room. Yes, his Nescafé prophecy had come true – the trip to Tuzla had been an amazing start to my research.

In the twilight car ride home, it struck me. Both of my chance encounters, with Kemal's physical bath and with Tülay's book on the history of hamams, were encounters with hamams as historical, antiquated remains to be dug up and written about. I was in Istanbul to uncover the vibrancy of an ongoing bathing culture. What was I about to walk into? Were today's hamams an 'unhygienic business,' in Kemal's words, or would I find otherworldly atmospheres of steam and glistening marble, private palaces to the body? Had the ancient communal baths been replaced by modern spa culture servicing the individual? I hoped not.

The very next evening, I called Marina from my new home in Ortaköy.

'You're not going to believe where I'm staying. I'm in a four-story town house with portholes for windows!'

'Excellent,' she said with breathy approval. 'Where?'

'In a little town along the Bosphorus called Ortaköy. It's only about twenty minutes from Sultanahmet,' I said, referring to the center of Old Stamboul where the Romans created Constantinople and the Ottomans Istanbul.

'Have you been to any hamams yet, the ones we talked about?'

'Not the ones we talked about,' I said, so ecstatic about my windfall living situation that I'd momentarily forgotten about my more pressing mission. 'It took two days to get settled, and then on the suggestion of Kemal and Baksim, I went to a place called Galatasaray. They told me it was the safest bet, but it was kind of sordid,' I said, remembering the *kese* scrub performed with a mitt that smelled like Gorgonzola cheese.

'Oh no, you didn't go to Galatasaray. That's the worst.'

'Thank God. I was getting worried that the best hamams are in France.'

'Go to Sultanahmet tomorrow, and try Cağaloğlu and Çemberlitaş. Both are very touristy, but will give you the flavor and scale of a real Ottoman hamam. So how did you end up in this apartment, I mean town house?'

'Marina, you won't believe this. The first morning I was in Istanbul, I met a character named Kemal who has an extra city house, of all things, that he's rented to me for as long as I want to stay here.'

'What do you mean, "as long as you want to stay there"?' Marina asked curiously.

'I mean if I decide to stay another week. Then, through one of Baksim's uncles, I met an architect and historian who wrote a history of Turkish baths and we're going to have lunch tomorrow.'

'This is all good, but you need to concentrate on living, breathing hamams, not people excavating or writing about baths. You need to visit at least two a day. Remember, there are sixty-seven registered hamams in Istanbul.'

'Got any bank weekends coming up?' I asked.

'In fact, I do,' she said, laughing. Marina had recently left her job in Moscow and taken a position at a London investment bank. Almost every weekend seemed to be surrounded by a bank holiday on Friday or Monday. Her suitcase was always in the hall; any time Marina had a three-day weekend she left the country. In fact, she traveled so often and to such exotic, borderline undesirable places that I sometimes wondered if she weren't a special agent or spy, not to mention that she liked to dance around in her underwear to the James Bond theme song. 'I could come over for a long weekend next week.'

'Perfect. But Kemal said I'm not supposed to have any slumber parties.'

'What?'

'You've got to meet this guy. I can't tell if he's a complete charlatan or a misunderstood artist. In any case, he's my landlord and I kind of like him.'

Earlier that morning and the day after we barged in on the tea party, Baksim and I toured the pink house alone. 'Wait, Kemal wants me to live in this whole house?' I asked, incredulous. On a cobblestone lane opposite the Ortaköy mosque, we had entered the chaotic mind of Kemal Orga. The basement kitchen was designed to look like the galley of a cruising yacht – a bilge pump toilet, plates moored to the walls using special vertical dish racks, and nautical instruments hanging from the rough cement walls. The next level was a small unlivable drawing room and dining room with an out-of-tune miniature piano, lumpy yellow furniture, and a grammar school writing desk strewn with antique fountain pens, inkblots, and letters in Turkish. It looked like an Agatha Christie crime scene. Painted across the wall in blue paint: 'the right feeling.' The third level resembled the ideal living quarters of a wealthy Oxbridge student circa 1910: French doors opened onto an enormous high-ceilinged, fustily furnished room with exposed brick and huge closets constructed out of tall bamboo reeds. This would suit me for the next ten years.

'One more floor,' said Baksim. 'You still haven't seen the bedroom.'

This final flight of stairs, the narrowest, led us through a homemade shoji screen and into a sunlit gabled room dominated by a king-size bed and two decks. One deck, like a widow's walk, peered down onto Ortaköy's main piazza, a row of restaurants looking across the Bosphorus to Beylerbeyi. The second deck, an outdoor living room with wicker furniture and potted azaleas, looked out onto Istanbul's famously surreal view. Ortaköy's flamboyantly Baroque mosque was pitted against the ultra-modern Europe-to-Asia suspension bridge.

The steps creaked and a deep-throated voice yelled, *'Günaydin!'* Kemal Orga emerged into his own attic bedroom.

Kemal was sporting three days of silver whiskers, and his apparel was more disheveled than his unkempt look of the day before. He wore a fluffy blue parka that would three weeks later be eaten by his puppy. He was definitely in costume. He looked like an aristocratic Turkish gangsta or a German hiker in need of a bath.

'Kemal, are you going for a hike in today's rain?' I teased, hoping to get to the bottom of the pose. I was starting to adore him.

He threw back his head with an English chortle. 'I'm about to confront my tenants, and I need to cultivate a raffish look.'

'Am I one of your tenants?'

'No, no. You're safe for now,' he said, reaching out to touch my shoulder. 'My family owns a building on the waterfront that we're trying to turn into a boutique hotel. A few tenants refuse to go, and since I'm the point man for the hotel, I have to take care of this.'

The point man? Baksim explained to me later that Kemal is the beloved black sheep of his affluent banking and real estate family. Kemal's older brother oversees a huge luxury housing project, but Kemal's interests revolve around antique boat restoration and painting. From time to time, the family put pressure on him to be the 'point man' on a project, but Kemal is cut from a fundamentally different cloth, and his forays into the business, according to Baksim, usually ended with another family member cleaning up after him.

'So what do you think of my house?'

'I'm speechless. It's a fantasy world.'

He smiled, looking pleased that I'd appreciated his porthole windows. I asked Kemal if guests would be a problem.

'Where would she sleep?' he asked.

'Well, right here. I've never seen such a big bed.'

'Like a slumber party? I don't want any slumber parties in my bed.'

'How's the excavation going?' I asked, not understanding his objection to slumber parties. I thought most men dreamed of slumber parties in their beds, even if they weren't invited.

'Yes, that's another reason I stopped by. I wanted to Xerox that book you were telling me about.'

'Oh, the ancient bath book,' I said. I had referred to it during our walk but hadn't thought he was serious about wanting to see it and put it out of my mind. 'Let me get it for you. It's a long book; you might want to look specifically at the section on the heating systems.'

'Thank you, and hopefully you can come back out to Tuzla this weekend,' Kemal said. 'We've cleared all the rubble and you can see the furnace now. Also, when you have time, I'd like to show you my other house in a planned community that my family developed. It's very beautiful and modern, and my living room is shaped like a hamam,' he said with a wink.

Our cab slowly snaked the congested seven kilometers from Orta-köy to Sultanahmet. Crowded buses were hard to endure when a cab ride cost only $1.50. We were going to the City. Say *Eis ten Polis* – Greek for 'to the city' – ten times really fast and you get 'Istanbul,' at least according to my college Greek professor. The city of Constantine, the city of Süleyman the Magnificent, where hamams were once so popular that bathing revenues subsidized libraries and a yearly parade of hamam owners drew crowds on the streets of Istanbul.

The cab dropped us off near the unimaginably large dome of the Aya Sophia, the minarets an afterthought to what was originally a Byzantine church. Marina and I scurried past rug dealers who roved the streets near the Divan Yolu, shouting, 'Nice shoes!' or 'Let me help you . . . spend your money' to us. Slightly lost, we asked a rug rogue, 'Do you know where Çemberlitaş is?'

'Yes, very close, but first come to my uncle's rug store for tea.' For once Marina was not interested in rugs; besides, she had her own personal dealers who e-mailed her when collectable *suzanis* became available.

Within a ten-minute walk of the Aya Sophia, the Blue Mosque,

Topkapi Palace, the vast dripping Hades of the Roman Cistern, the former site of the Baths of Zeuxippus (a second-century Roman bath), and the Roman Hippodrome (site of chariot races) – yes, just ten minutes from all these Roman, Byzantine, and Ottoman riches – are the last two great remaining monuments to the Ottoman hamam, Çemberlitaş and Cağaloğlu. Pronounced Chem-ber-lee-tash and Ja-la-lou. These are the hamams where foreign tourists end up after a day of sight-seeing in Old Stamboul and before the evening cruise along the Bosphorus with belly-dancing entertainers. There's something touristy and kitsch about these grand duchesses, yet if you want to see an imperial, still-functioning hamam, there's nowhere else to go in Istanbul.

Marina's pink scarf trailed in the warm breeze of this April day, her long brown braid wagging back and forth between her shoulder blades. She wore white netted heels with apparent indifference to the swirl of garbage on the street and stopped momentarily to consult a map. Marina had always been the map reader and I the second-guesser. While she traced her finger along the Divan Yolu, I thought about how this was our eighth year of visiting baths together. In college, Marina and I had a standing Friday night date: twenty minutes on the StairMaster, followed by thirty minutes in the college's sauna, disfigured by graffiti carved on every beam of wood. Our favorite graffito: 'Beware of Greeks bearing Trojans.'

We headed up the Divan Yolu, past Marina's beloved baklava-teria, past an English-language bookstore where the Turkish owner wrapped his inventory in Saran Wrap and suggested Irfan Orga's *Portrait of a Turkish Family* to every customer who walked through the door. A quick right on Vezirhan Caddesi, and there at number 8 is Çemberlitaş Hamam.

There was only a neon sign out front to tell us we'd arrived. Çemberlitaş's façade was not grand like a mosque's with a series of cascading domes and a parade of minarets. Hamams are always described as 'introverted buildings.' Gazing upon a hamam did not need to inspire awe in Allah; rather, hamams were places to

satisfy Allah's will by performing ritual ablutions. Hamam architecture always contained the same succession of rooms; the architectural challenge lay in adapting the traditional layout of
progressively hotter rooms to fit the constraints of a particular
lot. As a rule, though, the men's and women's sections were built
parallel to each other so the hot rooms could share a heating
system.

A lean man in his late thirties with black hair and a slight hunch
worked at the cashier's office. The listed prices, for a tourist hamam,
were reasonable. Roughly $8 for a bath, $15 if you added the *kese*
and massage. Certainly it was excellent value compared to some of
the fleecers and baksheeshers employed at Galatasaray and Cağaloğlu. But compared to a neighborhood hamam, where you could
have the works for $6, it was steep.

'*İngilizce biliyor musunuz?*' I asked in halting Turkish. This phrase
('Do you speak English?'), as far as I was concerned, was the first to
master in any language. It scored instant cultural diplomacy points,
spared me of being confused with an assumptive American, and
indicated subtly that I did not speak a word of Turkish.

He smiled. 'Yes, I speak English, of course I have to. It's not
Turks who come here after all,' he said as if it were a self-evident
fact.

'What do you mean, the Turks don't come here?' I asked. Had
Kemal's précis been correct?

Marina nudged me as if to say 'Spare us the theatrics, let's have a
bath.' But I needed to get to the bottom of whether or not Turks
still visited hamams. I was pouting and I knew it, but the cashier
obviously wanted to talk.

'I love the hamam,' he began. 'In fact, I love the hamam so much,
my wife left me because she said, "You love hamam more than me,"
and she was right.' Hmm, this struck me as unlikely. I had heard
about the law being a jealous mistress, but the hamam? He
continued, 'The hamam is regarded by many in Istanbul as an
old-fashioned ritual. Turks are proud of modernization, of all that

Atatürk accomplished.' He stopped and pointed to a wall hanging depicting a handsome square-faced man in a Western suit. The ubiquitous image of Kemal Atatürk, the closest thing this secular state has to a savior. After our moment of silence, the cashier continued, 'Atatürk modernized Turkey. No more veils, no more fez, everyone got a last name for the first time, Roman letters replaced Arabic letters, and we got plumbing. Turks are proud to be modern, and then, sadly, hamams became a reminder of life before modernization, before stability, before Atatürk. Now people think, Why do I need to go to a hamam if I have a nice bathtub or shower at home? They forget the history, all the significance of bathing together.'

'Do Turks *ever* come here?' I asked.

'Occasionally, yes. Especially if they have a foreign friend visiting.'

I shot a glance at Marina. She wasn't taking this as hard as I was. What came out of her mouth next shocked me. 'Excuse me, is that rug from the Caucasus?' she asked, pointing to a rug in the reception area. How could she be thinking about rugs when a hamam employee had just confirmed that the Turks no longer visit hamams?

'Yes, it's a nineteenth-century piece from the Caucasus. It's my most valuable piece. You have a good eye.'

'Does someone own this hamam, or is it property of the state?' I asked, steering the conversation back to what I was interested in and curious to learn if Çemberlitaş was part of a historic trust. It must be.

'I own the hamam,' he said, pushing back his shoulders. 'My family purchased Çemberlitaş twenty-three years ago. My name is Ruşen.' And he stuck out his hand in greeting. I've never known serendipity greater than Turkish encounters – owners and experts were always present instead of hidden behind screens of gatekeepers and bureaucracy. Right in front of us, the owner of a piece of Ottoman history. How strange to think that an individual could own a national treasure in Turkey. It struck me as the equivalent of a regular Joe owning Monticello or the Eiffel Tower.

'We want to open a hamam in America,' I told Ruşen. After a week in Istanbul, I was becoming as extroverted as the Turks. Withhold nothing, that was my new philosophy.

'An excellent idea. So many of my customers are curious Americans. Maybe we should go into business together,' he said, thinking out loud. 'Definitely you should come with me to visit my other hamam in Bodrum, where I use thermal waters.' Another joy of Turkish people, in addition to their extroversion, was their ability to think out loud – not imagining, as we Americans often do, that daydreaming leads to a commitment. Baksim had already promised to provide 5 per cent of the capital for our New York hamam, but I took his intention as a show of support instead of a number with five zeros attached.

I looked through the doorway into the large open-plan two-storied reception area, with a balustrade belting the private rooms and hallway on the second floor. A dark, bony man emerged from a changing compartment on the second floor, dressed only in a *peştamal,* a piece of plaid fabric worn like a wraparound skirt on men or like a beach towel on women.

'That's called the *camekân,* or reception area,' explained Ruşen. 'Men change upstairs and women have a separate locker room. After your bath, I invite you to come back here for tea and orange juice. You will be my guest.'

I peered into the *camekân;* mostly I saw corpulent Turkish women in baggy cotton dresses, smoking cigarettes.

'Those are some of the masseuses on break,' Ruşen explained.

Marina asked, 'This is one of Istanbul's older hamams, isn't it?'

'Yes, it's one of ten still-functioning historic hamams. It was commissioned by the powerful mother of Murat the Third. Her name was Nur-u Banu Sultan, and she hired Mimar Sinan to design it. You know Mimar Sinan?'

'The name sounds familiar,' I lied.

'Mimar Sinan is Turkey's most famous architect. He died at ninety-seven and not by natural causes. He was the Ottoman

Empire's architect under Süleyman the Magnificent; that is how you call him. In Turkey we call him Süleyman the Lawgiver. Sinan designed, or oversaw, the construction of over twelve hundred buildings, including thirty-two hamams.'

'So when was this built?' I asked, not familiar with the time of Murat III's reign.

'In 1584, near the end of Sinan's life.'

'This hamam is over four hundred years old,' I said, incredulous. Eighteen generations of Turks and two generations of foreigners had passed through these halls in search of water, gossip, rejuvenation, an afternoon without their veil, ritual ablution, a wife for their son, steam, heat, and, most recently, a living history museum.

'Yes, this hamam has seen a lot of sultans. You know, the sultan would make sure that his advisers stayed very close to the hamam owners. Why?' Ruşen was getting Socratic on us. 'Because revolutionaries conspired at the hamam. They would stand next to the *kurnas,* turn the water on full throttle, and plot a takeover of Topkapi Palace and the Seraglio Point; at least that was the legend. Hamam owners received kickbacks to watch the comings and goings of suspicious characters.' Nowadays, the Turkish men milling about in the Çemberlitaş *camekân* still look suspicious, but more likely than not they're discussing a new Türkcell phone plan or a hot new nightclub in Tünel rather than plotting Ankara's takeover.

We thanked Ruşen for the history lesson. So what if the only Turks in the room would be the masseuses; at least we could use this as a jumping-off point to plan our hamam. It would inspire us architecturally, and maybe we'd found ourselves an experienced business partner.

Ruşen had modernized the women's changing area so it resembled a gym locker room, and Marina and I wrinkled our noses at each other, hoping this would be the only modernized area. Wearing our *peştamals,* which looked like tablecloths we'd pinched from a Fourth of July picnic – blue-and-yellow checks for me, red-

and-black for Marina – and clomping along in *nalın,* wooden hamam flip-flops (think Turkish Dr. Scholl's), we felt like the miscast leads of a Turkish *I Love Lucy.* The shoes were two sizes too small, so we walked with the deliberation of dressage horses. Had it not been for Kemal's comment 'a very unhygienic business,' I would have ditched the *nalın* altogether.

First we walked through the *soğukluk,* a warm passageway that once served as the delicate appetizer to the hotter *sıcaklık.* Nowadays customers bolt straight to the *sıcaklık,* forgoing the more modest heat of the *soğukluk* altogether. But the *soğukluk* is an important place to remember if you're looking for the more banal outlets of a hamam – like the toilet – as it's invariably in this tepid hallway. Though I hasten to add that visiting the lavatory in a hamam can instantly kill the romance of a dreamy drift back in time.

We opened the warped wood door of the *sıcaklık* and a gust of humid air rolled over us. It felt as if we'd walked into a tropical cumulous cloud hanging over Barbados. The barometric pressure was so high that my contact lenses balked for a moment and then gratefully accepted the humidity. The mist cleared from my eyes. I suddenly remembered a line from the travel journal of Julia Pardoe, who visited a hamam in the 1830s: 'For the first few moments, I was bewildered; the heavy, dense, sulphureous vapour that filled the place, almost suffocated me.' Miss Pardoe had wondered whether the scene in the hamam was a creation of her 'distempered brain,' and I sympathized with the overwhelmed Englishwoman.

I clutched Marina's arm and we stood side by side, taking in the dimensions of this vast marble cavern topped with a Pantheon-size dome. It was enormous. Monumental and palatial. Big enough to accommodate the Hanging Gardens of Babylon and certainly a good climate for them.

The domes upon domes and tons of marble created the most astonishing acoustics. Again, I thought of Miss Pardoe, who was deafened by 'the wild, shrill cries of the slaves peeling through the reverberating domes of the bathing-halls, enough to awaken the very marble with which they were lined.' The halls still echoed with shouting, whistling, splashing, and laughing. Anyone sense-experiencing this room for the first time would be dazzled and overwhelmed; all five senses experiencing it in tandem were vying for attention amid sensory chaos.

Fanning off from the central octagonal room were small individual washing areas, *'halvets,'* said Marina, 'and the basins are called *kurnas*. One hundred years ago they would have had elaborate silver or brass faucets, but everything was stolen, now just basic spigots remain.'

We had arrived at 7:00 P.M., prime time, and Çemberlitaş was crowded with thirty or so women like ourselves, foreigners in Istanbul trying to resurrect an Ottoman lifestyle that sighed its last gasps a good eighty years ago. The *göbektaşi*, a.k.a. the bellystone, was a massive octagonal crater of interlocking marble slabs, five times the size of the quaint little bellystones we had seen in Paris. The *göbektaşi* is always in the center of the *sıcaklık* and lies directly over the hamam's heater so that it's the warmest spot, the place for tight, stressed shoulders to melt into the marble in preparation for a hamam scrubbing.

'Marina, look at that *göbektaşi!*'

'How many tons of marble do you think are in the room?' said Marina, similarly awestruck, though this was her second visit to Çemberlitaş. 'They must have emptied Carrara for this.'

'This must be Turkish marble,' I said, remembering that *marmara* was the generic Greek word for marble because so much of it came from quarries by the Marmara Sea.

Lying on the slabs of marble were ten women being worked on by ten hamam ladies, who undeniably looked rather similar. Baksim had told me there was an expression 'fat as a hamam lady.' At the time I thought he was being unkind, but he'd covered only the half of it. The hamam ladies all wore black bikini bottoms, actually underwear (why stand on ceremony?), and flip-flops. Nothing else bound their flesh. Their figures had long ceased to be girlish, and their breasts tumbled toward the floor. They possessed the build, uniform, and strength of sumo wrestlers. That might be my body in thirty years, I thought with a strange sense of calm.

We probably had at least a half-hour wait before jumping on the bellystone, but that was the perfect amount of preparation time. Other newcomers, without a Marina of their own, looked lost, confused, and overwhelmed. Arriving in the *sıcaklık* for the first time is slightly akin to showing up for your first therapy session. You enter a strange room and are told, 'This is your time.' And there's a paralyzing trepidation as you think, This is my time? What do you mean, it's my time? Ask me some questions, give me some tasks to perform, and I'll interpret, but don't make me invent. Time in a hamam is similarly unstructured. But hamam therapy has two big advantages over psychotherapy. First, there is no therapist to entertain with witticisms from your, hopefully, hilariously neurotic life. And second, being physically nude speeds you to a state of emotional nudity, a stripping away of pretense and Prada.

Marina and I found a *kurna* of our own in an unoccupied *halvet.* The words *kurna, göbektaşi,* and *halvet* were starting to roll off my tongue, I felt so much a part of their Ottoman world. The *kurna*'s deep marble basin overflowed with warm water, creating a continuous stream across the marble floor and into a gutter that circled the room. One could play a sophisticated game of bobbing for apples. Peering into the *kurna,* I noticed a faint green hue to the water created by the cast of the marble and the depth of the water. The gushing water created a feeling of largesse that in the old days, when water was something that came out of a well, bucket by bucket, must have felt like the ultimate luxury. I liked to imagine that Justinian built his cistern to feed the baths. We found a stack of turquoise-and-pink plastic hamam bowls, *hamam tasis,* that a hundred years ago would have been carved, perhaps even jewel encrusted, in expensive materials like silver, gold, or bronze.

Marina and I cleaned the floor and the bowls with a little soap. We doused ourselves in warm water to promote sweating and soaped the city grime off our faces and feet. Then we sat down next to the running water of the *kurna*. I looked at Marina and noticed that we had both lost weight since our pizza and sundae years at school in Iowa. The years after college were the lean years in every sense. Lean paychecks in large, expensive cities when dinner for one meant steamed broccoli and soy sauce. I filled another bowl with water and poured it over my head. Glancing around the room, underneath the dome, and in between the Corinthian columns, I saw every body type, every nationality, every pubic hair style on display. If people checked one another out, it was with a spirit of sisterhood. Comparison, perhaps, but not competition. Everyone in the room was more or less comfortable in her own skin, because the hamams draw adventurous, intrepid travelers without an assortment of body issues. No, the prudes were reading aloud from guidebooks down the street in the Blue Mosque, another of Sinan's tremendous creations.

The Blue Mosque's wealth of Iznik tiles – mostly blue, surprise, surprise – the elegant Arabic scrawl of verse from the Koran, the awesome expanse of the dome, and the daringly low candelabras inspired wonder and a shrinking sensation. Here in the hamam, each bather was an integral part of the tableaux. All the surroundings could be touched, used, and enjoyed. The *göbektaşi* was an altar at which I could comfortably be a supplicant.

One of the ladies came to collect first Marina and then me. Once you are under the hamam lady's power, you no longer have to move your own body. You are a car in neutral about to enter the most thorough, unrelenting car wash of your life. The hamam lady removed my ill-fitting *nalın,* positioned me on the bellystone, and doused me with warm water. We nodded hello to each other, and she introduced herself as

Nermin. I looked up to the huge dome, dotted with a constellation of skylights called *faunuses*. The coming twilight lit the room in competing lasers of bluish light, cutting through the *sıcaklık*'s steamy mist at jagged angles. A planetary light show for one. The hamam lady returned, her wooden clogs clanking noisily over the marble floor. In front of her pendulous breasts, she carried a round pink bucket with a washcloth and a coarse-looking mitt.

Our only possible communication was through pantomime and pointing. Tonight, I promised myself, I will study Turkish phrases at Kemal's. (*Nasilsiniz?* How are you? *Iyiyim tessukur ederim.* I am fine, thank you.) She grabbed the black mitt and started to rub my legs. She scoured me like a pot with stubborn burn marks. She pointed down at my legs. Little black balls of dirt gathered like a strange rash. She nodded approvingly, wanting me to acknowledge the efficacy of her treatment or just how dirty I had been. I bowed my bead appreciatively and said a tea-sugar thank-you. (Kemal told me that if you say 'tea-sugar' really fast, it comes out sounding like Turkish for 'thank you': *tesekkür*.) My amateur effort produced an amused look of comprehension.

It's a strange relationship between hamam lady and her client. I was not a regular and I didn't speak her language, so we couldn't swap baklava recipes or beauty secrets. Her large, deep-set eyes reminded me of green olives. The stretch marks on her stomach told the story of a large family. The scouring continued up my body. She took my right hand, and in order to stretch out my arm for easier scrubbing, she placed my hand on the top of her left breast with as little ceremony as if handing me a towel. What if I squeezed her breast by accident? How embarrassing.

She marched over to the *kurna* and refilled her bowl, returning to soap me with long, deep strokes of the washcloth. It no longer seemed strange that she scrubbed and massaged me under my armpits, behind my ears, between my breasts, and everywhere you'd think only to wash yourself in a windowless room. Turkish women, I'd heard from other travelers, think nothing of performing the most intimate ablutions in public, whereas Turkish men never even remove their *peştamals* inside the *sıcaklık*. Nermin tapped me twice on the hip — hamam sign language for turn over — and she scrubbed my backside with similar devotion.

'Marina, this is all clean, right?' I asked, lifting my head off the marble. 'They change washcloths after every person?'

'You can't think about that,' said Marina. 'When you eat at a restaurant, do you think about what's going on back in the kitchen?' Actually, I did.

I kept my eyes shut and gave myself over to the sensation of being soapy and slippery on warm marble. This is how pastry dough must feel as the rolling pin stretches it out on the baker's marble surface.

Nermin took my hand and guided me over to a *kurna*. She desudsed me with bucket after bucket of water. Then she shampooed my hair. She massaged my scalp, she pressed on my temples. I was melting. When she finally succeeded in removing all of the soap from my hair, she put her fingers on my eyes and pushed away the water so I could see. 'Rest now,' she said, and left me to find her next client.

'*Teşekkür ederim,*' I yelled weakly and gratefully after her. The *gobektaşi* was too crowded to take up our own post, so Marina and I returned to the *kurna* and leaned our rosy, scoured bodies against the wall.

'How long did that last?' I wondered.

'I don't know, maybe ten minutes, maybe half an hour. I feel rubbery and relaxed.'

'It's so different from an American spa, where something happens to you for a prescribed amount of time. That *kese* scrub and being in this dreamy, surreal room feels like . . . an unfolding process . . . like an experience that gets richer the longer you let it work on you. Not to mention the theatrics,' I said, thinking of the ongoing yells between the hamam ladies and the aggressive apple tea lady pushing her wares.

'I love the theatrics,' agreed Marina. 'Our hamam should be like a Fellini movie, a constantly changing cast of characters; show up on any given day and you might find a cellist playing Stravinsky in the steamroom or someone pushing through a tray of raspberry sherbet.'

'That's a brilliant idea. We could play silent movies along the walls one day, offer henna treatments the next. No two days at our hamam will ever be the same,' I said with a sudden burst of optimism that faded instantly. One minute the world seemed like our own tray of oysters on the half-shell, and the next moment our dreams seemed fenced off by insurmountable boundaries called money, connections, experience. 'Marina, what are we going to do with our lives? I feel like we're back in college, sitting on your bed and plotting our futures. Remember how sorted we thought we'd be by the time we hit thirty?'

'I know. Everything seemed so uncomplicated at twenty-one.' Then, out of the blue, Marina observed, 'You don't seem ready to go home.'

'I'm not, I'm only just starting to get this. I mean, of course I miss Charles, but what's another two weeks. He'll understand.'

'Maybe the baths of the world need your energies more than Charles right now.'

I wanted to change the subject. 'Marina, how are things with Colin?' Marina, unlike most women, did not like to talk about her boyfriend, and the moment, naked and relaxed, seemed opportune for prying.

'Same old, same old,' she said dismissively. 'I think our hamam should be alabaster instead of marble.'

'Fight, break up, decide you can't live without each other?' I surmised from 'same old, same old.'

'Exactly, the co-dependency continues. Three years of calling each other seven times a day.'

Marina would be the first to admit her relationship was dysfunctional. She envied the stability and honesty that Charles and I maintained effortlessly. I envied the passion that she and Colin had – they would fight, make up, then disappear for hours. While I accepted the universal rule always to side with your girlfriend, I knew Marina well, and I knew she was extraordinarily high-maintenance. I had been on the receiving end of some of her tirades. So I did have some sympathy with Colin's tribulations, though I would accept at face value any story that depicted him as an insensitive scoundrel bent on ignoring Marina's wishes. Marina's wishes, however, were many and very specific. Compromise to Marina meant meeting you one-eighth of the way. But she was a lovable bully.

We stayed at the *kurna*, staring up at the dome's darkening skylights that reminded me of Kemal's portholes. Both were windows that admitted light but offered no view of the outside world, nor did they provide the outside world a view into this intimate sanctum. It was getting late, soon we would have to leave this world.

'Are you hungry?' I asked.

'Famished. Let's get cheese borek,' Marina said. Cheese borek, a noodle pastry lined with filo, goat's cheese, and parsley, was her favorite Turkish food, second only to baklava.

'We had that for breakfast. Please let's have grilled fish,' I suggested. A fish restaurant wouldn't serve cheese borek and vice versa.

Marina adopted her open-eyed, beseeching look. Her eye-brows went up and her head tilted toward me. 'Oh, but I'm only here for three days. After I'm gone you can have fish every night.'

'Okay, fine. But we're supposed to meet Baksim for dinner. What if he doesn't want cheese borek?'

'I'm sure he won't mind.' Poor Colin.

Back in the *camekân*, our *peştamals* exchanged for jeans and sweaters, Ruşen brought over two orange juices and inquired after our bath. We were too deliciously spent for conversation. 'It's like a narcotic,' I said. 'I'm too messed up to say anything, and I'll be back tomorrow for more.'

We said good-bye to Ruşen, who again invited us to visit his thermal hamam in Bodrum and to stay in his house there. Bodrum is about six hours south of Istanbul and located on top of geothermal springs. Ruşen's Bodrum hamam is more spa than public bath. Because the waters are thermal, the Turks are allowed to soak despite the normal Islamic interdiction against soaking in still waters. For a Muslim to soak in a body of water, it must be continually flowing and replenishing itself. Otherwise it is considered unclean.

Ruşen's offer was kind and tempting, but it seemed much more friendly and forward than anything I was used to, and the suspicious New Yorker in me didn't quite know what to make of his generosity. I hadn't yet learned to recognize a good adventure from a bad, and I still regret that I didn't take Ruşen up on his well-intentioned offer.

Marina and I got busy. For the next three days, Marina put her textile obsession on hold and we racked up the baths, visiting ten different hamams. Sometimes we just stopped to peek in, like wine connoisseurs who just swirl and spit but won't taste a wine that doesn't meet their standards.

- **Çemberlitaş.** The best, most authentic of the big 'tourist' hamams, owned and run by a man who gets misty-eyed when he talks about hamam culture.
- **Cağaloğlu.** Designed in the Baroque style in 1741, so it's interesting for connoisseurs of hamam architecture. The bathing experience, however, will leave you desiring nothing so much as a hot shower and a bar of soap, since I think the place is dirty and neglected. Guidebooks that suggest this as a good first stop for the uninitiated are woefully out-of-date. It appears that the owners stopped caring about this place years ago.

- **Galatasaray.** One of the most famous 'tourist' hamams near Istiklal Caddesi. While the men's side is charming, an original from 1481, the women's side was a second thought built in 1963, and some of the women who work here are better at cleaning wallets than bodies.
- **Tarabya.** An excellent and faithful modern re-creation of a hamam in the Tarabya Hotel, an establishment favored by rich Arab businessmen. Though it requires a long taxi ride north along the Bosphorus, past Bebek and Etiler, it's worth the trip if you're looking for a mixed-gender bath – bathing suits required – and American levels of hygiene.
- **Bosphorus Princess Hotel.** A kitsch hotel bath. Small, clean, boring, architecturally flat. Might as well be in an American gym steamroom.
- **Baths of Roxelana.** Now a carpet store and the ideal place to see a Mimar Sinan–designed hamam without taking off your clothes.
- **Dolmabahçe Palace.** The most beautiful hamam in the world, adorned with honey-colored alabaster delicately carved so as to give the impression of snowflakes masquerading as lace. To see the sultans' former hamam, you must take the Dolmabahçe Palace tour while wearing surgical slippers over your shoes.
- **Beylerbeyi.** We peeked into this stunning gem of a neighborhood hamam on the Asian side, just next door the Beylerbeyi Sarayi (palace). It was about to close for the day.
- **Çinili** in Üsküdar. Marina and I arrived during the men's hours and were given a tour and invited to bathe. We declined, recognizing this as the 'bad' kind of adventure. This old-school hamam is a rare find, though. They have several styles of peştamals depending on whether you're bathing or resting.

- **Kalig Ali Pasa** in Tophane. We managed also to hit this
  old Mimar Sinan–designed hamam during men's hours and
  were invited to tour the *sıcaklık*. Immeasurably grand and
  sorrowfully neglected, this is the only hamam in which I
  saw a cockroach.

Marina and I had taken the measurements. Cağaloğlu had the best
architecture, Çemberlitaş the best management and a close second in
ambiance, Tarabya the nicest changing area and *camekân*. Galatasaray
was everything we didn't want to be (apple tea pushers and
baksheesh seekers), and the neighborhood hamams all had sweet
hamam ladies who acted like adoptive mothers.

Despite our action-packed three days, I felt that my work was just
beginning, my interest growing rather than satisfied. Getting a
handle on the hamam's architecture and accoutrements only raised
more questions. Where did the hamam tradition come from? Surely
from the Roman baths. The hamam, after all, was an Islamic
interpretation of the Roman bath. And where might I find an
enduring bath culture? A place where a visit to the baths might serve
the same social function as meeting at a restaurant for dinner. In
Turkey, the hamam no longer played the coffeehouse role, but
perhaps the Russians, Finns, and Japanese were still bathing with
frolicsome abandon. I needed to find out.

Midway through my stay in Istanbul, I was still looking for the
historic neighborhood baths I had read about.

Now and then, usually about once in a week, my grand-
mother had a sociable turn of mind and when these moods
came upon her she invariably went to the Hamam. Hamams,
or the Turkish Baths, were hot-beds of gossip and scandal-
mongering, snobbery in its most inverted form and the
excuse for every woman in the district to have a day out.
Nobody ever dreamed of taking a bath in anything under

seven or eight hours. The young girls went to show off their pink-and-white bodies to the older women. Usually the mothers of eligible sons were in their minds for this purpose for these would, it was to be hoped, take the first opportunity of detailing to their sons the finer points of So-and-so's naked body. Marriages based on such hearsay quite frequently took place, but whether or not they were successful few of us had any means of knowing.

          – Irfan Orga, *Portrait of a Turkish Family*

Where was this bath described by Irfan Orga? After Marina left I was determined to find it. The closest I came was my favorite neighborhood hamam, where once, no doubt, a crop of eligible women paraded for the mothers of eligible sons. A longtime resident of Istanbul whom I'd met at the rug bazaar told me about the Ağa hamam, describing it as an authentic old-school hamam with unpredictable, sometimes unorthodox activity, the kind of place rarely stumbled upon by travelers. Perfect, it was surrounded by a virtual velvet rope of anonymity. It was in an obvious enough spot, but it called no attention to itself and was the retiring younger sister of the evil, pushy Galatasaray hamam up the street. The hamam was on a small, tangled side street called Turnacibasi Sokaga, just south of Istiklal Caddesi, a buzzing pedestrian shopping arcade, where once all the foreign embassies were located until Atatürk made Ankara Turkey's capital (Istanbul had too much emotional baggage).

    When I first showed up at the Ağa hamam, the *hammaci,* the lady who takes your money at the entrance, examined me curiously. *'Hamami?'* she probed.

    'Evet hamami,' I confirmed, and I pulled out my own *hamam tasi* and *kese* mitt that I'd acquired at the Grand Bazaar's Hamam Store. She looked impressed – she obviously had thought I'd entered the wrong door – and called over some of the other hamam ladies. They nodded appreciatively that I'd amassed my own tools of the trade.

After my fourth visit, they stopped treating me like a lost animal but instead welcomed me with, *'Merhaba Alexia.'* Every visit, the same hamam lady would scrub me (her name was Neuron; at least that was how it sounded), and she liked to point out that we had the same color blue eyes. I'd even managed to make a friend, a Chinese film editor who had lived in Istanbul for two years. She invited me to a film screening. Perhaps hamam society was still alive.

One afternoon I invited Kelly to join me at the hamam; she was a thirty-year-old American dance teacher living in Istanbul whom I'd recently been introduced to. I had told Kelly how proprietorial the hamam ladies were, how if a man stumbled into the reception area during the women's hours, he was booted out the door, literally sent running down the street to the bakery where they make *simits,* a cross between a sesame bagel and a pretzel. I'm convinced this is why so many old, leather-skinned guys sat on chairs outside along the sidewalk. Watching the world walk by, sure, but also waiting for the latest installment of Ağa hamam drama.

I expected Kelly to be totally at ease with the nudity and physical license inside the hamam; she was a dancer after all. Luckily, she was a dancer who believed in regular meals, so getting naked together wasn't a skin-and-bones reminder of why I'd quit ballet at twelve. But despite her comfort with her own body, Kelly's jaw still dropped in shock when we entered the small, stunning *sıcaklık.* Nude splashing bodies, old withered breasts, mounds of flesh, friendly shouting, a woman sitting on her haunches scrubbing her undergarments, everything so carnal and so raw. It was a parade of humanity that you'd never be able to assemble. But here it happened every day.

A mother and her young daughter bathed together on this afternoon. There was nothing unusual about this. Kelly and I were lying next to each other on the small intimate bellystone, and the cries of the two-year-old daughter with long corkscrew curls grew louder and louder. Soap must have gotten in her eyes. The screams went on for longer than they should have. Kelly and I commented, 'Oh the poor little girl,' when what we were really thinking was, Get that little girl out of here. Just as we were having these wicked thoughts, a huge tall figure in a thick pink terrycloth robe burst through the door with a small terrier dog in tow. I didn't know which was stranger – the presence of the monstrously large woman or the dog. From my vertical vantage point on the *göbektaşi*, I looked directly at her hands – large knuckles, thick boxy fingers, and chipped coral fingernail polish. Unmistakably the hands of a man. 'Kelly, I think she's a man.'

The pink-robed figure raised her baritone voice and started scolding the young mother to hush her child. The child, scared or fascinated by the presence of the dog, was instantly quiet. The baritone's hair was in a turban, and as soon as the child stopped crying she turned on her heels and left the hamam, depriving us of a good look at her chiseled face.

The Ağa hamam, more than any other bath I visited, made me think of the greatest bath movie ever made, *Steam: The Turkish Bath*. In this Italian movie, a young, career-obsessed Italian interior designer arrives in Istanbul to settle the estate of his estranged aunt. He is embraced by the Turkish family his aunt lived with, and he sees the hamam that his aunt used to operate. Slowly, as he is seduced by the pace of Turkish culture, he begins to understand the peculiar magic of his aunt's life in Istanbul, the charm of Turkish people, and he discovers a calmer, more sensual part of himself during visits to the hamam. He decides not to sell the hamam, but rather to stay in Istanbul to restore it and possibly to reopen it. Every feeling in that movie resonated with me. The seduction of Turkish life, the desire to wake up every morning to the sound of a muezzin's call to prayer and walk, across the domed skyline, to work at a twenty-first-century hamam.

Kemal regarded all the time I spent in hamams with a blend of curiosity and suspicion. He used to drop by the house fairly often to pick up his mail or collect a book. Sometimes it seemed, or I flattered myself, that he dropped by more often than was necessary. Once he stopped by at 10:00 P.M. while I was out. He left a note: 'What goes on in these hamams at this hour? I must know . . .' I called him at his house in Tuzla to tell him about the drag queen, and he invited me to a record release party the next night at a club called, of all things, Hamam. The party reminded me of all that I wasn't homesick for. 'The DJ is from New York,' the crowd murmured with excitement, 'and Junior Vasquez is coming next week.' Everyone seemed perfectly happy that Hamam was no longer a place where people washed one another's backs. I would trade Junior Vasquez and the dreadlocked DJ for the fat hamam ladies in a New York minute.

Kemal, wearing a fisherman's sweater, didn't look as slick as the other partygoers, but he knew a lot of them and introduced me to a stream of people. 'I thought you might be homesick and enjoy a party like this,' he yelled over the noise.

'Actually, I prefer the tranquillity of Tuzla or drinking rakı somewhere quiet,' I said.

'Me too,' he said, taking my hand and leading me through the throng of bouncing, sweaty bodies.

The next morning, I accompanied Kemal to Tuzla to check on progress at his dig. The rubble and debris were completely cleared, and I noticed that the *pilae,* the short pillars of terra-cotta, were stacked in three piles in one corner.

'Kemal, why did you move the *pilae*?' I asked calmly, trying to mask my horror.

'We needed to clear the bath.'

'But the *pilae* are an integral part of the bath. I may have to call the authorities. These are highly erratic excavation methods.'

Kemal did not think this was funny. 'I wanted to get everything cleaned out,' he said again, seeming not to understand that he had essentially removed part of the foundation.

'You plan to turn this into a pottery studio, don't you?' I asked, remembering his original plan.

He looked away. Our notion of restoring the bath was dissolving in front of my eyes. Kemal stared at the middle of the floor and was, I guessed, imagining where he was going to place the throwing wheel and not the bellystone.

'I'm not sure yet,' he said. 'It depends if you stay and help me.' I shouldn't have been tempted, but I was, very much.

That afternoon, five of Kemal's friends arrived for another Marmara Sea tea party. Only this time, instead of feeling like an interloper, I helped prepare the tea and made sure Kemal remembered to put the sugar cubes on the tray. His friends were less soulful and more self-assured than Kemal. They had professions and children. One couple had just returned from three years in L.A. and wondered if there were any new bagel bakeries in Istanbul. In fact there was, a small chain called Tribeca. Another friend, an architect, had just launched a business where you design your own Turkish rug on-line and he has it delivered to your house a month later. Two of them had never been to a hamam.

'Never? Not even for a school trip or some sort of coming-of-age ceremony?' I asked, incredulous.

'No. I've been meaning to go for years, but I've never gotten around to it. Maybe I'll go down to Bodrum at some point and try the thermal hamams,' said the woman keen on Tribeca bagels.

'We should start a revival right here in Istanbul,' I suggested. 'The other day I was at a neighborhood hamam and the owner was there. He let me take pictures and I guess he sensed my interest, though we couldn't talk because I still speak only eleven words of Turkish. Anyway, he desperately wanted to relive the glory days of the hamam, so he disappeared for a minute and returned in this crazy green satin costume that he used to wear during the annual hamam owner's parade. It was a very bittersweet moment with him standing there pretending to march and wave.'

'Alexia, you should be a Turk,' Kemal said, defusing the situation so that no one had to humor me with vows of future hamam devotion or listen to any more of my hamam sentimentality.

After everyone left, Kemal invited me to dinner.

'Let's sail to the restaurant,' he suggested. I followed him down the jetty and we boarded a tiny sloop with a makeshift mast that was nothing more than a busted oar. With endearing effort to look effortless, Kemal managed to raise the enormous sail. The sail billowed, reluctantly at first, until the wind got behind us and pushed us around Kemal's jetty and a neighboring stone causeway. Once we'd rounded the modest causeway, Kemal turned the boat straight toward shore, forcing us to come about.

'What are you doing? I thought we were sailing to a restaurant.'

'We're there,' he said, smiling. I saw a seaside restaurant directly in front of us, basically Kemal's next-door neighbor.

'Couldn't we have walked?' I asked, wondering if maybe this was an island or somehow mysteriously separated from Kemal's compound not five hundred feet away.

'Yes, but what fun would that have been?'

The boat hit the pebbly shore and we stepped out. I liked life in Turkey.

Baksim walked by the restaurant as Kemal and I were nibbling on dolmas and eggplant dip. I hoped he wouldn't join us, so delightful was this dinner alone with Kemal. All my appreciation for Baksim's help and friendship was dwarfed by a desire to be alone with Kemal talking about sailing in between Aegean Islands. Baksim pulled up a chair and regarded us suspiciously. After a moment of uncomfortable silence, I cut a dolma in half and made a weak attempt at a joke.

'Did you know that Turkey has the richest kitchen in the world?' I asked, parroting a statement that Baksim had drilled into me over the four preceding weeks. Turks never tire of reminding foreigners that Turkish cooking is the apotheosis of countless traditions.

Baksim was not amused. 'What are you two up to?' he asked.

I had guilt written across my face, and so did Kemal, I suppose, though he always looked guilty. We weren't doing anything wrong – well, not really – yet there was something unmistakably complicit between us. Charles was far away in New York and would never know about this; and Kemal's on-again-off-again girlfriend, Şebnem, was studying in New York. Who knows, maybe they were having an affair. Neither Kemal nor I was being true to our New York flames, yet we were somehow being true to ourselves. I was exploring something I'd forgotten about – chemistry, longing, electricity. It had been too powerful to say no to, yet it wasn't enough to stay for.

Sitting across from Kemal, defending myself against Baksim's insinuations of infidelity, I felt as if I were witnessing my parallel Turkish life, an alternate reality in which I could be the wife of a profligate but very charming Turk. And in this one moment I had to choose – was it going to be life in Turkey or a return to the familiar stability of New York? How, I wondered, could I even compare Kemal to Charles? Charles was three times the person that Kemal was, yet it was Kemal who starred in my fantasies, whose face I saw at odd moments during the day. It was clear that I could stay in Turkey. But to do what? Well, actually there were a lot of things I could imagine doing in Istanbul. But I wasn't ready to unpack, not here, not in New York. No, I wanted to keep the furniture covered for a little while longer.

Kemal's bath, the proximity to antiquity, fueled my desire to wander back in time to the origin of bathing culture, the ancient world. The Greeks initiated and the Romans later perfected a cult of the bath that has never since been equaled. I at least wanted to wander through the ruins.

Remains of Roman baths dotted the Roman Empire from England to Jerusalem. The trick would be finding a dig and archaeological team willing to accept an interloper into their fold and where work was currently under way. From my days as a classics student, I still had a few connections, and a volley of e-mails directed me to dig near Korinth, once an important city in ancient Greece and later in Roman-occupied Greece. As luck would have it, a study tour was about to arrive for three weeks on-site, and if I didn't object to following to their rigorous twelve-hour-a-day study schedule with lots of housekeeping duties, I was more than welcome to join in the fun.

The bath in question was in Isthmia, one of the four Olympic sites that dotted the Peloponnese. It was a large Roman bath, called a *thermae,* built over an original, mysterious Greek bath, so I would get a taste of what Edgar Allan Poe termed 'the glory that was Greece,/ And the grandeur that was Rome.'

ancient korinth:
the emperor's new baths

Bring quickly from the cupboard oil to anoint him and towel to rub him, and other things necessary; and then bring my guest to the nearest baths, for I know he is weary of so long and difficult travel.

– Apuleius, *The Golden Ass*

In Greece the rocks are eloquent: men may go dead but the rocks never.

– Henry Miller, *The Colossus of Maroussi*

I flew into Athens on a dry, dusty day in May. This was my first trip to Greece, my belated 'semester abroad.' The plane's descent across the ancient port of Piraeus and through the shadow of Mt Olympus felt like a magic carpet ride into a 5th-century B.C. cityscape. I tricked my eyes into believing that one of the ships approaching the port was a homecoming Theseus with an unconsciously murderous black sail hoisted. And there – high on a precipice – was Theseus' father, King Aegeus, hurling himself into the sea.

My mythical fantasy was soon thwarted, however, by the apologetically ugly city of modern Athens. Archaeologists were expecting me in the city of Ancient Korinth by early evening, but the lure of the Acropolis and the urge to indulge my classics student curiosity was too great, so I stashed my bags at a luxury hotel near the base of the Acropolis and raced to the top of the citadel. I tried to exchange my Turkish liras for Greek drachmas, but there isn't a bank in the country that will swap these currencies. Two historic rivals spitting on each other's unstable money. En route, I dodged clusters of Greek, French, and English schoolchildren and families milling about in the heat: 'Can you identify this type of column, kids?' 'No, not euphoric, they're called Doric columns.' 'Can everyone say "Pentelic marble"?'

I had always imagined from pictures that I would be able to climb the three temple steps of the Parthenon and wander around the *pronoas*. I wanted to press my tongue against the Parthenon's Doric columns (the surest way to make contact with an ancient building, according to Charles). But fences separate the Parthenon from would-be tongue pressers like myself. So I retreated to the tiny benched pavilion, the windiest spot on the Acropolis and the best place to survey Solon's gifts – the fifth-century B.C. Athenian statesman who presided over this building spree with his master architect and sculptor, Phidias. Only the structural shells remain of the once elaborate precinct buildings: the Parthenon, the Temple of Athena Nike, the Erechtheion, the Propylaea. Most of the good stuff, Phidias' sculptures and relief work known notoriously as the Elgin marbles, is stashed 1,500 miles away in London's British Museum.

Staring down on these buildings I'd seen reproduced thousands of times, I was suddenly aware that I was in the middle of the physical embodiment of architectural innovation and the perfection of form. The very complex that still today is the international symbol of the classical ideals of proportion. Then I looked down, through the smog, to modern Athens, a city teeming with cabdrivers who audition you before stopping, a city blanketed by the insistent sizzle and lamb-led-to-slaughter smell of souvlaki. Block after block of gray, concrete crumminess posed the inevitable question: 'What happened?'

It's as if the Acropolis were the epicenter of a volcanic eruption and lava drenched the city in gray detritus, leaving only the original crater of the Acropolis unscathed. The Greeks themselves, even the Athenians, are the first to admit that Athens is an armpit of a city. Of course, temples and museums preserve pockets of riches, but overall, in order to see 'the glory that was Greece' one must hightail it out of Athens. Henry Miller wrote in 1942, 'I am in Athens . . . People are asking me – have you been to Delphi, have you been to San Turini, have you been to Lesbos or Samos or Poros?' And today, too, Athenians constantly ask you where in Greece you are planning to visit, as if to say 'Don't worry, there's more than this.'

My tour of Athens was truncated by a pressing need to reach Korinth before sunset. It felt strange to have places to go and people to see in a foreign country, not to be just a tourist with time to dillydally and sip iced Nescafé frappés, a vile concoction and the revered Greek summer beverage. After retrieving my roller suitcase from the left luggage area of the Acropolis Palace hotel (bellhops, as a rule, can't distinguish legitimate guests from storage freeloaders), I stood waiting for a bus that I only hoped would take me to the main bus terminal.

Right away I learned that Greek Adonises do exist. Alexandros swaggered over as I was asking a uniformed man to direct me to Korinth, which is like asking a random person on the streets of Manhattan to direct you to Rhode Island. In halting English, Alexandros explained that he too was en route to Korinth. I thanked the gods. Alexandros was what you might call strapping, and his appearance brought to mind a half-remembered fragment of Cavafy: 'Hair as though stolen from Greek statues, / always lovely, even uncombed, / and falling slightly over pale foreheads.' We transferred buses three times to reach the main station, and with each transfer I was more grateful for Alexandros's presence. He wheeled my suitcase, then translated for me while I bought my ticket, and we raced to the final bus just as it was boarding. Two bus drivers argued over who would take this route. Alexandros explained that last minute haggling over routes was standard bus driver protocol. 'He try to trade him Korinth for Mycenae.'

The driver who ended up with Korinth acted like the winner. He took his seat grinning, and as I sat back in mine, I hoped all my travel karma would be this good. Alexandros sat next to me on the bus, and I admired the gap between his two perfectly straight front teeth. His English was good enough to explain that he was in the army and wanted to be a veterinarian. When he found out I was twenty-seven (he was nineteen), he became deferential and asked me if I had children. I had been demoted from Aphrodite to Hera. I tried to smile and asked him how to make tzatziki, thick yogurt with garlic, cucumber, and lemon. The trick is to strain the yogurt three times.

After thirty minutes, when we'd made it beyond the industrial factories on Athens's periphery and the bus chugged along stony beachfront highways, Alexandros asked, 'Why you go to Korinthos?'

'I want to learn about the baths.'

'Bath. What is bath?'

'You know, *thermae, gymnasium*. An ancient bath.'

'Oh, gymnasium. Yes, yes. I know. They are all gone. That was ancient Greece, not Greece now.'

'Yes, I know. I will visit ancient gymnasium.'

'Ahhh, you archaeologist?'

'Not exactly. I'm a student,' I said to simplify matters.

Now he understood, but seemed to think I was a rather old student. Fine. It was clear Alexandros and I had no future after this bus ride. I was an old student looking for baths that no longer exist.

I got off the bus at the Isthmus of Korinth stop, which sounded more like a movie Kirk Douglas might have made after *Spartacus* than a bus stop. The Isthmus is a narrow, seven-kilometer-long sliver separating mainland Greece from the southern Peloponnese. All north-south traffic in Greece once had to pass through the

Isthmus, making Korinth, within ten miles of the Isthmus, the second most important Greek city after Athens during the classical period. Pausanias, the ancient travel writer, referred to this part of the Peloponnese as 'well-watered Korinth' and home to one thousand sacred prostitutes on a hilltop. Yet I was completely alone on a long stretch of silent, dusty highway. I needed another Alexandros to swoop down and guide me to the Rooms Marinos.

'The Rooms Marinos, Ancient Korinth,' was all I had scrawled in my notebook, and I cursed my idiotic optimism that I would stumble onto the place. Several hundred yards away stood a high-way truck stop where leather-skinned men sat outside on plastic patio furniture, drinking beer. The gruff proprietor called me a cab. Five hours into my stay in Greece and I was already noticing something that would be confirmed again and again: Greeks, in general, aren't nearly as friendly or hospitable as Turks. (The Turks make better baklava, too). A silver Mercedes showed up to collect me (most Greek cabs are in fact Mercedeses, but I didn't know that at the time and worried that I would be seen as uppity for arriving in what I assumed was a higher-priced cab).

The tiny village of Ancient Korinth, only five minutes away, centered around a cluster of creatively named restaurants – Nikos's Place, Themis's Place, Panagiotis's Place – that served identical menus and guarded the entrance to the fenced-off archaeological site. Hidden behind the barbed wire were small, privately owned neighborhood baths called *balnea,* but we were to study a larger, grander, imperially owned bath called a *thermae* at the neighboring Isthmian site. Tourist buses were parked along the small street leading to the site, and it was clear that Korinth was a brief afternoon stop during a three-day Peloponnesian tour. The Rooms Marinos, the campus compound for anyone attached to Dr Greg Christopher's retinue, was farther up the gentle slope of Ancient Korinth, removed from the fray of the archaeological site.

I unloaded my things from the taxi and walked into the gated concrete courtyard of the Rooms Marinos. The sun was setting over the pines, and the hooting of owls replaced the cooing of doves to welcome the oncoming darkness. Fuchsia bougainvillea climbed the walls of the main house. Two dried-out fountains crowned with white plaster statues of boy gods decorated the concrete esplanade. Someone with bad taste had lavished a lot of love on this place. One hundred yards away, near some temporary goalposts, I spotted a group of doughy college students and two middle-aged men milling about. The two men regarded me curiously. I experienced a moment of buyer's remorse, and I had yet to learn that they were all Southern Baptists.

The more dominant of the two older men was thick-limbed and heavyset, his thinning black hair combed forward in a Caesar. He looked the part of a patrician and possessed an air of irritability that seemed to have nothing to do with the very pleasant circumstances – warm May evening, pines swaying gently in the breeze, the faint smell of rosemary and lamb being prepared for dinner. He took an impatient swig from a water bottle that was holstered around his waist. His nose was fried to a crisp and looked as though it might fall from his face at any moment, thereby morphing him into one of those dime-a-dozen noseless busts, the kind that litter third-rate museums. I knew immediately that this must be Dr Christopher. The other had a gentler affect – a kind, soft-contoured face with a gap between his front teeth. I'd found my grown-up Alexandros. He wore rimless glasses and had salt-and-pepper hair that made it hard to age him – anywhere from thirty-five to fifty-five. This must be the southern professor, Dr Garrett Greene, the one Dr Christopher had palmed me off on when I'd inquired the week before about digging opportunities.

It was too late to turn back. Now was the moment of awkward introductions. I barreled ahead, reminding myself that I was a confident New Yorker who'd dealt with much worse than morose professors. My arrival was welcomed with as much effusion as grisly academics muster for anyone who doesn't make tenure decisions. More accurately, Dr Christopher seemed to tolerate my presence,

whereas, by comparison, Garrett Greene seemed warm and inquis-
itive. I was shown to my room and introduced to my roommate (I
hadn't been expecting that). She was a heavyset girl named Janet
who'd brought a thick stack of Nora Roberts novels and enough
anti-everything medication to run a MASH unit for a month. Our
shared room with two cots and a barely functioning bathroom was
the size of Kemal's smaller deck. The library tour and modern Greek
lesson were in an hour, followed by a family-style dinner. I was a
freshman again.

That night at dinner, Dr Greene, who insisted I call him Garrett,
and I drank red wine, while the students sipped water and regarded
the tzatziki and spanikopita (spinach pastry) suspiciously. On the
page, Garrett was someone whose curriculum vitae would have
intimidated me, but in person he was open, accommodating, and
thoroughly unpretentious. Garrett had as much enthusiasm for tae
kwon do (he was a red belt) as for the New Testament – his area was
Paul the Apostle – and he had a knack for saying and doing the right
thing at the right time. Throughout dinner he continuously refilled
my glass, a profound gesture of understanding.

Dr Christopher was another story entirely, a man less given to
banter and the normal lubricant of social discourse than anyone I've
ever met before or since. I tried to dismiss his temperament as an
occupational hazard, remembering a description of an archaeologist
written by Francis Henry Taylor: '[He bore] all the complexities and
difficulties inherent in the true archaeologist – jealousy, infallibility
coupled with a sense of persecution and a madness for his own subject
. . . the very essence of the archaeological character and temper.'

Dr Christopher's reputation preceded him. According to sources
in the surprisingly lurid and gossipy world of academe, Dr Christopher was reputed to have a 'dig girl' each summer and to be
charming and irascible. The hard-drinking, womanizing classics
professor is practically a Jungian archetype, at least where I went
to college, so I had a ready mental image of Dr Christopher. His
reputation, however, was based on the pre–happily married man.

He was not, I discovered, just your run-of-the-mill harmless asocial misanthrope.

I suffered through the first bizarre dinner listening to Dr Christopher obsess about his cistern. It was clearly a pet project with which he'd been boring Garrett for years. Garrett nodded and responded appropriately: 'I thought you solved the sealant issue last year.' Dr Christopher wasn't quite a drone – he wasn't forthcoming enough – and he wasn't a bore because he was too elliptical. He was dismissive yet careful – without ever saying anything overtly cruel, he could shovel scorn in any direction. He was the kind of guy who emitted infinitesimally brief rays of charm only to retreat back into his tortoise shell of academic arrogance for hours.

Luckily for me, there was Garrett, with whom I felt an instant camaraderie. After dinner, he invited me to accompany him to the Platea, the town square, for a beer. It was only 9:30. We walked down the hill, inhaling the heavy honeysuckle air, past a convenience store and a small church with a cross like a tall antenna. The Platea was almost triangular. Along the base were the shops – the cluttered laundry, the village grocery store, and a bread and baklava store. The main road, congested with tour buses during the day, was lined with restaurants and souvenir shops. The tourists stayed in hotels in the modern city of Korinth or farther down the Peloponnese. That night, like most nights, was quiet. After 5:00 P.M., only the locals and the rival packs of archaeologists remain. And the locals have a second siesta between 6:00 and 7:00, when the surprisingly sinister Greek version of *Who Wants to Be a Millionaire* is shown.

Garrett and I sat outside at Nikos's Place. Nikos's was the favorite that summer; Themis, the owner of Themis's Place, had hit the ouzo hard, and his taverna had fallen to seed, or so went the local lore. And Nikos was Ancient Korinth's youngest, most charismatic taverna owner, and he spoke the best English, which made his place the taverna of the moment.

We ordered two Mythos beers, a watered-down version of Heineken. In the six years since I'd graduated from college, the experience of sitting across from a professor had changed completely. I no longer worried about saying the right thing or asking the right questions. When Garrett noticed a horde of the students coming down the hill toward Nikos's, he said, 'Ugh. The kids. I hope they're not coming over to ask about tomorrow.' I was now considered adult company. Between the teetotaling Baptist students and our acerbic host, Garrett and I were set up to become the best of friends.

'So what *are* we doing tomorrow?' I asked, using my adult dispensation to ask the annoying question.

Garrett smiled. 'Christopher's going to give us an overall introduction to the Olympic site: the athletic stadium and track, the theater, and the Temple of Poseidon. And, of course, the bath. In the coming weeks we'll devote more specialized attention to each structure. And there'll be some housekeeping duties at the dig house.'

'I can only imagine,' I said, thinking of Christopher's cistern. My mind rushed to the bath, which I imagined as a vast marble, labyrinthine structure with various chambers containing plunge pools, benches, mosaics, and columns. Finally I would see an example of the stunning bath architecture and brilliant engineering I had heard so much about. The imperial baths, after all, had been used as architectural laboratories to test wider and wider vaults and domes. Why anger the gods with faulty temple architecture when a few bathers can be sacrificed during a test run?

'I've read so much about the Roman devotion to bathing, and still it's hard to wrap my head around the extent of the obsession.'

Garrett nodded. 'Yes, it's difficult for us to imagine what an integrated role the baths played in the life of the average Roman. We live in such compartmentalized worlds by comparison. The baths were a daily pleasure, the setting in which they washed, exercised, socialized, relaxed, gazed upon art, politicked, scrounged-up dinner invitations, had sex . . .'

'Had sex?' I asked. I'd read contradictory accounts about the level of overt sexuality in the baths.

'Yes, there's a delicious body – or collection, I should say – of bath graffiti. For example, a duo from Herculaneum left many explicit clues at the Suburban Baths. Apelles and Dexter were their names, and they'd write subtle things like "Apelles and Dexter had lunch here most pleasantly and fucked at the same time."'

'Hmm, a full-service *balneum*. Who did they "fuck"? Men or women?'

'Good question. They left us a more specific line: "We, Apelles the Mouse and his brother Dexter, lovingly fucked two women twice." Also from the same room at the Suburban Baths, we find: "Two companions were here and, since they had a thoroughly terrible attendant called Epaphroditus, threw him out onto the street not a moment too soon. They then spent 105½ sesterces most agreeably while they fucked."'

The distinction between bathhouse and bordello has always been murky. Eight erotic frescoes were discovered at another of Pompeii's neighborhood baths in 1986. Scholars can't agree on what the two-thousand-year-old porn aims to suggest. Depicted in exaggerated, and some argue comical, form are various sexual acts, including the only known rendering of cunnilingus from Roman times. Are the eight sexual scenarios a menu of services available upstairs? Or, as other scholars insist, were they meant to be funny and even to serve as a mnemonic device (e.g., it's easy to remember that you left your toga under the man with the engorged testicles)?

Most baths, however, were wholesome places that often doubled as healing centers. Based on medical and nonmedical writers, we learn that the Romans considered visiting the baths indispensable to good health. Vitruvius explained that 'sulfur springs cure pains in the sinews, by warming up and burning out the corrupt humours of the body.' Galen, the ancient physician, prescribed sweat bathing to all his patients, most famously to Emperor Augustus, who apparently recovered from a life-threatening illness after frequent visits to the baths. *Placebo* does come from the Latin word for 'I will please,' but placebo or not, sweating out illnesses in the baths proved efficacious for many and was probably an excellent antidote to all the lead they were consuming. Roman aqueducts contained lead piping, and wine was stored in lead vessels; the mental instability of later Romans (think Caligula) has often been blamed on lead poisoning.

Prostitutes were not the only people pushing their wares. There's convincing evidence that medical masseurs, eye doctors, dentists, and possibly surgeons plied their trades at the baths. Lunch, a quickie, and a molar extraction could all be found under the same roof.

Garrett explained that the baths were the great social leveler in Roman society. What went on behind the scenes at the Roman baths varied and depended on that bath's specific clientele, the neighborhood, and the proclivities of the emperor at the time. Early on, during the disciplined days of the Republic, the baths were single sex, or so the architecture and literature indicate. During the second century B.C., a social revolution was under way in Rome, and women enjoyed greater liberty.

The gravitas and severitas of the Republic slowly yielded to the comparatively lighter, frolicsome mood of Augustus' empire. The first-century Stoic philosopher Seneca complained bitterly of this new laxity and effeteness. 'Yes, pretty dirty fellows they evidently were!' he said, referring to his idea of the 'good old days' when men were men. 'How they must have smelled! But they smelled of the camp, the farm, and heroism. Now that spick-and-span bathing establishments have been devised, men are really fouler than of yore.'

Ultimately, the baths were the death of Seneca. At one point, Seneca had lodgings over a bath where he daily suffered the noise from below. He describes in one of his famous letters from *Epistulae ad Lucilium,* 'the hair remover, continually giving vent to his shrill and penetrating cry in order to advertise his presence, never silent unless it be while he is plucking someone's armpits and making the client yell for him!' At the end of his life, when ordered by the emperor to commit suicide, Seneca first cut his veins. When this did not kill him, he tried hemlock. Still alive, he was brought to a bath, where he finally suffocated on the steam.

During the long, colorful period of Augustan succession, business at the baths boomed. Spa towns like Baiae near Naples boasted floating hotels on stilts, and baths were built with such care and grandeur that archaeologists later confused them with temples. Roman life was more permissive than ever, and men and women bathed together – indeed, during this period after the Republic until the time Christianity took hold, the female sex enjoyed a greater personal, sexual, and economic freedom than would be known again until the latter half of the twentieth century.

Martial, the high-living wit of late-first-century Rome, wrote of coed bathing establishments as if they were a common part of life. He wrote to Galla, the object of his quest, 'When I compliment your face, when I admire your legs and hands, you are accustomed to say, Galla, "Naked I shall please you more," yet, you continually avoid taking a bath with me. Surely, you are not afraid, Galla, that I shall not please you?' Need we greater proof of coed bathing establishments? Whereas previously scholars assumed that prostitutes were the only women to frequent the baths, literary evidence of concerns about adultery and illegitimate children proves that married or marriageable women must also have frequented the baths. Augustus even banned coed bathing temporarily because of the number of illegitimate children sired at the baths who were abandoned on the Aventine Hill.

Garrett explained all this while I sipped my Mythos and ignored the attention-seeking ploys of Nikos, the proprietor. It was amazing to have Garrett synthesize all this information, and I wondered if academics had differently wired brains.

'How is it that we end up with a Roman bath here in Greek Isthmia?' I asked.

'The Romans built baths as far as the Pax Romana extended. During the go-go days of the Roman Empire – say, the first and second centuries A.D. – the Romans had brought the Greeks to heel and conquered most of Asia and Africa. After the fall of the Greek city-state, Greece itself became a Roman province, though it always maintained its cultural superiority. But one area where the Romans excelled with just the slightest germ of Greek inspiration was in their enormous *thermae* complexes.'

'And did all Romans get to bathe or just the wealthy?'

'Everyone went, even the slaves. Not to bathe would be un-Roman, so barbarians, philosophers, and Christians were often considered fringe citizens. The imperial *thermae* were dubbed "people's palaces" or "pagan cathedrals." It was the one way that even the poor could share the empire's wealth. There's no equivalent in today's society.'

God, Garrett was clever. He was a virtual encyclopedia and yet also capable of insightful commentary. And he never sounded bored with what he was saying, the way professors so often do. I could be happy with a man who possessed Garrett's knowledge, Kemal's physicality, and Charles's emotional depth, I thought, suddenly realizing the truth of the Russian saying 'A woman needs three men: one for her mind, one for her body, and one for her heart.'

We stared at our empty beer glasses. 'Do you want to see the Odeon? It's just down the road,' said Garrett.

'I'd love to.' We settled up with Nikos ('Don't leave – it's so early') and strolled down the dark, deserted street past shuttered souvenir shops. Shortly we came upon a barbed-wire fence with a hole just large enough to accommodate a human body, and we both climbed through into the Odeon. The theater, a semicircle with at least forty rows of steep seating, was a smaller and more intimate venue than a coliseum. Here the Romans staged mock naval battles (a favorite Roman entertainment) and the latest works of the playwrights Terence and Plautus. Garrett and I sat high in the nosebleed seats and stared down at the steppes of vine-covered farmland. From underneath the stage, a testament to marvelous acoustics, we heard dogs loudly nuzzling each other.

'Why did the baths die out?' I asked. It seemed an appropriate question in the darkness.

'In the case of the Isthmian bath, and the baths of Rome, for that matter, everything changed in the fifth century. The Roman Empire's influence, especially in the provinces, was waning. The Goths, Visigoths, and Vandals were attacking from the north and destroying the aqueduct system in the process. Paganism's end was at hand. Zeus and Hera and the entire Olympian family went into exile, and the Christian Church began demanding a lot more than hecatombs of cattle from its subjects. The church mandated a certain standard of behavior in which bathing nude each afternoon was not a part.'

'The beginning of the Dark Ages,' I offered.

'Exactly,' said Garrett, and he explained that in Isthmia, the Temple of Poseidon and the Roman bath both display unrepaired cracks, broken pipes, and fire damage from around this time. In fact, the abandonment of the temple and the bath occurred simultaneously in roughly 400 A.D. The bath-and-banquet lifestyle that the security of the Pax Romana allowed was a thing of the past.

Conversation had at last exhausted itself. Tomorrow would be a long day on-site. We headed back up the hill, stopping to peer through the barbed wire protecting the other side of the Korinthian site. The moon bathed the forty-foot Corinthian columns in dim yellow light. We listened to the crickets hiding in the flowers and inhaled rich bouquets of honeysuckle.

Early the next morning we set out for Isthmia, walking single file through tall grass and prickly scrubs, past groves of orange blossom and lemon trees. I was filled with the giddiness of anticipation. I'm not sure exactly what I was expecting, but I was expecting a kind of clarity, a visual image of a bath, remnants of *something* for my imagination to riff with. While most people go to Rome to glimpse Roman baths, I'd ventured all the way to the Peloponnese, in search of something richer: a Roman bath with Greek roots.

All my rosy expectations were shattered, however, as we made our way through an opening in the pockmarked fence and tramped down a long, gentle slope that led into the valley of the Isthmian ruins.

Garrett pointed to a southern part of the valley. 'There it is.'

'Where?' I asked, seeing only an empty valley with odd clumps of stone overlooking a ravine. 'There?'

'Yes, there,' he said comfortingly.

I could tell that he was used to dealing with students disappointed by the fragmentary remains of archaeology. But why hadn't he told me last night that this was all there was? I'd seen aqueducts in southern France and wandered into decaying coliseums and always been dazzled by the remains. But Isthmia's Olympic Village was nothing more than a field of rubble. My mind was spinning. Where were the marble riveted walls I'd read about? Where were the furnaces, the columns, and the plunge pools? In short, where was the bath? These couldn't even be called ruins; they were more like the ruins of ruins.

Students in T-shirts and Tevas wandered around under a sun so scorching hot that we were like ants under a seventh grader's heat lamp. My throat felt as parched as the cracked ground, and I had no water to tide me over until lunchtime. I'd finally arrived at the much-anticipated bath and all I was thinking about was saliva generation. Around Dr Christopher's waist hung his trusty holster of water; every time he took a swig from his one-liter jug I got thirstier.

I should say a few more words about Dr Christopher and the perils of asking him questions like 'Where is the bath?' I'd never met a real-life Jekyll–Hyde personality until now. His actions, allowing students rare access to his site and research facilities, displayed an altogether Jekyll-like good intention. His insuppressible Hyde side emerged in his disdain for those less intelligent than himself, which was just about everybody. What began as cute, witty stories and charming Socratic questions turned taunting and degrading when the students lacked his intuition or the confidence to venture an answer.

Christopher might point to some circular cuttings in the earth and say, 'What do you think caused these cuttings?' Loud silence. 'Was it a spaceship?' he'd ridicule. 'Perhaps, but probably not.' Long pause as everyone examined their shoelaces. 'Well, of course it was a door! Those are the grooves caused by the door opening and closing.' Of course! He floated in a transmillennia bubble. 'Look at me,' he'd exclaimed. 'Archaeologists can walk through walls.' And as he'd walk from room to room, where once there were walls, I wondered which period, antiquity or the modern day, was more alive in his mind. Who was more real, Herodes Atticus, the man reputed to have built the Isthmian bath, or the twelve of us standing in front of him on this sweltering May day?

Christopher took us on a dizzying tour of what would have been the *tepidarium* (warm room), *caldarium* (hot room), *frigidarium* (cold plunge pools), and the underground alcove where the hidden slaves fed the furnaces. I took notes in my small orange notebook, citing the irregularities in where the drain channels connected, the mystery surrounding the destruction of the bath. Fire? Earthquake? Christian destruction? We simply don't know. Dr Christopher addressed all the questions raised by physical remains of the bath.

So relentless was his attention to evidence, evidence, evidence, that when he asked, 'Does anyone know what this room would have been used for?' I answered: 'The *frigidarium*?'

'Why?' he asked.

'I don't know, it just has that . . . *vibe*.' Garrett suppressed a laugh, and Christopher curled his lip. I knew it was a word he'd hate.

'Lucky guess. You're right, because this was a ring-style bath, where the bather would progress in a circle from warm to hot to cold. From the placement of this room, we can deduce its purpose.'

'What did the Romans do inside the bath?' I asked Dr Christopher, hoping he might detail Roman habits and lifestyle and not just their brilliant engineering.

Dr Christopher informed us that they had found strigils inside the bath. Strigiling, in addition to sweating, was the main *caldarium* activity. The strigil was an odd device used for cleaning the body that the Romans copied from the Greeks. A strigil, usually wrought in iron so it wouldn't bend, looked like a cross between a sugar spoon and a meat hook. After working up a healthy glow, the bather would rub a sand-and-olive-oil mixture onto his body. Rubbing this gritty substance on the body exfoliated all the dirt and dead skin, then the bather would start scraping the sand mixture off his body using the strigil. The sand and olive oil scooped up by the strigil was then flicked onto the walls, where it was believed to add a curative effect to the surroundings. Even though modern medicine might tell us otherwise, I would have preferred ancient levels of sanitation to the present-day bathrooms of the Rooms Marinos.

We walked through the banquet room, covered by a protective tarp weighted down with pebbles, and stepped over the fifteen-inch remains of a wall into room one. The archaeologists have assigned numbers to each room. 'Everything must have a name,' Dr Christopher would repeat six times daily. If you had no idea what an object was used for, it might become 'piece five found in basket four of trench two.' Rather than make any assumptions about what a ceramic shard or a room was used for, everything was classified according to location. Archaeology is an art that doesn't allow for editorializing.

Room one, Dr Christopher explained, was probably the *apodyterium*. Athletes and Poseidon's pilgrims – Isthmia's main customers – would pass into this room after paying the *balneator* at the door, who, if he was a nice guy, would bid them the customary *bene laves* (bathe well!). In the *apodyterium,* a large rectangular room with benches and overhead cubicles, street tunics or competition garb (unlike Greek athletes, Roman athletes did not compete in the nude) were replaced with lighter cotton bathing tunics and wooden sandals to protect feet from the hot marble floors. Bathers would deposit their valuables, street sandals, and sesterces in the cubicles. Rich customers could afford to leave slaves to watch their belongings, but most people had to take their chances, and theft was common.

This Isthmian bath was surprisingly grand and ornate considering its backwater location. Yes, it lacked the epic proportions of the Roman imperial *thermae* (the Baths of Caracalla in Rome were a thirty-acre palatial waterworld!), but Isthmia wasn't Rome after all, it was an Olympic outpost used every two years as well as a destination for Poseidon-worshiping pilgrims. Like the three other Olympic sites – Olympus, Delphi, and Nemea – Isthmia had to have a large bath complex for athletes, spectators, and pilgrims alike. But where the Isthmian baths surpassed the other Olympic baths, and raised so many questions among archaeologists, was in its enormous banquet hall with a magnificently wrought monochromic mosaic, the largest and most accomplished in the eastern Mediterranean.

Tomorrow we would be indulged in our only 'digging' responsibility. We would shovel away the pebbles, remove the protective tarp, and water down the mosaic to reveal the enormous rectangular nautical tableaux. Depicted in tiny black-and-white squares were a small army of Nereids riding Tritons. In the center, Eros drove a dolphin while other dolphins playfully leapt about with eels, lobsters, squid, and octopi. The subject matter was standard stuff for a bath situated next to a Temple of Poseidon, yet the execution and scale were quite sophisticated. More romantic theories suggest that after Herodes Atticus' younger lover drowned, Atticus was looking for an appropriate tribute.

Isthmia's gargantuan banquet hall also pointed toward the future role of baths in the eastern Mediterranean according to ancient bathing scholars (a surprising hotbed of study) like Fikret Yegül, dubbed Mr Roman Bath. The Roman *thermae* evolved differently in different regions of the empire. In the East, the *thermae* was slowly transformed into the more introverted hamam, an inward-looking building suited to a modest religion. The central room of early Islamic baths, aka hamams, was a large banquet hall used for socializing or cultural activities. Here in Isthmia's luxurious banquet hall, with its decorative mosaic and massive statues – a room obviously designed for social instead of athletic interaction – we see the first hint of a changing bath architecture, a small nod to future hamams.

Studying the Isthmian dig's field notebooks was fascinating intellectually, and for a day or so I even fantasized about enrolling in archaeology graduate school. But the study of baths wasn't as interesting as the practice. As John, the only hothead among the Baptist students, said after Dr Christopher waxed for forty minutes on exactly what the Temple of Poseidon would have looked like 1,800 years ago: 'Well, it's not here now. Let's go eat.' I was starting to relate to that sentiment; there was only so much time I could give to suspending my disbelief about walls, arches, and domes that no longer existed.

I realized that my trip had reversed the flow of history – from Istanbul to the Roman world. I was time-traveling back through the empires: Istanbul to Constantinople to Byzantium; then, sidestepping down the Dardanelles, I'd encountered the destruction of the pagan world, the riches of the Roman-occupied Peloponnese, and the innovations of the Greeks. I had arrived two thousand years too late. The Roman bathing scene was in ruins, and the Turkish scene wasn't far behind.

It was time to leap ahead to the contemporary havens of public baths, where spa culture was still communal: to Russia, to Finland, to Japan. And why not? I no longer had a job, and Charles promised to come and visit. Yet again I extended my return, enjoying the continued liberation from the trivial worries of home – Did I lock the door? Is it garbage night? All of life's business was in able hands with Charles. Bills would get paid; the apartment wouldn't burn down. I was free to explore my fascination with public baths, the physical spaces, the swirl of activity around them, the secret parts of people that emerged when inside. This was no longer just 'taking the measurements,' as Marina and I had done in Istanbul. This had turned into, well, the search for the perfect bath.

russia:
vodka, sex, and banyas

A banya without steam is like cabbage soup with no grease floating on top.

— Old Russian proverb

Perhaps the march of time would be less marked in Russia. The Russians are certainly proud of their Russianness, and perhaps this nationalistic pride translated into holding on to village traditions like the banya. I had always heard that there were four prerequisites to being Russian: weekly visits to the banya, drinking either too much vodka or none at all, easy access to cheap caviar, and the right to enjoy your suffering. Russians suffer with style. In America, suffering veers toward self-pity; the Russians, however, manage to imbue suffering with nobility.

My great-grandfather Isidore Sirota was born in Belarus, often referred to as 'White Russia,' before immigrating to New York City at sixteen years old. Izzie was not the vodka-drinking, caviar-eating, long-suffering variety of Russian. He did, however, carry with him, from old country to new, a lifelong appreciation of the *shvitz*, the

Yiddish word for a banya. The banya, which translates as 'bathhouse,' transcends its literal definition and its humble architecture – a
dark-wooded hut containing a furnace of hot rocks. Moreover, it
inspires a distinct way of life with its own menu, accoutrements,
appointed hour, ceremony, and ritual.

I lived with a Soviet TV journalist turned fiction writer turned tour
guide named Irina. No patronymic, just Irina. According to Irina,
journalists shed their fathers' names in classless togetherness. Irina was
a miniaturized aging Bond girl of the Ursula Andress school, a petite
blond with wide-set small brown eyes and cheeks that resembled
split-open peaches. Twenty-five years ago she must have been a
knockout, and there was still an unmistakable feistiness in her eyes and
the way she sashayed around in her high-heeled black boots.

Irina had perfected the art of spin. When I stepped into her tiny
fifth-floor walk-up apartment, hyperventilating and disoriented, she
greeted me with a Cheshire cat smile and the loud impersonal boom
of a tour guide: 'Welcome to your beautiful home.' Of course, I
couldn't help but smile back, grateful to see my first friendly Russian
face and to have a place at last to put down my suitcase. I ignored the
moldy beer factory smell and quickly slipped off my shoes, as the
guidebooks instruct. But the guidebooks also say your host will offer
you slippers, and Irina didn't. I was stumped.

She toured me through the apartment, smiling like a delirious
Vanna White: 'This is the kitchen, where I will serve you a delicious
breakfast every morning. Now come, I will show you to your
beautiful room.' I followed her down the short, narrow corridor
with peeling rose-patterned wallpaper. 'And this is your wonderful
room. Now I leave you to put away your things.' I looked around
my beautiful, wonderful room, with an old, fusty leather sofa you
might find in a 1890s train station, dusty bookcases, and a bed
designed to produce instant insomnia. I flicked on the switch to the
crooked chandelier. Only one bulb illuminated. Thank God for
white nights. I looked at the solid oak writing desk. Home office.

Sweet. Then I looked at the bed more closely: a one-inch-thick foam futon on top of a blue plastic frame. I sat down and the frame teetered and almost buckled under my weight.

How did I end up in this person's home? I wondered to myself. It was disorienting for me to be here, but I imagined how scary it must be for Irina to open her home to random foreigners. It's not as if the host organization that brokers these home stays does any sort of background check on those of us drifting through Russia.

Irina bounced in and wanted to give a tutorial on locking the front door and using the bathroom. If there was ever a time to be happy I was doing research on public baths, it was when I saw Irina's bathtub: small and stained reddish brown by the rusty water. I knew my search for the perfect bath was not going to end in Irina's apartment. At first I took the water stains as a good sign, a sure sign that there was indeed water, but when I saw the rate at which water trickled out of the faucet, I realized it was a miracle that this tub had water stains at all.

My banya research must start straight away. The next morning, I showed Irina my list of St Petersburg banyas that I had heard or read about (a dozen or so of the fifty-eight listed banyas in St Petersburg): Kruglye, Banya #50, Banya #51, Banya #24, Banya #45, Nevskie, Yamskiye. During Soviet times, all banyas were state owned and operated and were identified by numbers instead of jazzy names like the Comrade's Hot Rocks. Indeed, under the Soviets the banyas proliferated in much the same way the Roman *thermae* had two thousand years before. Down at the Politburo, the Soviet leaders joked, just as the Romans had, that the decline and fall of the Soviet empire was directly related to the explosion of banyas and the ensuing debauchery and heat-induced laziness.

The reason behind the 'banya for the masses' plan was quite simple: Going to the banya was a classless weekly pleasure enjoyed by all Russians. Building palatial sweat lodges with tiled pools for comrades to sweat together helped perpetuate the myth of the utopian Soviet state. Not to mention that the banyas were an ideal environment to purge oneself of the toxins that sadly became a fact of life under communism.

Irina scanned my list, smiling, looking nostalgic, and nodding her head.

'So many banya memories. I haven't been in years.'

'Where should I go, Irina?'

'You really want to go? These places not Western. Nobody speak English.'

'Well, maybe I'll pick up some Russian.'

Irina cocked one eyebrow at me. Over breakfast that morning, she had labored to teach me some simple Russian phrases and was less than dazzled by my linguistic abilities. I had studied Romance languages in school – French and Italian – but the unlikely bunching of consonants in Russian was unutterable for me.

'Go to Tchaykovsky,' she said with characteristic certainty. 'Walk down Nevsky Prospekt to the Fontanka River. You'll see two bronze horsemen, there should be four, but two are getting fixed. There take a right and walk for a long time, past Anna Akhmatova's house, past Peter's Palace in the park, then you'll see it on your right. Wait, first I call and make sure it's not free day.'

'Free day? Free day sounds good.'

'No, not good. Not pretty. Each banya once a week have free day for poor people. Not nice time to go.'

She called the banya, and it was a regular fee-paying day.

'Watch your dress.'

'What?'

'I have my dress once stolen at Tchaykovsky banya. Oh, it was a terrible picture. There is me, after banya, naked and looking like a duck, and the banya lady she steals my new flower cotton dress. Oh yes, a very terrible picture. I walked home naked in my coat.'

I hit the Nevsky Prospekt with a backpack full of banya essentials: little plastic bottles filled with soap, shampoo, and conditioner, and my faithful green rubber flip-flops. They had trudged through nearly fifty hamam visits in Turkey, and now they were about to be exposed to serious banya heat.

I walked up the east bank of the Fontanka River, a seven-kilometer river that draws an arc around the heart of St Petersburg and comprises the popular tourist stomping ground known as 'within the Fontanka.' The Fontanka is a wider, more magisterial tributary than the shaded, ambling, canal-like Moyka, where Tolstoy had his home. I reached the point where the Fontanka flows into the Neva, the huge river that hems the city to the south. In the winter, Russian parents still dunk their newborn children through holes in the icy Neva in an ancient rite, a pagan peasant baptism reputed to improve the child's heartiness if it doesn't kill him first. Just before the vortex of the Fontanka and the Neva, on the western bank, I saw the gardens of Peter the Great's humble brick-and-stucco Summer Palace, his first imperial dwelling just an unpretentious cut above the wood cabin he lived in previously. It would take only four years for him to bury his peasant values and build himself the Versailles-inspired Peterhof at enormous expense.

With no time to dawdle at cultural relics, I promptly took a right on Tchaykovsky Street and right there, just as Irina promised, was a sign advertising Banya #17. Despite the end of communism, the banyas still lack more individual names, though people refer to them by their location. But I was learning that this is a common Russian phenomenon. Russians don't devote thought to coming up with clever names for commercial establishments. Instead of christening one's private business with a catchy, memorable name that might lead to an identifiable client base, Russians settle for names like *obuf* or *producti,* meaning, respectively, 'shoes' or 'products.'

No bustle or vestige of human life animated Tchaykovsky Street, and I feared that the banya inside would be as abandoned as many of the hamams I visited. Once off the city's main boulevards, St Petersburg felt empty and desolate, like people inhabiting the set of a movie that finished filming long ago. I walked into an enormous darkened lobby with what has to be the world's largest coat check.

Rows and rows of naked hangers wound back into emptiness. But there was no attendant and there were no coats. Directly in front of me, an old woman sat scrunched up on a stool behind a plate-glass window. She was the only life form in the lobby. I couldn't read the Russian sign, so I just walked up to her and whispered, 'Banya?' in a way that sounded unintentionally conspiratorial.

'*Da, banya.*' She nodded while staring down at the pages of a thick paperback. I expected her to name a hugely inflated price. Most Russian institutions, like the Kirov Ballet and the Hermitage Museum, have a separate set of prices for Westerners, and it's often ten times the Russian price. But at the Tchaykovsky banya, the price was 3 rubles (roughly 10 cents) for everyone.

After collecting the tiny fee, she waved me upstairs, as if our transaction were an ordinary occurrence. I expected her to recognize how far off the beaten path I'd traveled or at least to act mystified, as the hamam ladies had, when I turned up day after day. But the Russians are as introverted as the Turks are extroverted.

I wandered upward in this cavernous building, like the colossal public schools built in the 1950s and later demolished because they were lined with asbestos. Signs in Cyrillic bounced me from room to room until I saw two women in their mid-twenties with flushed faces and damp hair. 'Banya?' I asked.

'*Da, banya,*' and they pointed to a door on my right and walked on.

I had reached my destination. My first Russian banya. Fifteen women were staring at me. Fifteen people giving me the once-over, glancing at my purple shoes and khaki capri pants and registering my otherness. Having satisfied their curiosity, they went back to their preening.

I disrobed quickly. Once naked, my otherness disappeared. I wanted to be one of them. I had read about the Russian ideal of *sobornost,* roughly translated as 'togetherness.' Travel writer Colin Thubron in *Among the Russians* explained how this concept of *sobornost* goes back to the *obschina,* the old Slavic village assembly, in which decisions had to be unanimous. To dissent was to proclaim yourself a heretic. Collective unanimity prevailed over the individual. I remembered one of the slogans of the Communist revolution: 'If you are not with us, you are against us.' Perhaps I was being too literal to view the banya through this lens, but there is something of the town assembly in the banya proceedings. And as I was about to learn, if you deviate from banya etiquette, the Russian women are not shy about correcting you.

The whole washing room, the *moechnaya,* as it's called, was abuzz with incredible female energy. Mothers braided their daughters' hair. Women walked nude and purposeful about the room. They tended proprietarily to silver buckets, fed their bodies or large bowls with a hose, stood for long intervals under showers, or washed the soap from their bodies using bowl after bowl of water. Women shaved and masked and plucked and preened. Every woman demonstrated what seemed to be her own intricate and personal ablution. The comforting country smell of hay fields after a long rain pervaded the room. I traced the smells to herbs and branches stewing in plastic buckets all around the room.

I showered (rule number one, 'Wash before bathing,' prevails everywhere) and watched people look at me. Mostly they were trying to figure out how to talk to me. One old babushka came up and started speaking a flurry of Russian. I gave the polite universal shrug for 'Forgive me, I do not speak your language,' and she started pointing to my watch and shaking her head no. I tried to mime, 'It's waterproof.' Still she would not let it rest. This was my first taste of the Russian fanaticism for rules and strict protocol. The watch came off.

After showering underneath a rusty spigot and washing St Petersburg off my sandaled feet, I followed the flow of women into a room with a heavy planked wooden door such as one you might find at a remote log cabin in the Adirondacks.

'Banya?' I asked.

'Da, banya. Parilka,' a young woman answered emphatically.

More lessons from the Russians. So this was the parilka, the fabled interior *hot hot hot* room where all the banya action happens. It wasn't so much a room as a state of mind, a treehouse on stilts in a concrete box. The treehouse was constructed with planks of dark, auburn wood the brownish red hue of cellos and violins. Strewn across the floor, as if a hurricane had just blown through, were birch leaves and twigs. The slow wheeze of steam and the incessant chatter of the women completed the illusion of a gathering of *Macbeth*'s witches in this St Petersburg banya.

I stared at the disarray, clutching my water bottle. The only water bottle in the room. More otherness. Many of the women stopped talking for a moment to look at me curiously. They were all wearing felt hats or kerchiefs in their hair, and almost all of them were holding veyniks, bouquets of leafy twigs twined together. Trying to act nonchalant, I sat on the lowest bench and breathed in deeply, pulling the heat close to my body. I imagined my body as a cappuccino machine, a vessel heated and pressurized and bursting with steam. The first beads of sweat started to form on my forehead, hairline, and the small of my back. I thought about Irina's spare room and decided that sleeping on the floor wouldn't be so bad. I even imagined that Irina and I might visit a banya together. I glanced out the small window in the parilka. The evening sun at nine o'clock still glared in. I noticed that my nose tingled and burned when I inhaled, a stiff shot of wasabi to the brain. Nowhere on my body was as hot as my toenails. The heat was massaging my body everywhere and all at once. My brain was slowing down, no longer bothering me with its constant critical interior monologue. At last, the inner voice was shutting up for a while.

The peace was short-lived. A woman with a gold-capped front tooth sitting next to me began to talk at hurricane speed and gesticulated madly to my hair. In the international code of female vanity, I made out that she was concerned that my hair would fry in the heat. She gathered a small fistful of my hair, took the ends in her hand, rubbed them together like sandpaper, and somehow managed the English: 'Split ends.' Ahh, beauty magazine, spreading a veritable Esperanto. Words like *cellulite, split ends, exfoliate,* and *Wonderbra* are almost universally understood. Why she should have cared about my hair enough to spend three minutes lecturing me in the heat, I didn't know. But Russians do have this fanaticism about their superstitious rules. I was the banya dissenter, the banya heretic without a kerchief and veynik.

I bobbed my head and clicked my tongue, '*Da . . . da . . . da . . . da . . . da,*' to her instructions at appropriate intervals. Then the *thwack*ing began and spread like hiccups to all the other women. First the lady with the gold-capped front tooth, the queen bee of the parilka, lifted her birch branch bouquet and began flagellating herself like a penitent Christian at Easter. She arched her neck and beat her breast, décolletage, and back in quick, snapping wrist motions. A mottled red design slowly tattooed her torso, and she moved her staccato brush strokes onto the legs. Meanwhile a chorus of other self-flagellators had begun. A young woman next to me said, '*Paritsa nye staritsa.*'

'What's that?' I asked.

'Old Russian saying. If you *paritsa* like this,' she said, indicating the beating action, 'then you don't *staritsa* – get old.' Eternal youth through leaf-whipping welts.

'Veynik – for you,' she offered.

'Really, are you sure?'

'Yes, I am done. And you need veynik for your first Russian banya.' So I took the veynik from her and plunged it into a bucket of warm water, and when the women started their next chorus of self-flagellation, I lifted my veynik with them. As the fresh birch leaves danced through the hot air, they released the smell of forest walks after a rain. The leaves were warm and supple from soaking, and the self-flagellation, while it sounded like punishment, delivered the same relief as a good back scratch. Was I doing it wrong? Shouldn't it hurt? This was Russia after all. Suffering is the goal. But the nose-singeing heat was punishing enough. My skin soon mottled into red

Rorschach tests. The capillaries widen when exposed to the banya's heat. The veynik *thwack*ing had pulled all the blood to the surface and created blotchy tattoos, red badges of pride.

The other women smiled at me encouragingly, as though I were a young student who had surpassed their early low expectations. I was one of them, one of the banya witches. Ask a Slavonic peasant where is the most dangerous place for magic and divination, and she will reply, 'The bathhouse at midnight.' Village bathhouses were dangerous, dilapidated places and were superstitiously avoided when not in use at the appointed bathing hours.

And here I was among the banya witches in their felt hats, stewing their mystery herbs and spitting three times to the left (okay, not quite) as they passed the threshold of the parilka. This was the surest transport to the witches' refrain *'Double, double, toil and trouble; Fire burn and cauldron bubble.'* Any one of these women around me could have been the dreaded *bannitsa,* the most hostile of the Russian goblins and a threat to newborn children.

The *bannitsa* was the reason that the midwife would walk naked three times around the bathhouse with the newborn child. Most women, including the czarina, gave birth in the village bathhouse, but always in the company of at least two others to fight off the scourge of the *bannitsa.* In Russia, 'The banya is your second mother' was a common saying, not only because the banya nourished people throughout their lives, but because until the twentieth century most people entered the world on a banya bench. The banya was roomy and the benches clean, and the hut itself was removed from the rabble and clutter of the family and house. (The logic there was that if the banya burned down, as it frequently did, the house and hearth would not also catch fire.) If given a choice today between having a baby in a banya or in one of the virulent Russian hospitals, the choice would be obvious, at least for me. From what I had seen and read so far, this was one country not to have an appendicitis attack in.

I burst out on the street ecstatic from the sisterhood of my first banya visit. I'd been accepted into the sorority. I didn't speak their language. I didn't have the right accessories. But I had enthusiasm. I understood banya ethos. I will admit that there was part of me that thought upon entering the parilka, Is this all? After the grandiose marble halls of Istanbul and the crumbling yet majestic baths of antiquity the rustic village aesthetic felt, well, too drab and coarse. But the banya had one huge leg up on the hamam: it still pulsated with conversation and laughter. Inside Tchaykovsky I found a vibrant little village. The voices – at turns secretive, authoritative, soft, and warm – the sloshing of water from a discarded bucket, the sharing of branches, the not minding one's own business. A free-for-all parade of banya shoulder-rubbing *sobornost*.

Reveling in this quintessentially Russian ritual connected me in a mysterious way to a place where I was the ultimate foreigner. It was as if I'd come to Russia to partake in the ritual and liturgy of the Russian Orthodox Church. I would be accepted. I would find a community. Banya life is no different. I could walk the streets of St Petersburg with a stronger notion of belonging, a greater sense of sympathy and understanding for the people around me, because I'd just bathed with them or their mothers or sisters.

By the time I left the banya it was 10:30 P.M., but with white nights it looked and felt like 2:00 P.M. on a Sunday afternoon. Throngs of people traversed Nevsky Prospekt, giddy with a night that refused to fall. At a bright corner along the Fontanka, a large ensemble street band pounded out Louisiana blues, while nearby fashionable St Petersburgers chain-smoked at the cafés. In front of a captivated audience, a lanky young man with pupils dilated so wide that they threatened to flood the whites of his eyeballs held a microphone to his yellow teeth and sang a slow, sultry version of 'Light My Fire.' For him the night was about to end unless it was chemically resurrected. I watched him, enchanted and vicariously drugged, through his three-song set. Then I moved on, past vendors of AC/DC bootlegs, past the sherbet pink-and-purple buildings still shadowless in the 11:00 P.M. sun. Everybody was smiling, enjoying the freakish sun of the fifty-ninth parallel, the insomniac lunacy of another sleepless night. No darkness to signal dinner, to signal sleep, to signal the end of the day.

In addition to the delirium of white nights, St Petersburg was preparing herself for the three hundredth anniversary of Peter's founding of the city in 1703. It felt rather like walking in on an over-the-hill, half-naked woman of ill repute exchanging her tattered, faded imperial clothes for something more practical. Construction crews gussied up all the main boulevards. Sidewalks were torn up and expanded, roads repaved, grime-coated pink-and-purple buildings finally getting their faces washed. The rivalry between the oft and loudly lauded mayor of Moscow, Yuri Luzhkov, and the underdog mayor of St Petersburg, Vladimir Yakovlev, was waged in this rather overzealous, frantic fight to restore the Tolstoyan luster to St Peterburg in time for the tercentenary galas in May 2003. St Petersburg has always been Russia's most liberal, urbane, and self-proclaimed 'European' city. The Kirov Ballet at St Petersburg's Mariinsky Theater is superior to Moscow's Bolshoi Ballet, though the Bolshoi has the better brand name in the West. And Tolstoy, Turgenev, and Dostoyevsky were all St Petersburgers. Now I was going to do my own St Petersburg–versus-Moscow banya comparison.

Marina was to arrive tomorrow, and I couldn't wait. So far I'd been asking random people – the man who sold rabbitskin hats at the market, the lady at the Georgian pastry shop, a Versaced-out girl who looked like a Memorex version of herself – 'Where can I find a good banya?' I learned the Russian carefully: *'Kakaya vasha ljubimaya banya?'* I received the oddest stares. This was the one sentence I could speak in perfect Russian, and the randomness of the request struck many of my polling victims as funny. Yet every single person I asked had an opinion on the subject. The rabbit-hat seller went every two weeks with friends. A rowdy group of his male friends would rent out the entire luxury section of the banya for an evening of bachelor party antics. The lady who sold me my breakfast pastry every morning was a fan of Nevskie Banii (just around the corner from Irina's), which had been closed for repairs for the last year; now she hiked out to a 'village banya' in the St Petersburg suburbs, where there was a pond to swim in between parilka sessions. And the Memorex girl claimed that Moscow banyas like the Sandunovskye were far superior. On the banya question, as on any subject, every Russian had an opinion that was always expressed as fact.

Irina's English was pretty limited. After a dazzling display of sisterhood when I first arrived, we had settled into a state of mutual toleration. My stock skyrocketed when Marina arrived five days into my stay. Just in time, too, because breakfast had degenerated into hardened cream logs covered in chocolate. Not exactly how Lance Armstrong started his day. Also, Irina had started smoking her Capri cigarettes after breakfast while bemoaning with every puff how 'unclean' it was to smoke. I had given her a box of chocolates upon arriving, and she would dutifully eat one after her cigarette every morning. 'Not good for your figure,' she decided for me.

'Irina, my friend arrives tomorrow. Stay for three nights. Then we go to Moscow together,' I told her in simplified English. This is why foreigners speak fragmented English, I'm convinced, because we native speakers trim away all the grammatical subtleties in speaking to them like deaf preschoolers.

Her face lit up and she kept repeating, 'Not a problem. Not a problem.' I soon realized that it was not a problem because she was charging another $15 a night for Marina to sleep on the cracked leather couch. In Russia at this time, $15 went about as far as $100 in the States – that's if you're buying from the Russian economy, and there are two distinct economies.

The next afternoon, I brought Marina back to our little Nevsky Prospekt pied-à-terre. Irina happened to be there, coloring her hair. 'Irina, I thought you were giving tour of Peterhof?'

'No, group from Caucasus never came,' she said, somewhat annoyed and put out that we were seeing her in a plastic hairnet.

'This is my friend Marina from London.'

Then Marina greeted her in flowing Russian – as I listened to her, I imagined a Cyrillic thought bubble floating around the room – and Irina's annoyance turned to shock, then enchantment, and immediately she started plying Marina with questions. Marina tolerated the barrage of questions that ran the gamut from 'How did you learn such lovely Russian?' to 'What do you like to eat for breakfast?' Then Irina turned to me and said, 'Oh, Alexia, you did not say friend speak Russian. And such beautiful Russian. What can I fix you for breakfast? Anything you want.' In Irina's world, there was unmistakable causality between personal approval and performance of household tasks. For the next three days, she served all of Marina's favorite Russian delicacies, like tvorog, sweet milk curds. She even did our laundry for free, where previously she'd quoted me $5 a load.

On top of all the food bounty, old maps of St Petersburg were dusted off. Irina then drew us little walking tour maps and made lists of places for us to visit – Anna Akhmatova's house, Dostoyevsky's house, the Engineer's Palace at midnight. Irina was suddenly the full-service host mom, all because she thought my friend was an exiled Russian princess. 'Where did she learn such beautiful Russian?'

The next morning at breakfast, Irina, who now understood my banya mission, decided that she must weigh in. As we drank our second cup of tea, Irina gave us an unsolicited list of inconvenient places we shouldn't miss.

'And after all this activity, which banya should we visit, Irina?'

She took a deep breath and looked dreamy. Marina and I glanced at each other with raised eyebrows. This would be our third dramatic monologue by Irina. Last night we'd sat through a forty-five-minute exegesis on the tempestuous relationship between Turgenev and Tolstoy, and yesterday afternoon it was twenty minutes on the noble life of long-suffering Russian poetess Anna Akhmatova, whose Modigliani portrait hung in the kitchen.

Ever the drama queen, Irina looked at us with the mysterious smile of a woman about to confide. 'I collect banyas in my heart.'

I dared not look at Marina for fear that we would fall apart laughing. Get ready for *Banya: The Miniseries,* I thought. By injecting her favorite English word, *turmoil,* often enough, Irina could make any story sound like an epic melodrama.

'Many, many banyas I visit, and I store in my heart. Beautiful memories. All my life I visit banyas. But then there was much turmoil.'

She paused, as if to steady herself for an outpouring of emotion. 'The banya was my muse. Picture this, Alexia, I used to go skiing with my ex-husband outside of St Petersburg at our dacha. We skied very long and got very cold. After skiing we light banya fire and the hot banya on my cold skin felt very nice. There we would stay many hours, telling stories, eating, using the veynik, ex-husband and other men drinking, always drinking. Then I would come home. I would try to sleep but couldn't. I would get up and write all night until dawn, my head clear. All worries removed by the banya.'

Before we could say anything, she continued, 'I remember well my first trip to the banya. The year was 1945 and I was living in Leningrad with my mother and her sister and her daughter during the war. Such turmoil. All the men away. Victory is announced and we go to the banya to celebrate. I remember this banya on Nikravsava Street. It was built before the revolution in the 1890s, so it was well built, with marble floors and a beautiful cast-iron staircase. I remember a huge line to get in. Finally we get tickets for the first class on the third floor. There's an enormous bathtub for children there. It's my first time to see a bathtub like this, and I cannot believe it. Our mothers leave us there for hours, and still my cousin and I do not want to leave.

'In the 1950s more banyas open, only they not so nice. No more bathtubs, just parilkas and pools. Everything very common. Nothing beautiful. Stalin very bad man, so bad banyas. In the 1960s less turmoil. Khrushchev opens the borders and we meet the Finnish sauna and soon many banyas add Finnish sauna.'

'Why?' I ask. 'The banya is so lovely.'

'It's foreign. It's chic. Who knows. Maybe because sauna is dry heat and cleaner than the wet banya with leaves all over the floor. Alexia, rule one for journalist, Don't interrupt my story. I used to go to the Palace during Soviet times. It was a very beautiful banya, much marble and many statues, and it cost three rubles to get in. A lot of money! But I don't drink vodka, so I put money other people spend on drinking to the banya. But my favorite is the Sandunovskye Banii in Moscow. Have you been there?'

'No, not yet, but Marina and I will go next week.'

'Oh, you must go. This thing I really cannot describe, the statues, the carpets, the paintings, the luxurious waiting room. And then inside enormous plunge pool next to banya, just like prerevolutionary banya down on Nikravsava Street. And when I leave this place, I feel more beautiful.'

After all this outpouring of banya emotion, I asked, 'Irina, how come you don't go to the banya anymore?'

'It's bad for my hair,' she replied, and lit another Capri cigarette.

Marina's Version of Russia

I was so glad to have Marina, expert on all things Russian, to guide me through the slippery streets. It's one thing, when you lack language skills, to amble your way through a comparably sane city like Istanbul. Chaotic as Istanbul was, the people and their behavior made sense. But here in Russia, I couldn't find my center of gravity. The cabs were private cars with no meters, and on a particularly *Twilight Zone*–ish ride, I almost got kidnapped by a scar-faced driver who kept asking me if I wanted to go out for shashlik (shish kebab). I watched a businessman in front of the covered market alternate bites of his ice-cream Popsicle with a bag lady. A band of teenagers rode through the streets on horseback at midnight. And I was tactlessly bounced at the ballet for impersonating a Russian and ordered to pay the $65 foreigners' surcharge.

Marina is not Russian, but after a childhood in Moscow and a two-year stint at a Russian investment bank, she both speaks the language perfectly and understands the peculiar post-Soviet style of getting things done. We had booked tickets to Moscow on a new private airline. Hours before the departure, my passport was still being registered by the authorities. When my entreaties were shrugged off, Marina knew exactly whom and how to bully to get my passport back. So we kissed Irina good-bye, thanked her for the tvorog breakfasts, and headed off for four nights in Moscow.

The first and last time I visited Moscow, in midwinter 1994, I came to see my then boyfriend, Josh, who was teaching English at a private school and living in a shabby satellite city. It was a dark, depressing, vodka-drenched visit. Josh had taken Pushkin's famous verse much too literally: 'We drink to escape our woes/Where is the cup? Our hearts will be more gay.' Beyond the drinking, there was a lot of Russian posturing. He and all his expat friends put a ridiculous amount of effort into pronouncing 'Pushkin' (Pwohush-kiin) and glorified their street barters for butter and eggs.

Anything would have improved on my last poisonous visit. The weather was the first surprise. I arrived in July, when Moscow was bursting with sunshine. The second great leap forward was in lodging. Staying at an airy, elegant loft five minutes by foot from the Kremlin obliterated all previous negative associations of the city. The gargantuan and sumptuous loft belonged to Marina's friend and former colleague, an aristocratic Frenchwoman named Simone, who was tall and elegant and spoke impeccable English with charming trilled Ls. I had no idea how splendid the life of an expatriate banker in Moscow could be.

From my vantage point in her blue, airy guest room, Simone had mastered the art of expatriate living. Her maid and chauffeur both adored her and said she was 'like a sister.' Pictures of her travels across Russia, looking ravishing in fur, dotted the apartment, as did little treasures from her excursions. Somehow, in a completely uncontrived manner she transported 16th Arrondisement opulence to the Volga. Aesthetic harmony reigned in the loft's luxurious, eclectic blend of bear and zebra skins, Russian folk art, black-and-white prints of pouting ballet dancers, and the odd piece of furniture upholstered in French fabric. Despite her tailored, perfectly accessorized appearance, Simone had no princessly airs. She was warm and engaging, yet just aloof enough to remind me that she floated in a different orbit. Irina in St Petersburg and Simone in Moscow were both perfect representatives of two very different stratospheres in contemporary Russia.

With just a small taste of its high life and with introductions to interesting people who didn't belabor the names of Russian authors, Moscow was proving a most enticing destination. Marina was happy because she could buy cheap fox furs and see old friends. I was happy because we were going to pay a visit to the Sandunovskye Banii, the most famous and stately of the Moscow banyas, where Pushkin went for inspiration until his untimely death at thirty-eight during a duel with his wife's lover. And there is no better tour guide than 'Pwohushkin.' Truth be told, though Pushkin is the Sandunovskye's most famous patron, he never actually visited it. He died fifty-nine years before Sila and Elizaveta Sandunov opened the Sandunovskye Banii in 1896.

The 104-year-old Sandunovskye Banii was right in the middle of Moscovian action near Teatralnaya Ploshchad. The banya was originally a country institution. Each village had at least one banya built on the banks of a lake, river, or pond. This ideal of a village banya endures today in a more personal form. Despite the fact that the majority of Russians live in cities and that the Communists tried to make everything communal, most Russians dream of having a country house, or dacha, with their own banya. This dacha-garden-banya scenario for them is the embodiment of an idyllic existence.

For centuries, effectively until Peter the Great took power, the cities in Russia were nasty, crime-ridden places. City dwellers preoccupied with trade didn't spend time or energy improving their quality of life with frills like banyas. The earl of Carlisle noted in his *Relation of Three Embassies,* written for Charles III in 1663, that banyas 'were as rare at Mosco as hunting.' Seventeenth-century Moscow must have smelled like a vodka-spiked sewer, and deliberate measures were taken: banya owners were exempted from taxes.

Our driver in an old smoky Lada took a 50-ruble note, about $2, and would take us only as far as the inner ring road. Marina knew the way and guided me through the steep, cluttered streets toward the Sandunovskye. Construction crews were everywhere, and scaffolding swayed in the breeze. Of course, one doesn't walk under scaffolding in Russia; it is like having unprotected sex – a big risk for a nominal inconvenience. So Marina and I were walking down the middle of the street, when suddenly we heard choral chanting emanating from a small onion-domed church.

The ethereal melody and vague scent of incense drew us into the tiny, crowded nave. Rows of bowed congregants stood in front of an altar with a diptych of Russian icons gleaming gold and magenta in the darkness. The women sang one verse and then alternated with the gathering of priests near the altar. After a few minutes, the congregants started to form a line near the altar. They approached the priest, received his blessing, and bent to kiss their favorite icon. One right after the other, the women pressed their lips to the painted wood blocks. All of the women, wrapped in shawls, heads covered in scarves, seemed possessed by a deep-felt fervor, whereas the men, shifting in their seats, seemed to tolerate the proceedings. A few women near the back turned to look at us. Their lack of a welcoming nod or a small movement to accommodate us in the pew was sufficient notice that we were not wholly welcome.

It was starting to rain, and we rushed down the small street to where a caravan of shiny black foreign cars, Mercedes and Lexus SUVs, was parked. As the hoity-toitiest banya in all of Russia, the Sandunovskye was a magnet for 'New Russians,' which is synonymous with an entire class of people who became rich, generally through questionable or shady means, in the freewheeling wake of perestroika. The men's side of the Sandunovskye is known to cater to a devoted clientele of Russian Mafia; for this reason, some people avoid the place. For a vicarious experience of a banya filled with Russian mobsters, read the book or rent the video *Gorky Park;* the 1982 thriller depicts the protagonist visiting the Sandunovskye in order to eavesdrop on Mafia deals.

First, I must say another word about the nature of banyas. After many sessions with the St Petersburg witches, I had a banya epiphany. I realized how banyas are different from the Roman thermae and Turkish hamams. Banyas, unlike hamams, aren't paved with marble. Nor do banyas have the soaring, curvilinear architecture of hamam domes studded with skylights that glisten like diamonds. Hamams are gently heated with soft, vaporous steam that lulls the body like rich cello notes bowing across your body.

Banyas are pure village. The wooden-beam architecture is dark and coarse. The banya is a mad wizard's treehouse with a forest inside. Banya heat is infernal, the pure Stravinsky staccato notes of a violin piercing rays of heat through a prostrate body. Banya heat purges and punishes. Banyas are about suffering, the release from that suffering, and the joy that comes from the resultant equilibrium. Inside the hamam, ladies in flower-patterned cotton dresses ply you with tea and oranges; they use soap and washcloths to clean and massage you on a warm marble slab. Hamam life is soft and sweet and altogether feminine. In the banya, the *banshitsa* whips you with branches and then leads you, dizzy, blood pressure dropped to 80/50, to the cold pool to shock your body back into consciousness.

Yet despite the externally more pleasurable, indulgent aspects of the hamam, hamam culture, at least in Turkey's largest city, was in a sad state of decline. Visiting local hamams in Istanbul was like walking through a cemetery, visiting a stone marker to a former epoch. A remembrance, a deserted monument to a previous age.

Here in Moscow, the banyas were packed. Russians, like the Romans before them, believed in the simple recipe for political stability: bread and banyas will keep the people content. A well-fed, well-bathed citizen is a happy citizen. And I remembered Irina's banya treatise that, consciously or not, evaluated banya developments through the different Soviet leaders: 'Before the revolution, banyas very well built. Stalin's banyas not so good. Khrushchev build very nice banyas indeed. But Sandunovskye best of all.'

Once out of the church, we hurried past the fleet of expensive black cars. Most cars had drivers taking a nap or reading the paper and having their thirtieth cigarette of the day. My heart quickened as we searched for the entrance, weeks of anticipation coming to fruition. The women's entrance is hard to find, around the corner and up the hill from the more stately men's entrance. My suspicion is that the owners don't want the women to spend too long gazing jealously at the men's swimming pool encased in stained glass. Rule three of bath culture: Men *always, always, always* get the superior facilities.

Drenched in acid rain, Marina and I approached the cashier at the foot of a staircase that curved up for two stories.

'This isn't what I pictured,' I said to Marina as I noticed the prevailing design aesthetic of Versace meets Roman decadanza. In the lower atrium and in the recessed nooks leading up the staircase stood fake white statues from Roman mythology better left on a Miami lawn and beveled mirrors better left in Tony Soprano's house. This was a prime example of the prefabricated opulence so distinctive of Russians flaunting their money.

'Yes, I know, but this is what the New Russians consider classy.'

'What, it's five hundred rubles?' I said, looking at the sign.

The $20 fee was a near fortune in most pockets of Russian society. I had gotten used to living in the Russian ruble economy in St Petersburg with Irina. Ten cents for the banya, 50 cents for coffee and a pastry. The hard-currency economy for foreigners and New Russians runs about the same as New York City prices. The fee to get into the Sandunovskye was the same as my East Village *shvitz* back home in Manhattan. But in this context it seemed like a czar's ransom. Of course, for $6 we could have purchased tickets for the second class of service. But, paradoxically, here in Russia the highest class of service is the norm, and choosing the regular class is like choosing standing room only at the theater. Even parsimonious Irina in St Petersburg told me she chooses only the highest class of service.

We pulled ourselves up the balustrade and walked into the brightest, nicest banya changing room I'd ever seen, and my spirits lifted. In fact, it was more of a reception room with six banquette areas designed for sitting in small groups and sipping tea. Overhead there were hooks and shelves for storing clothes and bags. Several uniformed attendants buzzed around the wide rectangular room, delivering glasses of tea and water. Most of the guests were twenty to thirty years old, younger than the average St Petersburg banya-goer. Marina noticed this too and said, 'Oh, of course, it's *devushki* night. Simone said it might be.'

'*Devushki* night?' I asked.

'I'll explain inside. But be on the lookout for silicone.' *Devushki*, I later learned, means literally 'young women' in Russian, but among expats it's used to describe a particular genre of young woman – the attractive, hard-bodied chattel of the rich New Russians.

I did a cursory silicone scan, and everywhere I looked gravity-defying breasts reached skyward. Russian implants don't just enlarge breasts, they actually levitate the breast to within inches of the owner's chin.

'There's Gallia!' said Marina.

I looked toward the entrance and saw a thin, wiry woman with wide green eyes and an anxious face that melted into a smile when she saw us. Gallia raced over to Marina and kissed both her cheeks. Gallia, I learned during the introductions, was a banya-phile and used to be the office manager at the bank where Marina sold Russian equities during the heady times before the crash in 1998. Until eight years ago, Gallia struggled with chronic bronchial problems and caught every virus being passed around the office. Finally a friend suggested that the banya would alleviate the pains in her chest. She tried it; it worked; and now she never missed her weekly session.

Gallia undressed quickly and pulled a pink bowl out of her bag just like the hamam taṣis. The wide shallow bowl contained a bar of soap, loofahs, washcloths, and a packet of herbs – she was a banya insider. All business, she said, *'Devushki, paritsa'* (Girls, it's time to steam), and led the way hurriedly through a wooden door to the wet room. This wet room, with its white-tiled floor and enormous elevated plunge pool, was the largest, most modern banya prep room I had yet seen. The brightly lit, high-ceilinged room also had two soaking tubs overflowing with water near the door to the parilka, one made in wood in the Japanese soaking style, the other white marble with ornate rosettes on the side, no doubt a leftover from the original 1896 furnishings. The only other furnishings were the requisite rows of benches for resting in between sessions and for placing buckets stewing with herbs and other salubrious unguents.

I soon learned that Gallia was an old-school banya-goer, and like other Russian women, she did more than advocate for her method. When Marina and I headed over to the shower stalls along the wall to wash ourselves before going into the parilka, Gallia did not even try to hold back her sneer. She was crouching in front of a spigot that poked out from the wall, dumping small buckets of water over herself. 'This is the traditional way to clean yourself before banya,' she said meaningfully. I vacillated between wanting to wash myself in the 'correct,' old-fashioned manner and wanting to stand up to a bossy Russian woman. Soon I was crouching next to her, throwing steaming buckets of water over my back and listening to Gallia tell me, 'This country has no future.'

'Why do you say that, Gallia?'

'Don't listen to Gallia,' Marina yelled from the showers, 'she's in one of her moods.'

Gallia continued, 'As long as men prefer to drink vodka and make one hundred rubles a month selling potatoes instead of having good job and an occasional bottle of wine, this country has no future. Russian men, they don't care about job, about family, they just want to drink vodka.'

There was nothing to argue about. Russians, according to the World Health Organization, consume on average 15.5 liters of alcohol per year, beating out every other European nation. Getting drunk is perfectly acceptable social behavior; in fact, drunkenness is glorified among most Russian men, so temperance movements have difficulty finding a foothold. Gallia's life had clearly been affected by vodka. She spoke proudly of her nineteen-year-old daughter, whom she had raised alone. Gallia, I was shocked to learn, was forty-four. In general, Russian women don't age that well, or as Marina pointed out, they age overnight. Gallia, however, looked to be in her late twenties. Her daughter studied at an American college, and Gallia said, beaming, 'I'm so happy she has a future. In this country she would have no future.'

Gallia was well-known to the Sandunovskye's *poddavshitsa,* the 'mistress of steam.'

'Come meet Natasha,' said Gallia. Then she whispered, 'She's a witch.'

'Who is Natasha?'

'She heats the banya and announces new sessions. She also stews magic herbs, makes the best steam, and is an artist with the veynik. You'll see.'

Just then, a stout young woman with dirty blond hair wearing a thick pink cotton bathrobe and a pointy felt hat emerged from the parilka. Underneath her elfish hat was an elfin, small-featured face, pink and glistening with sweat. In her right hand she held two veyniks, one made of birch and the other of pine, and with the other hand she held up the limp, red body of a young woman who looked as though she needed to be revived with smelling salts. Everyone stood out of the way, as if gathered around a road accident, while Natasha brought the red woman to the marble tub and drenched her with water to remove all the leaves and pine needles from her body.

Then she helped the woman step into the cold tub to cool off after the treatment. Only then did she remove her own hefty robe and revive herself with cold water. After she'd had a chance to resuscitate herself, Natasha noticed Gallia and gave her a kiss.

'Are you next?' Marina whispered to me.

'No, I think I'd rather give the treatment. Why don't I learn on you? C'mon, it's not as if I'm practicing a medical procedure. Natasha looks like a good teacher.'

Gallia had told us earlier that when Natasha performs the veynik treatments, it looks more like a shamanistic ritual or a Martha Graham dance than a mere beating with twigs. I glanced over at Natasha again. She was young, maybe thirty or so, and had a natural, earthy look compared with the other silicone women. Her breasts sagged slightly, and her hips were wide and sturdy. In short, she was normal looking, whereas the young Russian patrons had the svelte, statuesque Slavic build. I noticed another, more subtle difference. All of the women under fifty had shaved or waxed off all of their pubic hair save for a narrow Mohawk. Natasha hadn't. Even Gallia, who was unequivocal on her position that Russian men were swine, had a tidy Mohawk. Later I asked Marina why Russian women groomed themselves so specifically. 'It's pretty standard for young urban women. They don't do it for men, they prefer the hairless feeling themselves. We can have it done tomorrow if you're curious. I think Simone knows a good place. I used to get it done when I lived here, and, trust me, Russians are gifted waxers.'

After Gallia and Natasha had finished catching up, Gallia rejoined us on the benches. 'Gallia, has Natasha always been a *banshitsa*? I mean, is it a profession that you are born into?' I asked, remembering that half the hamam ladies came from the village of Tokat.

'No, no, no.' Responses are always emphatic in Russia, as if you've asked a stupid question. 'She used to be a Russian-to-German translator, but when she lost that job she started working here.'

'What kind of wage do you think she makes?'

'Well, her actual wage is probably very low, like fifty dollars a month, but because there are so many hard-currency clients she probably does really well with tips.'

'Do you think she'd give me a lesson on how to use the veynik?'

'Yah, I'm sure she would be flattered that you are so interested in what she does.'

But I would have to wait a while before my lesson. Natasha puts on her robe and mittens to perform her veynik dance only once an hour. 'I have to pace myself, otherwise I'll get too dehydrated and maybe pass out,' she explained.

It was time to get the parilka ready for a new session. Banyas, unlike saunas, are not left continuously at the same heat. The biggest banya surprise was how much structure and discipline was applied to the sweating ritual. You don't simply shower, sweat, shower, and leave. Having a real banya involves partaking in several rounds of carefully moderated heat – ideally 140 to 180 degrees Fahrenheit with a 20 to 40 percent humidity range – and submitting to the will of the *poddavshitsa.*

At the Sandunovskye, along with the other Moscovian banyas of the highest echelon, heating the parilka is a formal affair compared to the haphazard heating up that takes place in St Petersburg. At the 3-ruble Tchaykovsky, there is certainly no paid *poddavshitsa,* so the queen bee of the moment heats the parilka to the loudly voiced specifications of the other bathers. If she does a bad job, if the steam doesn't disperse evenly, or if she pours too much water on the rocks, thereby smoking out the room and sending the women running from the parilka, they will yell, *'Khvatit! khvatit!'* or 'Enough!' and it will be a long time before this banya amateur is allowed to pick up the ladle again.

Natasha, a self-described *lyubitel* (die-hard fan) turned professional, has a more formal and exacting approach to heating up the parilka. To label Natasha a mere *poddavshitsa* would be ridiculously unfair. Rightfully she is a *banshitsa,* part herbalist, part homeopath, part performance artist, and part witch, in the words of one Sandunovskye regular. The women rush up to her. 'Natasha, Natasha, is the parilka ready? What herb is stewing in the red bucket over there?' Banya devotees schedule their sweats around her working hours.

First she cleared the parilka of bathers, telling them it was time to start a new session and she needed it empty to do her work. When Gallia explained to her that I too was a *lyubitel,* Natasha let me accompany her into the banya to observe the heating process. So I stood next to her, both of us naked, holding ladles and wearing pointy felt hats. I thought of the priest's holding icons for the faithful down the street.

Once the room was empty, she unhooked the furnace's metal doors using the butt end of the ladle. Inside the massive furnace was a platform holding a pyramid of round metal balls that looked like miniature cannonballs. She began to scoop warm water from the bucket into the furnace. She counted forty ladlefuls of water in Russian. 'Why warm water?' I asked, the dutiful pupil.

'Because cold water makes a weak steam. The steam from cold water falls directly to the floor. The steam from warm water is spread throughout the room evenly.'

Then she shut the oven door and replaced the latch. Next she grabbed the black garden hose from outside the parilka door and dragged it in. She sprayed the ceiling and the walls of the parilka generously but without getting water on the floor. The temperature of the room was rising by the second. The walls and ceiling exhaled steam, and, as if I were captive in a stormcloud, beads of precipitation began forming on my body.

'Natasha, I think I'm getting dizzy,' I admitted.

'This is nothing yet.'

She led me out of the parilka and shut the door firmly behind her. We waited for exactly two minutes outside while the steam dispersed evenly throughout the room. The forty ladles of water sizzled on the cannonballs and fired rays of heat and steam through every square inch of the parilka's treehouse structure. As I peered through the window, I felt that I was witnessing the process of some profound chemical decomposition process, even though it was just water molecules bursting from liquid to vapor. After a few minutes, Natasha walked out to the reception area, where many of the bathers were drinking tea or eating salted sardines called volba to replenish all the salt lost through sweating. From the other room, I could hear her calling out the now familiar, 'Ladies, it's time to steam.'

Devushki and *babushki* alike rushed to make a line outside the parilka. Gallia, Marina, and I were first in line, and about ten penitents were behind us. Everyone adjusted their hats to make sure no stray hairs would get fried by the heat. Each of us wore flip-flops to protect our toes from the hot cement floor.

Natasha opened the door, and in total silence, with all the seriousness and sense of purpose of facing a firing squad, we entered. The heat above three feet was so unbearable that the women walked in doubled over. Everyone immediately carved a niche for herself. Some spread their towels on the floor, prostrating themselves on this lower level of heat as quickly as possible. The alpha women who assumed positions sitting or lying on the benches brought their hands to their faces in order to filter and soften the steam before it hit their nostrils. In America the heat would have required a billboard-size notice reading 'Please consult your doctor before entering.' This truly was nostril-singeing steam.

I crouched low and spread my towel next to Marina, who had her knees pulled in tight to her chest in a banya fetal position. The less skin you expose, the less painful it is. I tried this, too, and it helped a bit. My toenails hurt from the heat. Growls and groans rose up, a chorus of approval from the other women.

'This is too hot, isn't it? Everyone is suffering. My toenails are going to fall off,' I whispered. At serious banyas like Sandunovskye, there is a prohibition against talking midsession. If you speak above a whisper, some bossy Russian woman will invariably hush you with a 'Be quiet. We are trying to relax here.'

'I know, but for Russian women the more excruciating the better. Look at Gallia,' said Marina.

I looked at Gallia, lying two feet higher on a bench. Her eyes were closed, and she wore an intent look of concentration. 'She looks miserable,' I said.

'No, that's her Buddha look. She's in heaven.'

'Well, I have to get out of here. I can't take it.' I crawled down the stairs as if escaping from a burning house. Just as I was about to stand up and bolt through the door, three women shouted, 'Nyet,' in unison. Natasha, who was sitting on a bench by the door and rocking back and forth with her eyes closed, explained in a whisper, 'You can't leave this early in a session. You'll ruin their steam. Just sit it out for another two minutes.' My skin felt as though it would begin melting any moment, but it was slightly cooler out of the treehouse. I sat next to Natasha, closed my eyes, and thought about Seneca, who died in a Roman steam room. I could imagine worse ways to go. Then, to my utter amazement, I heard the cracking sound of leaves hitting skin. Just when I thought this woman was the lone masochist, four others joined in. These women were out of their minds, or else they redefined warm-blooded. I asked Natasha a question that occurred to me after watching so many Russian women revel in what were brutally painful circumstances: 'Why are the Russians so fond of the banya?' I asked.

'Well . . .' She paused. 'I think it's because Russians like extreme situations.'

Finally Natasha nodded at me, essentially dismissing me from class. I slinked out of the parilka in shame. Now the heat-immune Russian women would all have a story for dinner about the weak American girl who couldn't stand the heat.

Water. Water. Where was the cold water? I grabbed hold of the side of the Japanese soaking tub and splashed water onto my face and into my mouth (bad form, but I didn't care at this point; I had already humiliated myself as a banya zero). I took a few deep breaths and tried to steady my heat-addled brain. Then I climbed the stepladder into a soaking tub that looked like an enormous wooden wine barrel. I bobbed up and down like a cork in the fifty-degree water for a couple of minutes before the other women started to stream out of the parilka. They were smiling radiantly, as though they had just suffered through a terrible ordeal but had escaped alive.

To make room for others more worthy than myself, I got out of the tub and caught a glimpse of my body in a mirror on the opposite wall. My skin was gone. I was red and blue and purple, I was a medical experiment gone terribly wrong. I could see the veins in my breasts. I had X-ray vision.

Natasha came out with Gallia and Marina and said, 'In a few minutes I'll show you how to use the veynik,' and then she went out to the reception area to smoke a cigarette. Ten minutes later she returned, carrying her pink bathrobe and white felt gloves.

'Marina, you hot-blooded Kazakh, are you ready?' I asked. Marina stood up, stretched like a cat, and doused herself with cold water. There was the undeniable sense that we were about to embark on something difficult and painful, but a necessary and worthy endeavor. The banya, especially when you add a veynik treatment, is a three-day juice fast crammed into three minutes. The sweat, while 99 percent water, also contains about 1 percent hard metal, and the heat speeds up your kidneys so that waste and toxins are processed and released more quickly.

Natasha put on her uniform: pink bathrobe, woolen mittens, and pointy white hat, and she scooped up the silver basin with two birch veyniks soaking in warm water. She looked like a baker, a house-wife, and an elf. I, her apprentice, wore just a felt hat. The parilka had cooled since the height of the last session's heat. Marina, our sacrificial lamb, lay on a bench with a cold wet towel wrapped around her hair.

Natasha took a veynik in each hand. She raised the bouquets of birch to the ceiling as if lifting two huge torches to the sky and shook both hands gently so the leaves trembled and shed drops of water. Then she dropped her arms to her sides and began moving them in wider and wider circles on top of Marina's body. I crouched next to Marina. I could smell the fresh, tannic aroma of a damp October morning in Vermont. With each circle, Natasha circulated the parilka's hot air and coaxed the steam onto Marina's body. All this before any skin-to-leaf contact.

And then – *thwack*. The first blow was to Marina's feet. The feet contain nerve connections to every organ in the body, so it's a good place to lay that first blow of heat. It sends waves of heat throughout the trunk of the body and allows the body to prepare for the onslaught to come.

After her feet had absorbed the initial shock, Natasha began beating the branches in quick, rhythmic movements up Marina's calves and thighs and across her back. She played her shoulders as if they were snare drums. Cha, cha, cha-cha, Cha, cha, cha-cha. The sweat streamed down Natasha's face, but she showed no signs of heat fatigue. She tapped Marina twice on the hip, and Marina turned over. Before repeating the same series of lashes on her front side, Natasha dunked the branches in a bucket of cold water and gently brought the branches to Marina's face so that the cold water streamed down her neck. Marina sighed with gratitude. Those small injections of cold water are the only thing that makes it possible to endure lying there passively while heat and steam are heaped onto your body and birch leaves slap your skin, removing the toxins. Or so the folk wisdom goes.

It felt as if the veynik treatment lasted an hour, though it was probably more like four minutes. It seemed I was going to learn by watching. For her final coup de grâce, Natasha shook the branches, a shamanistic call to the spirits, and then shimmied the two bouquets down Marina's body to lock in all the purifying steam of the parilka and all the organic goodness of the birch leaves. Finally, she poured a little more cold water on Marina's face and then helped her to sit up. Marina opened her eyes; the whites of her eyes were completely clear, and she gave us a weak smile. We helped her down the stairs and revived her with buckets of cold water before depositing her in the marble tub like a small child.

'I feel at peace,' Marina managed to get out.

'You do this once a week and you never get sick. Really, it burns all the germs right off your body,' offered Gallia.

'Gallia, what time is it?' Marina asked.

'About seven-thirty.'

'We've been here two hours, unbelievable. Alexia, we need to hurry. Simone is expecting us any minute.' Marina then pulled herself out of the cold pool and proclaimed triumphantly, 'Well, I can end my search for the perfect bath. How about you, Brue?'

'My perfect bath won't possess the Nietzschean "What doesn't kill you makes you stronger" guiding principle,' I said.

We dressed in less than five minutes, which was in great contrast all the young women around us, who were spending five minutes just coloring one eyelid. We rushed toward Simone's loft apartment. The rain had stopped, and we walked by the small Russian Orthodox church. The courtyard was empty, and I pondered how different the rituals were – the pomp and regalia of the liturgy versus the peasant and the profane at the banya. Inside the Russian Orthodox church, the women piled on the scarves to cover their shoulders and their hair. The faithful require so many accoutrements – icons, robes, vessels for drinking water and wine. Inside the banya, all that is stripped away and the soul is truly bared.

Simone threw a dinner party to welcome Marina back from her exile. She and Andrew, her dashing English war photographer boyfriend, had just flown in from Rome with pasta, fresh pesto, and raspberries. Andrew was such the perfect Central Casting version of a globe-trotting, passport-as-thick-as-a-novel war correspondent that I wondered if Simone hadn't ordered him from a top-secret Magnum personals catalog. But they had met, I was told, at a banya birthday party that a mutual friend had thrown at the Sandunovskye. Andrew was instantly smitten and called Simone a few days later. After they'd arranged to meet for a drink, Simone, ever the ingénue, said, 'Will you recognize me with my clothes on?' Andrew, though he photographs fighting in Chechnya and Iraq, was mysteriously based a block from the Campo dei Fiori in Rome, but he spent as much time as possible with Simone in Moscow.

An eclectic assortment of friends showed up. First was Sasha, a tall and gangly Russian who told me almost immediately, 'I don't work, I travel, and I'm not interested in guidebooks that tell me how to live on fifty dollars a day.' Sasha's girlfriend, Svetlana, cat-walked in five minutes later wearing something gold, shimmery, and strapless. Svetlana was a certain kind of Russian woman – that perfect cocktail of DNA: the tall, trim, leggy figure of a uniquely well-endowed ballerina and the softly chiseled face, wide-set eyes, and painted, pouty lips of the typical Slavic stunner. She was gorgeous, and in her mysteriously quiet way, she spent dinner politicking and power brokering at her end of the table. Then there was Nigel, a dipsomaniac Englishman who gulped wine, chain-lit cigarettes – his own and Svetlana's – and smiled and purred involuntarily.

As Marina had explained to me earlier, Svetlana was Sasha's *devushka*.

'So *devushki* are prostitutes?' I had asked.

'No, I mean, well, not really. They aren't paid to perform sexual acts, but it is understood that in exchange for being supported in high style, they'll perform, service, satisfy, you get the idea . . .'

'So the *devushka* is like a kept woman or a mistress?'

'Yes, precisely, but with a little geisha thrown in.'

'And is this relationship between *devushka* and patron exclusive?'

'Well, from the woman's end it is. Like last year, Sasha supposedly spent fifty grand on Svetlana's needs, and this buys him exclusive rights to her affections.'

'How do you know all this?'

'Sasha tells Simone everything, especially since Svetlana's gotten rather more demanding lately. Last year Sasha bought her a Range Rover. Now she wants to be sent to an art and auctioneering school in London for a year, which would kind of defeat the whole purpose of a *devushka* relationship. At least from Sasha's end.'

'Yes, a long-distance mistress is hardly a desirable situation. And do they act like boyfriend and girlfriend?'

'Well, you'll see for yourself tonight. Sasha is "physically obsessed" with her, but in public they seem rather indifferent to each other.'

And throughout the dinner party Svetlana seemed to pay more attention to Nigel, while Sasha regaled me with a delightful body of banya jokes and stories: 'A cell phone is ringing in the banya. Boris picks it up and says, "Yes, of course, dear, buy yourself the mink coat." The phone rings again, and Boris answers it and says, "You want a diamond ring? Anything you want, dear." For a third time the phone interrupts them, and Boris answers, "A Mercedes SUV, of course, buy it." Then he holds up the cell phone and addresses his banya buddies: "Whose cell phone is this, anyway?"'

While Sasha was telling me another story about a bachelor party he'd attended at the Sandunovskye banya that turned into an orgy, as well as a national scandal that erupted when a foreign minister was caught on camera cavorting with a prostitute inside a banya, at the other end of the table Svetlana was contributing to Nigel's purring.

I asked Marina later about the bedroom eyes flying back and forth between Nigel and Svetlana. Marina explained the *devushka* logic: 'Well, Svetlana picked up on Nigel being from London and being unemployed at the moment, which she translates into "independently wealthy Englishman." She was sizing Nigel up as a new patron, one more likely to send her to art school in London. Nigel could never afford her, though.'

Throughout dinner, talk of the banya animated the conversation. All of the foreigners in the room had their own connection to the banya and had been introduced by Russian friends, rather than seeking it out as a touristy lark the way foreigners in Istanbul did. Andrew told a story of a macho *New York Times* war correspondent who was 'wounded' in Chechnya. Some Chechen sources had invited him to join them for a banya. After four rounds of heat, probably eight rounds of vodka, the correspondent tripped and fell toward the banya's hot rocks and burned his leg. The burn was bubbling, and he had no choice but to visit the makeshift military hospital. Too embarrassed to admit it was a banya injury, which is really an admission that you can't handle your alcohol, he told the doctors he'd tripped over a land mine.

Village Banya for Rent

Colin, Marina's raffish boyfriend, arrived the next day. While he met with his banking colleagues, Marina and I played *devushki* and got waxed to within an inch of our lives at a fancy place Simone suggested. 'Let's make you look like a Russian woman,' teased the masochistic Russian depilator while waving a tongue depressor of hot green wax. I left, my body smooth and hairless, a little less of a mammal. Suffering in the name of good health and vanity was, I was learning, a common theme in Moscow.

Our plan was to visit the Golden Ring cities of Vladimir and Suzdal and as many others as we had time for. The Golden Ring is the tourist trade name of the fabled constellation of nine cities that form a ring east of Moscow. They constitute the historic core of ecclesiastical Old Russia, the Russia of the eleventh century and onward, when the patriarch had the ultimate power.

On the highway leading out of Moscow, we saw women sitting in lawn chairs just a few feet back from the rush of cars. They were surrounded by their wares: ten-gallon bags of cheese puffs. When they have no revenue, or when all the money has been skimmed off the top, Russian companies pay their employees in goods, but you can't pay the rent or buy potatoes with cheese puffs. Just as we were discussing all of the injustice in Russia, we got pulled over by a police car. It wasn't our speed that arose suspicion, but rather a blend of our obvious foreignness and the car that transported us, a new Volvo sedan, the car (and driver) of an out-of-town banker friend of Marina's. (Note to self: Learn more about banking.) The uniformed police officer was obviously bored with no one to harass but the ladies selling cheese puffs. To amuse himself, he wanted to check our papers and get a better look at Marina. Then he waved us on.

Vladimir, 130 miles due east of Moscow, is the logical first stop on any Golden Ring tour. Historians are fond of pointing out that had the Mongols not sacked Vladimir in 1238, it might well be the capital of Russia today and Moscow a small provincial backwater. Vladimir was founded by the Slavs in 1108, 350 years before Moscow's Kremlin was a glimmer in Ivan the Great's eyes, and was the Slavs' major cultural and religious center after the eleventh century. All of the Golden Ring cities, which rose to prominence from the eleventh to the thirteenth centuries, had one thing in common: They were located along the river that connected the Black Sea to the Baltic Sea.

The massive arches of Vladimir's Golden Gates were our introduction to the Golden Ring; however, Vladimir today doesn't have much else to recommend itself. Communism has transformed this once glorious, cathedral-dotted countryside into a gray, concrete strip of unappetizing restaurants and overpriced, junk-filled tchotchke shops. Most of the churches have long since been demolished by Communist decree so the brick could be used for other more utilitarian buildings. Marina, undeterred by the blight that was Vladimir, was soon trolling through an antique shop with an impressive collection of Russian icons.

Suzdal is the Golden Ring city with the greatest draw. This tiny fairy-tale hamlet is often described as what Russia would look like if communism hadn't happened. Suzdal is laid out on the banks of the narrow, meandering Kamenka River. Little wooden footbridges make it possible to cross the Kamenka, more brook than river at this point, and look down on the lush water lilies below. The Kremlin on the hill is enclosed with white stone walls built in 1299, and inside the Kremlin walls are prime examples of every type of ecclesiastical architecture for the last eight hundred years. In the eighteenth century, Suzdal had four hundred households and fifty churches, and I doubt this proportion has changed much today. Suzdal owes its bounty of churches to two local historians who, when the Communists demanded that cathedrals across Russia be demolished for the bricks, sacrificed only the least valuable buildings and saved the masterpieces.

We toured the town, a merry band transported into an Arcadian fairy tale of clover and sheep, starry pink churches and bell tower concerts, and villagers selling pickles and pancakes. The Russia of ten-gallon bags of cheese puffs, shabbily constructed concrete blocks, and soot-covered façades was conspicuously absent. In short, this was the Russia of a Marc Chagall painting; I looked up half expecting to see a green unicorn floating upward toward the stars.

We pulled into the Central Tourist Complex (CTC), which was about as beautiful as the name would suggest. A Soviet monstrosity, it was the one blight on Suzdal's horizon. It hadn't been our first choice, or second choice, for that matter, when we booked from Moscow the day before. We had wanted to stay in one of the little *izbi* (wooden cabins) at the famously charming Intercession Convent but were perfunctorily told by the Central Booking Office that the convent was fully booked and we would have to stay at the CTC. Now at the CTC we were told that the CBC had been mistaken: there was no room for us in this impersonal aircraft hangar hotel, but that we could find a room at the convent before they closed. 'But quick, hurry.'

The 'fully booked' convent turned out to be empty except for the three receptionists nursing tea next to a samovar inside the reception cabin. 'Yes,' they said, laughing, 'we have many rooms.' Our cabin was the fifth in a circle of identical *izbi*. Along the stone path we saw several nuns who nodded to us. Were any of these nuns Romanov descendants? I wondered. This fourteenth-century convent was once famous for housing discarded noblewomen like Evdokia, the first wife of Peter the Great, and the wife of Ivan the Terrible.

'Is there a banya in the convent?' Marina asked, as I stood next to her in silent gratitude.

'Well, yes, normally, but it's closed this time of year.'

It was the part of summer, we were told, when all municipal water in Suzdal was shut off for two weeks while they cleaned the pipes.

'Can we rent a banya?'

'No one has ever asked to rent a banya, but I think something may be possible.'

She looked up a phone number and made a call with the rotary phone.

I winked at Marina to thank her for the ongoing translation services and for indulging my village banya excursion. She and Colin loved baths as much as me, besides what else were we going to do at night in Suzdal?

'Are we going to wear bathing suits?' she teased.

'I have three people who'd like to use your banya. How much would it be?' asked the Russian receptionist into the phone.

She paused.

'Yes, *how much*?' she said emphatically and rather leadingly. It was obvious that the person on the other end had never rented out her banya and hadn't the first idea how much to charge. Had Marina and her fluent Russian not been here, undoubtedly the convent receptionist would have sized up the cost of our luggage and suggested a steep price to the banya owner. The price that was finally suggested was 1,000 rubles, or roughly $32, which seemed a bit excessive to borrow someone's banya in the Russian countryside, but by the end of the evening it would seem the ultimate bargain.

A rusty blue Lada sat idle outside the tall gates of the convent at 8:00 P.M. A man sat slumped in the driver's seat, smoking a filterless cigarette. It was not a very prosperous-looking picture. 'Marina, what will this guy's banya look like?' I pictured benches with cigarette burns and flies buzzing about the place.

'Trust me,' she said, 'it will be the nicest part of the house. Remember what Gallia said about building her banya before her dacha in the country?'

Colin sat in the front seat, earnestly trying to make conversation in Russian. Marina had gotten huffy today when Colin, who according to Marina speaks perfectly serviceable Russian, left all the duties of communicating and translating to her. She said she was feeling like the *devushka* of two foreigners, though I am forgiven because my efforts at speaking Russian were, frankly, embarrassing.

After a five-minute drive through the sleepy streets of Suzdal, we pulled into a one-door garage. The garage's interior resembled a dismembered forest. Hundreds of veyniks hung from the rafters, and cords of firewood lined both sides of the garage. The driver, who turned out to be the master of the dacha, smiled, revealing a gold tooth, and said proudly, 'Enough veynik to bring us through the winter. Pick out a veynik for tonight. Any one you want.' I picked one that looked thick with foliage and tightly wrapped. 'Oh, you have a good eye. This one's very full, like a good head of hair, and will not fall apart no matter how hard you hit him.' He laughed and pointed to Colin. This was translated for me later. Often people spoke Russian to me because I looked white Russian, and because I played along, nodding my head and saying *'Da'* at appropriate intervals, it was assumed that I understood what was going on around me. This is a fine impression to give, as long as people around you can translate and bail you out if you get in over your head and accidentally say *'Da'* to the wrong question.

His wife came out to greet us. She was a lovely plump woman with gorgeous skin and bad teeth. 'Welcome to our banya,' she gushed. We were treated like important guests, and I suppose that to them what they were charging us was a small fortune. They led us around the side of the house, past a small, tidy garden where potatoes and turnips grew and into a separate dwelling. 'This is our banya,' they declared, 'but tonight you should treat it as your own.' They gave us a proud tour. First the lounge, a modest, clean room with two cots and a dining room table covered with a flowered cloth. On the table stood a huge samovar to pour ourselves endless cups of tea, with a pot of apricot jam. A savvy twist on saccharine. The room was decorated with framed embroidered scenes: grandmothers drinking tea in front of a samovar, the omnipresent symbol of Russian culture, and a scene of bathers beating each other with veyniks. Another enduring image. The man demonstrated how to use a little boom box in the corner with the one-tape collection of Russian pop music that would grow on us with every glass of vodka and in the end sounded like Stravinsky. It was modest, but it also was charming and clean, and it felt like a privilege to be inside their banya. It was like being led into a writer's study, an artist's studio, or a cook's kitchen. In other words, a sacred place where a lot of time is spent and much attention is given to the details.

Then the man, who was forty-two but looked seventy, showed us the parilka. First he led us into the antechamber where one derobes and showers. He pointed out a small door that I thought would reveal a cubby filled with banya hats and mittens but instead was the blazing mouth of the parilka furnace. He showed us a stack of firewood that we should use throughout the evening to keep the parilka stoked up. 'It's been heating for over an hour,' he said. 'It should be just perfect now.' Then he brought us inside the parilka, where we saw a bed of fist-size rocks heaped on top of the furnace. He threw a ladleful of water on the rocks, and they sizzled like pancakes on a griddle. *'V parilku!'* he said, which literally means 'Into the parilka' but idiomatically means 'Time to steam.' Colin said something to him in Russian, and he replied with a cocked eyebrow and seeming confusion.

'A for effort, Colin,' I said.

'See, I don't really speak Russian,' Colin said. 'I don't know why Marina thinks I do.'

From behind him Marina said, 'Colin, you do speak Russian, you're just too lazy to try.' Marina and Colin had the kind of constant squabbles usually reserved for people who have been married upward of fifteen years. It wasn't uncomfortable to be around them, say, the way it was to be around a couple truly at war. Their bickering became white noise, and after a while I learned to watch it like a low-grade boxing match in its twenty-ninth round.

The tour complete, the lovely couple excused themselves to do whatever Russian couples do at night when they are not using the banya. A few weeks ago, I wouldn't have understood the implied protocol and the assumptions that were made after they gave us a tour of our borrowed banya kingdom. It was assumed that we weren't coming just to have a quick steam and then leave. It was assumed we had come for several hours of entertainment, unwinding, and intimate conversation. It was assumed that we'd be having a party and that they would cater it. It wasn't considered strange when we intercomed the main house (a bizarre interloping of technology) to ask for a liter of vodka.

First we undressed. Normally one wears not a stitch of clothing inside a banya. *Nothing comes between me and my banya.* A bathing suit is thought to be an insult to the sweating process. Only a banya heretic would wear a swimsuit. I suppose the normal protocol of unmarried men and women together at a banya party would be to politely drape sheets over now hairless parts, but toga-style sheets were not part of this village banya package. So that left us in a wardrobe quandary. Colin was my friend's boyfriend. Much as I liked him and occasionally thought of him like a brother, I certainly didn't want him to see me naked. I am like the majority of people who look much better in clothes. Marina is in that small minority of people who look best in a state of nature, and since she was with her boyfriend and best friend, she felt perfectly comfortable being naked. She tossed her clothes in the corner and said, 'Come on, guys, what are you waiting for?' Of course, she knew what we were waiting for. For a cold day in the banya.

There was no way either of us was getting naked. I was a prudish New Englander, and Colin was a prudish English bloke. I could see getting naked in front of a bunch of gregarious, chilled-out Italians, but not in front of someone who managed to dot his i's during casual conversation. We both pulled bathing suits out of our bags; apparently we'd had similar thoughts on how to handle this delicate situation. And we all burst out laughing that, despite our best intentions to the contrary, we simply weren't swingers.

Then the sweating sessions began. At first it was about intensive sweating and steaming. We'd go in for one session, sweat till we couldn't take it anymore, then drench ourselves in cold water and recuperate until we had just enough strength to face the parilka again. Believe it or not, this sends endorphins flying, and after about an hour we had the insane high associated with six-mile runs. We were hungry for life. We were thirsty for vodka.

After our third session, during which I demonstrated my skill with the veynik – gleaned during my apprenticeship with *banshitsa*-goddess Natasha – the wife brought in a steaming plate of boiled potatoes sprinkled with a thick coating of dill. I thought fondly of Irina and her folded-up newspaper with dill drying in the sun. There was also a plate of half-pickled cucumbers covered in garlic and dill and thick slices of rye bread. All the carbs you crave after a good sweat. We thanked her profusely, not expecting such a beautiful feast, and complimented her on the magical powers of her banya.

'Oh, you make me happy,' she said.

'How long have you lived here?'

'Oh, not long, maybe ten years. This is our son's house. He built it for us. He is a New Russian.' This was how Irina had proudly referred to her son as well.

We finished the liter of vodka. Our faces were soft and flushed, the whites of our eyes completely clear. We talked ourselves hoarse on everything from what makes a person Russian – Colin's take: 'Russians are united by suffering. Once they gain material well-being, they want to leave Russia. They are no longer Russians' – to the final scene of *Anna Karenina,* which Colin managed to spoil for me since I was one hundred pages shy of finishing it. The intercom crackled and the husband asked if we wanted another liter of vodka. Only then did we realize it was well past midnight. We thanked our hosts and gladly paid them the $32 that would easily cover their living expenses for a month. The husband drove us through the silent streets of Suzdal, depositing us in front of the darkened convent. No one had told us about a curfew.

The gated compound had been locked for the evening. The huge wooden doors were fifteen feet high, and even though we were drunk enough to think we could scale a wall without injury, there wasn't even a foothold to get us started. We soon realized that we'd never get through the main gate, that no one was answering the bell, and that our yells were going unanswered. We walked around the walls, hoping to find a less imposing door. Finally Colin located a ten-foot padlocked door that we could climb. He hoisted Marina over. 'Colin, be careful of my bag!' Bang. The ground was hard, but it didn't matter.

The next morning I woke up bruised all over. Russia is an obstacle course, but this had been our first physical barrier. Usually you can talk yourself around barriers in Russia: 'Closed on Wednesday . . . That's not my job . . . Please fill out this form in triplicate . . . We're out of every item on the menu that you want.' So it was funny, and quite frankly refreshing, to be confronted by an actual physical barrier.

A few days later, I was back at Irina's door. Irina was ecstatic to see me. We hugged. 'Irina,' I said, 'what are you doing for the next three days?'

'A couple of tours, not too much.'

'Let's go to some banyas.'

'You invite me? Does that mean you pay?'

'Yes, Irina. You are my guest.'

'Oh, it is so wonderful.'

Irina found her long-ignored banya hat, and we made the rounds of St Petersburg's more offbeat banyas. We hit Smolni, the favorite banya haunt of the KGB, in a four-story concrete block decorated in vinyl and dim lights. To Irina's glee, we rented a private banya suite, where we bobbed up and down in the cold pool together and Irina told me about weeping caryatids in her short story that was anthologized with Pushkin.

Our most memorable outing was to a village-style banya in the ugly outskirts of St Petersburg. Locating this place was difficult, though Irina had heard about it and wanted to visit for years. A taxi driver with a mouthful of gold teeth found it for us, while regaling us with better banyas we should try in the meantime. This was typically Russian, the desire to point out that you're not going to the best place, that the best banya, cheese, church, can be found at X inconvenient location. Finally we came upon three women walking along a dusty road in beach towels asking one another out loud, 'Have you ever seen anywhere so beautiful?' I remembered Irina's first greeting: 'Welcome to my beautiful apartment.'

After getting settled and undressing, we ventured into the parilka and Irina complained, 'Oh, it is too cold in here.' She grabbed the hose and started 'giving water to the walls.' I realized that I had been spoiled by the protocol and propriety of the watering process in Moscow. In St Petersburg it's often pandemonium. Irina sprayed everything, everywhere, and everyone. I felt the room getting hotter around me. The other women started to moan – at first, I guessed in approval of Irina's aggressive watering tactics. All of a sudden the air in the room disappeared, my shins and toenails became painfully hot, the walls seemed to be coughing scalding steam. Afraid to face the fate of a steamed wonton, I jerked upright, covered my face with a damp towel, and crawled out of the room on my hands and knees. The other women were right behind me this time and spoke quickly to Irina, who still held the garden hose and looked very guilty. 'Too much water,' she admitted.

Only temporarily humbled, we headed out to the lake for a swim. It had been a cold summer in St Petersburg, and the lake wasn't more than fifty-five degrees. Irina was red-faced and happy.

'Oh, I like this banya very much. I'm getting clean inside out. For two days I haven't smoked, and now I never smoke again. Yes, I become pure again.'

'Were Soviet times very hard?' I asked.

'Oh no, very nice times, Black Sea vacations twice a year, always enough money. I was a journalist, and I make as much as a doctor.' I wondered if the banya had produced such a state of euphoria that

Irina thought only of the good. Perhaps she was so high that she couldn't remember the lines for food, the repression of the free press.

After the banya, we walked through a mangy park where afternoon strollers examined curious mushrooms and the houses of New Russians were loudly being constructed along the shores of another small lake. Irina told me the cost in dollars of each upcoming monstrosity. Finally we reached the subway station; a huge platform outside had at least twenty stalls selling food and drink.

'I want to buy you a snack to thank you for the wonderful banya,' said Irina.

'No, it was my pleasure, really.'

'You try this special doughnut and coffee,' commanded Irina, and we entered a prefabricated silver edifice on wheels. Irina ordered, and we were handed two cups of instant cappuccino and a plate of fried dough. Irina told me how clean she felt after the banya, how she would never smoke again, and how she would start work on a novel. As I wiped the grease off my lips with a coarse napkin, I noticed that I was starting to love all the contradictions of this country.

The next morning, I left at dawn for Helsinki. Irina came down to the street with me and hailed a cab. She surprised me by getting into the car and riding to the train station. 'I want to make sure nothing happens to you on your last morning.'

She walked me onto the Repin's platform. As I hugged Irina good-bye, I realized that I didn't know her last name.

finland:
saunatopia

There is nothing that Finns have been so unanimous about as their sauna. This unanimity has remained unbroken for centuries and is sure to continue as long as there are children born in their native land, as long as the invitation still comes from the porch threshold in the evening twilight: 'The sauna is ready.'

– Maila Talvio, 1871–1951

[V]oluntarily they torment themselves, acquiring pain instead of cleanliness.

– Nestor of Kiev, writing about Finnish saunas in 1113

I boarded the Russian Repin, an old Soviet train, for the six-hour ride from St Petersburg to Helsinki. The crisp, sunny early August weather seemed to mirror my destination: Lutheran sauna country. 'How was Petersburg?' asked an English family on the train. They had ridden overnight from Helsinki but had been denied access into Russia because of incomplete visa paperwork.

'Even better than *Anna Karenina*' I said, already missing the tarnished sparkle and mysterious happenings of St Petersburg. 'How was Helsinki?' I asked in return.

'Rather too perfect, really,' the mother replied in clipped Oxford English. A prophetic comment, as it turned out.

I had my own compartment for most of the ride. Watching the forests roll by, I calculated how many veynik could be made from each swath of forest. This grove of birch would yield at least three hundred veynik, five from that one tree alone. Responsible deforestation − veyniks require only a few leafy outer branches − all in the name of a good banya. I'd heard the Finns used veynik, too, but they called them vastas or vihtas, depending on whether you're in the east or west. I thought about Irina, en route to a writers retreat in Optima, no doubt soon to be terrorizing the nuns in the abbey. In the end, she had shown herself to be a true mensch.

I tried to picture my boyfriend, Charles, whom I hadn't seen since a week-long stopover in Budapest two months earlier. As the Repin chugged west through the seemingly pristine Russian countryside, on the other side of the world Charles was probably snapping pictures of shy starlets. That was his job, and being a celebrity photographer required a rare blend of social and technical skills. His effortless stream of provocation and self-effacing humor produced marvelous responses and spontaneous pictures.

Charles loved the baths of Budapest and had wanted us to visit them together. He is at his happiest soaking up to his chin in water, and we passed many languid summer days sampling the ubiquitous hot spring baths on the Buda side and looking at Roman and Ottoman ruins (my obsession). But Budapest scored low on bathing culture because the atmosphere in the baths was more German Kur than New Rome. The German, Czech, and Hungarian brand of rejuvenation involves enemas, medical massages, and carbon dioxide treatments in which a rubber bag is cinched tight around your waist and filled with CO_2. Talk about the placebo effect. While some of the Buda baths were tucked away in architecturally interesting places and had a romantic old world grittiness, these are not joyful places to be.

Next week, Charles would arrive in Helsinki to enjoy the waning days of summer with me in a country he wasn't particularly curious to see. Work and visa restrictions had made it impossible to visit Russia, a place that held more fascination for him. I felt a definite pressure to make Finland come alive.

I heard a sudden knock on my cabin door, and a stone pillar of a man, a statuesque, uniformed blond who looked like Dolph Lundgren on high-dose steroids, entered the compartment. Thirty minutes earlier, two dark Russian men had come through, grabbed my passport, and stamped it. Now, at the Finnish border, Dolph, in heavy boots and with perfect English, asked, 'And how was your stay in Russia?' as he looked under the seats for stowaways. This question, when asked by someone in uniform, can never sound casual. 'How was your stay in Canada?' sounds nonchalant, but a deliberately slow articulation of 'And how was your stay in Russia?' can make even an Omaha dentist feel as though he's jumped onto the thrilling pages of a John le Carré novel.

I was grateful that Dolph didn't have a German shepherd like the guards at the Slovakian border, but he didn't need a salivating dog to be intimidating. Concentrating on looking blasé, I said, 'It was very pleasant.' He stared at me like a pit bull sizing up the fight of its prey before attacking. 'Are you carrying anything valuable? Jewelry? Works of art? Icons, perhaps?'

The last question rattled me. I was prepared to say no to 'Do you have anything to declare?' but when Dolph asked so pointedly about icons, religious paintings that adorn churches and homes across Russia, I struggled to maintain my composure. Two exquisite renderings of St George slaying the dragon were buried in my suitcase. Should I lie outright, or should I massage the truth and say, 'I picked up some little paintings at a junk store, but I don't think they're valuable'? He would then ask to see them, inform me that they were icons, and I would act shocked and say, 'What? You call these little dragon pictures icons?'

I went for the big lie. In my mind's eye, these icons were already hanging on the wall next to the fire escape in our apartment. Besides, what were the chances that Dolph would dig to the bottom of my suitcase? And even if he did unearth the icons, the outcome would be the same as if I confessed right now. The icons would be sent to the Russian authorities, who would either seize them or charge me an enormous 'tax.'

'No? You have nothing?' he asked skeptically. 'Well, let's have a look.'

A crimson wave washed over my face; I felt seasick. At that moment, I knew I'd make a terrible spy. I'd sing at the mere mention of Siberia. What would Marina do? She and Colin had smuggled two icons back to London without incident. I opened the huge suitcase that I'd spent two hours packing late last night. Dolph and I both stared down at the neatly packed contents.

He took pity on me. 'It would be a shame to ruin your perfect packing job. What's in the yellow bag?' I unzipped the bag. 'A computer. What do you need with a computer?' he asked, as if carrying a computer qualified me as an intelligence agent. 'Is it an iBook?'

'No, it's a ThinkPad,' I said. He seemed disappointed. The interrogation was over. Dolph welcomed me to Finland, and a moment later I heard a muffled, 'And how was your stay in Russia?' from the next cabin. I was officially an art smuggler.

Arriving in Helsinki with ten hours of daylight still stretched before me smoothed over any anxiety about my usual predicament of not having a place to stay. My icons were intact; the weather promised to be perfect for the next month; I was in a foreign country of fluent English speakers, where public bathrooms were clean, sanitation was an obsession, and taking a sauna was the state religion. What wasn't there to smile about?

My only Finnish acquaintance, Reeta (pronounced with a trilled R and transformed into a five-syllable word), was at a wedding in Turku, Finland's original capital on the west coast. But at this point I didn't want help. I preferred to put myself at the mercy of a city, to see what unfolded. Entering a city for the first time is like meeting a person – you form a first impression that is generally correct. And my first impression of Finland was of a utopian fantasy land where quotidian business happens with unprecedented ease and no one gets too excited about anything.

The train station, conspicuously missing the general splattering of bird droppings and broken bottles so common in Russia, had a lodging office catering to poor planners like myself, where I picked up a list of Helsinki brokers with short-term rentals. I knew better than to hope for a four-story town house (I would never equal my Istanbul digs in this lifetime), but a small studio with a kitchen and, who knows, maybe a sauna would be an ideal home base. Helsinki, with its stunning esplanades and cobblestone streets and the sleek, frosted-glass modernity of its countless bars and restaurants – each, it seemed, stolen from the pages of a *Wallpaper* design fantasy – was the obvious place to unpack my bags.

Not only was Helsinki absurdly picturesque, it was also easy to navigate and decidedly provincial, especially considering that it is a European capital. The Gulf of Finland, the same gulf that St Petersburg perches on, acted as a guiding North Star, and nothing was farther than a fifteen-minute walk. Helsinki occupies a small peninsula with two different centers of gravity, depending on your personal tastes. Some might call the harbor area of Eteläsatama Helsinki's hub, with its thriving market square, the *kauppahalli,* and the nearby fish market where you can buy gravlax soaked in everything from cognac to vodka to honey. Others stake the center of Helsinki at Stockmann's doorstep. The Finns are fond of saying, 'If you can't find it at Stockmann, it doesn't exist.' And that's not hyperbole – the ten-story Stockmann sells everything from truffle oil to sauna rocks to Aalto-inspired furniture to *Tom of Finland* books. The center of my Helsinki universe, I hoped, would be the Finnish Sauna Society headquarters, a sauna sanctuary on the island of Lauttasaari, just west of central Helsinki.

. Twenty-five minutes after arriving in Helsinki, I was at Maarta's real estate office in Kaivopuisto, a chic neighborhood crammed with boutiques and chocolatiers. Four-dollar cappuccinos, $40 pedicures – gone were the $2 champagne-and-caviar snacks in St Petersburg. Gone also were the flies on the food, the swirl of garbage on the street, and the charming Russian surliness.

I did my New York best to negotiate Maarta's only available apartment down from $80 per night. Since the owner in question, already at her country house, was trying to rent it at the last minute, I figured she might be willing to negotiate, and she was. I rented the apartment for $50 a night, sight unseen. Checking the apartment seemed unnecessary in a country where, I was quickly learning, cleanliness bordered on sterility and functionality bordered on obsessive. I hoped I hadn't just rented the one exception.

An hour later, Maarta, a relentlessly chipper fifty-year-old wo-man, helped me collect my bags at the train station and gave me a car tour of Helsinki: the sloping parks and gardens of the embassy area, different views of the Gulf of Finland, and the massive island military fortress of Suomenlinna, forbidding even from three kilometers away. Finland, I soon learned, is a one-metropolis country. The Helsinki metropolitan area – if you include Espoo and Vantaa – is home to nearly 1 million of Finland's 5.2 million people; the next largest city, Tampere, lags at 195,000. The city's prosperous, meticulously manicured atmosphere was worlds away from St Petersburg's grime-encrusted façades and chaos. The layout, the perfect vistas, the seamless transportation systems (a web of trams, buses, subways, and free bikes), the garbage-free shaded streets, all seemed to suggest a metropolis designed in one all-encompassing scheme of Utopia. The people also seemed like refugees from

Stepford. They walked purposefully, looking contented and sane, smiling into their shiny Nokias.

'You've picked the nicest month of the year to visit Helsinki. Perfect weather and long days,' Maarta congratulated me. 'What will you be doing in Helsinki for the next month? Are you here to enjoy the festival?' she asked.

'What festival?' I asked, my interest piqued. My arrival seemed so auspicious that perhaps I'd been lucky enough to arrive on the eve of a bacchanalian sauna festival. Maybe the Helsinki equivalent of the running of the bulls involved Finns running naked by moonlight through the streets to the nearest sauna.

'Every year Helsinki hosts a summer festival, but this year it is a little more special because we have been selected as a European City of Culture.'

'What does that mean, European City of Culture? It sounds like a great honor.'

'Well, really, it means nothing. It's just a marketing ploy.'

I wrote this comment off as Finnish self-effacement. 'Are there other cities of culture?'

'Yes, though I'm not sure what they are.' Then, remembering something important, she added, 'But I do know that no city in Sweden was selected.' Her glee in conveying Sweden's failure was thick with schadenfreude and was my first taste of the rivalry between the Nokias and Ericssons, the inventors of sauna and the usurpers of sauna.

We pulled up to my new home just off of Korkeavuorenkatu, a street name I wouldn't, even after a month, be able to pronounce. Next door to my new home was an Alko, a state-run liquor shop, the only blight in the area. The tastefully furnished two-bedroom apartment, stuffed with books and classical music recordings, was a gem by Manhattan standards. Maarta took me to the basement to show me the laundry facilities and the common apartment sauna.

'Here is the sauna sign-up book. You can reserve a sauna time for yourself. Most evenings are filled in, but there are some free slots during the day.' I examined the sauna appointment book, the same narrow-lined schedule used in American offices, filled in with names like Tikkanen and Ruusuvuori. I peered inside the sauna, window-less and drab like a prison cell in light wood. It smelled like the inside of a tree.

'My friend lives next door, and maybe you can take a sauna with her. Lenin hid in that building before sneaking back into Russia. So you can use the same sauna as Lenin.'

I appreciated Maarta trying to provide a cultural experience for me, but I had made it a point not to visit Lenin's tomb in Moscow, and I had no desire to walk in Lenin's Helsinki footsteps. No, I had shifted gears. I wanted to see Sibelius's and Alvar Aalto's saunas. The renowned composer and designer had both taken great care with their saunas, and Aalto had designed some curious, curved sauna benches.

There were only six days until Charles's arrival. Six days to complete the bulk of my research. Six days to declare a winner in the unspoken banya-sauna rivalry. Six days to uncover enough offbeat Finnish delights to keep Charles entertained. Of course, Charles's entertainment was not my responsibility, and we could discover things together; but in a way, he was a guest on my fantasy trip. This wasn't a vacation we were taking together. Rather, he was visiting me on an odyssey that had spiraled out of a vacation to Istanbul. That made me the de facto host and tour guide. I looked forward to getting caught up in the swirl of wonder and curiosity that characterizes Charles's approach to life. Yet I loved the greater spontaneity and serendipity of traveling alone. Was this an approach to travel or an approach to life? I wasn't sure.

The next morning, I pushed through the line of silent, red-nosed alcoholics waiting for the 10:00 A.M. Alko opening, on my way to the exclusive, members-only Finnish Sauna Society. I had secured an invitation by passing myself off as a bathing expert, though any foreigner can make an appointment to visit the society. Part of the society's mission is sauna education, which foreigners need more than Finns.

Gaining membership to the Finnish Sauna Society is like gaining admission to the French Academy – you need a combination of manners, breeding, and political clout. First you must be recommended by a member with a solid five-year standing in the society, and from there you must produce various documents and letters of recommendation to prove that you are truly a stalwart friend of the sauna. Membership itself is inexpensive, not more than $250 per year, but the bragging rights are priceless. The society was founded in 1937 and now has 2,800 members.

The society's mission is to record and promote sauna rituals, history, and architecture. They vigilantly guard sauna integrity and protect against the forces of sauna denigration. If a feckless company tries to market a body tent or substandard heating unit as a sauna, the Finnish Sauna Society swoops in, vanquishing anyone who has taken the sauna's name in vain. With the Finnish Sauna Society as a watchdog, the Finnish sauna will not be the setting for any blue movies or euphemistically named 'massage parlors.'

I expected a massive building for the headquarters of such a venerable group, a huge cedar log cabin with a sauna for giants. I expected something that screamed authentic Finnish sauna. I expected, at least, a sign out front. But I was not yet in touch with the understatement that is quintessentially Finnish. As I walked down a recently tarred narrow street surrounded by woods, I thought that surely this couldn't be the Finnish Sauna Society headquarters. Then I inhaled the rich, smoky smell of a birch-and-alder bonfire hanging in the air like a rolling mist.

Ahead of me, amid the birdcalls and racing squirrels, was a modest wintergreen compound plopped down in a clearing in the woods. I followed the line of a long jetty down to the water. I noticed several women breast-stroking languidly through the water; one climbed out of the water, without a stitch of clothes, and wrapped herself up in a pink towel.

Before I could join them and swim naked in the Gulf of
Finland, I had to locate Sinikka Korvo, my entrée into this
pink-toweled world. Soon enough, I found myself in a strangely
conventional office. This was the bureaucratic nerve center of the
Finnish Sauna Society. Its archive looked large enough to launch a
good fifty sauna Ph.D's. The society also publishes its own
quarterly magazine, as well as medical research articles with
alarming titles such as 'The Influence of the Sauna on Histami-
nopexy, Histamine, and Its Discharge Through the Urine' and
'Experimental Exposure of Rats to the Sauna.' Whereas I had
taken banyas a lot more seriously than most Russians, I couldn't
hold a candle to Finnish fanaticism.

Sinikka, a tidy blond woman in her mid-forties with an air of
competence and resourcefulness, was sipping coffee and planning for
the next congress of the International Sauna Society. She greeted me
with a warm smile and lively blue eyes shining behind her square
wire-rimmed glasses. An executive assistant all her life, she enjoyed
the sauna as all Finns do but never imagined she'd have a full-time
job tending to sauna business. After two years as the society's
secretary, talking shop meant talking sauna, and her eyes sparkled
every time she worked the word *löyly* into the conversation.

'Wait, how many syllables does *löyly* have?' I asked, pronouncing
it like *lowly*. 'I'm saying it with two syllables, and you're saying it
with six.'

She smiled understandingly. 'This is a difficult word for foreigners
to say, just as it is a difficult concept to understand. *Löyly* sums up the
spirit and mysticism of sauna, even though literally it refers to the
steam produced when water is thrown on the rocks. Here, try saying
it with me. Looohleee.'

I followed Sinikka back into the sauna wing of the society. My
arms had goose bumps – I was about to see the sauna in its purest,
most authentic form. Sinikka sensed my reverence and smiled. We
walked into a café with a large-stoned hearth that opened in the
middle of the room. Its menu consisted of beer, juice, sausages, and

salads. 'We always try to have salads on ladies' day. The men just eat sausages and drink beer,' Sinikka said, and we exchanged knowing glances: Ahh, men and their sausages.

'Here's where members sign in and pick up towels.' She handed me a generous helping of pink towels. This was rather a steep step up from begging the Russian banya ladies for an extra hand towel. Sinikka continued, 'Downstairs you'll find the locker rooms, but first let me give you a tour of the sauna compound. It can be confusing.' She slipped off her shoes, and I did the same.

'Here you have your showers, self-explanatory, I should think,' she said while we padded barefoot through the gray-tiled chamber containing two rows of showers, with a picture window overlooking the placid bay. The Finnish Sauna Society's setting was so rural, tucked away and sheltered from civilization, that a picture window in the shower room posed no threat to privacy.

'Over here,' Sinikka said, pointing to an alcove with a massage table, 'a washerwoman will give you a traditional scrubbing with pine soap, and because today you are our guest, I invite you to try this special washing free of charge.' Sinikka introduced me to Aino, the washerwoman. Aino was in her sixties and wore a dress and apron. She could have as easily been a waitress as a sauna scrubber. 'We'll leave the cupping for next time,' Sinikka teased. Cupping, also known as bloodletting, was still practiced into the early 1990s at some of Helsinki's public saunas. The premise, that off-balance humors in our blood lead to illness, goes back to Empedocles, a Greek. After bacterial ointment is spread over the body, the cupper makes small incisions, then attaches the horns (small bulbous glass containers) to pull out the blood. After the bloodletting, the client goes to the sauna to add dehydration to anemia. It's still popular with older Finns.

'Last month we were the Sauna of the Month, and we had five hundred people a day coming through here, with huge lines out the door,' Sinikka said on our way through the showers and down a dark-wooded passageway with latticed windows.

'Sauna of the Month?'

'It's a special program because we are a European City of Culture.'

'That sounds like a great honor – European City of Culture.'

'No, it is nothing, just a silly EU marketing ploy.' All Finns seemed equally skeptical about this City of Culture business. Sinikka continued, 'Sauna of the Month allows access into normally private saunas. You see, Finns all have their own saunas at home or in their apartments, but sauna is such an obsession that we are curious about private saunas.' In America, we are curious about how the rich and famous live; in Finland, they are curious about how the rich and famous sauna.

'Where is the featured sauna this month?'

'A very unusual one on the island of Suomenlinna, the so-called Fortress of Finland. It is probably the world's largest sauna, designed to fit an entire company of one hundred and twenty men. Though up near Lapland you can visit the world's largest savusauna.'

Savusauna? This was a new word for me, and Sinnika explained its meaning and history. *Savusauna* means 'smoke sauna' and refers to the heating process of the oldest saunas. Some would argue that a sauna by any other name is not a sauna. Originally, saunas were nothing more than holes dug into the side of a hill where the ancient Finno-Ugric people would essentially have indoor campfires, take off all their clothes when it got hot enough, and pour water on the campfire rocks. This gave way to building a structure, generally a rectangular one-room log house, for the express purpose of bathing, as well as salting meats, brewing beer, giving birth, and preparing the bodies of the dead.

Early savusaunas contained an open stove piled high with rocks and a raised platform with benches. In a process that takes three to four hours, the rocks in the stove are heated, while smoke from the burning wood fills the room before escaping through a vent in the wall or ceiling. Black soot covers everything – the walls, benches, and ceiling – but the charcoal, though messy, is bacteria-resistant and makes the sauna an even healthier environment.

Slowly, saunas with chimneys were introduced at the beginning of the twentieth century. For all their magic, savusaunas had several drawbacks: They frequently caught fire, they took four hours to prepare, and the soot from the smoke required constant cleaning.

Sinikka explained my options. 'We have five saunas here. The first, and least popular, is a futuristic electric sauna with self-producing *löyly*. It is state of the art, but people don't come here for electric coils, they come for the smell of smoke. Back here are the two most popular saunas, the savusaunas.'

I peeked through the window into the darkness of a room lit by the faint red glow of the hot rocks and a few small windows that created silhouettes of the blackened benches. 'How are they different?' I asked.

'Number four is hotter than number three, and you are only allowed to use the vasta in number four.' So many rules, I should probably have taken notes.

'Who heats the savusaunas? It sounds complicated.'

'Oh, it is. Our sauna major, Hanu, heats the savusauna. He arrives at seven in the morning to have it ready for the two o'clock opening.'

Sauna major? Then Sinikka showed me the continuous wood-burning chimney saunas, which fall between electric saunas and savusaunas on the continuum of sauna purity. Again, they were heated differently, and one allowed vastas and the other didn't. I tried to imagine all these rules in Russia. I couldn't.

It was 2:00, opening time for the society, and women were starting to arrive in droves. Sinikka handed me a vasta, the most beautiful green leafy bouquet of birch leaves I'd ever seen. It was thick and verdant and smelled as if it had been cut just moments ago. A far cry from the anorexic veyniks in Moscow, which at the time I thought were perfectly acceptable.

One of the ladies in the dressing room said to me, 'Feel free to ask anyone inside the sauna for help.' Who needs help inside a sauna, I wondered, though at a place with an official 'sauna major' anything was possible. If I survived the St Petersburg banya witches, nothing inside a tranquil Finnish sauna could possibly trip me up. I remembered the flavors of saunas as explained by Sinikka: Saunas two and three are cooler, and vastas are not allowed; saunas one and four are hotter, and you can whisk yourself to death. What I didn't yet know is that inside a sauna there are as many subtle rules as there are kosher dietary laws.

I had too many saunas to choose from, so I just stood indecisively in the hallway, like a Soviet at the grocery store choosing between recently unveiled brands of toothpaste, until I heard a voice ask, 'Can I help you?'

'I don't know which sauna to go into,' I confessed.

'You should try the savusauna. If this is your first time, maybe you should try the milder one.'

'No, the hotter the better.'

'Okay, well then, come with me,' the pink-toweled stranger said, smiling, and I followed her.

'These are the savusaunas,' she said, ushering me inside.

I put down my towel and sat across from the enormous *kiua,* the sauna stove that assumed the position of an altar. The five other women in the room were all silent. I looked around, hoping to make eye contact with someone. A lifelong member of the society welcomed me. She was in her late sixties and told me that her father had been a founding member of the society. This tidbit was presented as if she were a Daughter of the American Revolution. Teaching me the subtleties of sauna behavior, it was obvious, was both a pleasure and a burden to her. She touched her cane, which she had placed next to the stove, and said, 'In Finland we have a saying: "In the sauna you must behave as in a church." ' Here's a summary of her imparted gems.

1. Ask permission of your sauna sisters before making *löyly*.
2. When leaving the sauna, ask the other bathers if they would like you to pour water on the rocks. This is akin to asking anyone if you can get them a refill while you're up.
3. Do not discuss business, politics, or malicious gossip.
4. Do not discuss your job.
5. No bottles of water or any other liquid are allowed in the sauna.
6. Herbs and essential oils may not be poured on the rocks, lest someone is allergic.

It is common for sauna sisters who have been saunaing together for years not to know one another's last names or professions. It is even considered sacred not to know these things, because inside a sauna, profession, rank, last name, and address simply do not matter.

I watched my sauna sisters wiggle around the rules. My presence raised their curiosity. They wondered, 'Have you ever been inside a *real* sauna?' I could honestly answer:

'No, not like this.'

I asked someone if *sauna* is trademarked by the Finns. It is, after all, the most popular loanword from Finnish. Aside from *sauna*, the only Finnish word I knew was Nokia. One word for communing, the other for communication. A woman in her thirties told me that it was the more market-savvy Swedes who trademarked the word *sauna* and who now run a large *kiuas* export company using this generic name.

She shook her head in dismay. 'Everyone knows the Finns are the world experts on all things sauna. And the Swedes are trying to steal Santa Claus, too. Santa's official address is in Lapland, and now the Swedes are building a Santa's village of their own.'

I didn't care who got credit for Santa Claus, but I thought it criminal that the Swedes would hijack sauna, and a Finnish word to boot. The Finns lavish such unrestrained love and fanaticism on their saunas that they deserve exclusive use of the word. Modesty and understatement don't help in global marketing.

I commiserated with an understanding nod and looked around. The savusauna was perfect – the dark wood beams, the smell of recently departed smoke, the low-key conversation. There was no average member. The women ranged in age from their early thirties to early seventies. They all had practical, no-nonsense haircuts. No indulgently long hair or carefully tweezed eyebrows. This was not a culture that valued preening, manicures, pedicures, or body waxing. The bodies were different from those in Russia, not at all what I had expected. For some reason, I visualized Swedish, Norwegian, and Finnish women as cut from the same genetic cloth – six feet tall, thin, blond, and symmetrically featured. Walking clothes hangers. But the Finnish women were actually quite *lumpy,* to use Reeta's word.

The sauna's grande dame ladled water onto the rocks, and the five of us inhaled the resultant wave of *löyly* while staring out the windows in silent satisfaction. Contemplating nature is a huge part of the sauna ideal, and all good saunas have well-placed windows. When people get too hot they leave, careful to shut the door behind them, and either sit outside in the cool, crisp air or rush down the jetty, leaving their towels on the dock, to plunge naked into the gulf. A little while later I took the plunge, and diving off the jetty, I half expected to hear the sizzling sound of a hot pan being rushed under cold water. It may have been August, but the water was unbearably cold, and I swam for only a few minutes. A woman in a pink towel said that I must come back when the gulf is frozen to swim in the ice hole. Finns are universally macho about their beloved polar swims.

I returned for round two. The number of times you go back and forth between sauna sessions and cooling off distinguishes the Finnish sauna experience from the American gym variety. A German travel magazine explained the masochistic routine thus: 'If you want heaven and hell at the same time, go to a Finnish sauna.' Real sauna aficionados repeat the hot-cold cycle as many as ten times, at which point their endorphins are ricocheting off the timbered walls.

When endorphin levels increase – remember, *endorphin* literally means 'the morphine within' – we feel euphoric and carefree. Endorphins flood the brain after a jog, after sex, during daredevil stunts, and after an intense sauna cycle. That familiar postsauna glow prized by all Finns comes from the prolonged exposure to hot, dry heat followed by a sudden plunge into cold water. The president of the Finnish Sauna Society, a medical doctor, wrote, 'The increase of cardiac load in the sauna is similar to that seen during brisk walking.' While sweating in sauna, the blood pressure decreases as the major flow of blood moves from the internal organs to the skin level, the capillaries. A sudden dive into cold water reverses this cardio output, and the bather's blood pressure suddenly increases. All the while, endorphin levels are mounting.

During my second of four sessions, and having absorbed all the sauna knowledge one, even very sauna-curious, person can absorb in a day, I began to muse about Charles's arrival next week. Even though e-mail made it easy to know what he'd eaten for dinner, I had no idea if his state of mind was as anxious and foreboding as mine. In the background, there has always been a silent disappointment about what doesn't pass between us. The months away made me wonder if we hadn't moved in together rather too quickly. And when I thought of playing house back in New York when I returned the felt like a hurried, forced situation.

Time-consuming activities began to take shape in my head. We would return to Lauttasaari one morning to watch the sauna major smoke up the savusauna, we'd make that northern pilgrimage to the world's largest savusauna in Kuopio, and we'd figure out how to finagle an invitation to an Alvar Aalto–designed sauna. I would keep us so occupied, we'd have no time to ask ourselves whether we were in love.

On my way out, I stopped by Sinikka's office to thank her.

'Please let me know if you wish to drop by again. I might not be able to arrange another washing, but you can certainly use the saunas.'

'Actually, I have an odd favor to ask. Could I come back one morning and watch the sauna major heat the savusaunas?'

'Yes, of course. Hanu would be delighted to teach you how to smoke up the savusauna. Try to arrive by seven-thirty. He'll have coffee brewed.'

I stepped out into the early evening air of Helsinki to find an emissionless bus that seamlessly transported me back to city center. Life in Finland was exceptionally easy after all the challenges of Russia, and the women of the Finnish Sauna Society were a much tamer bunch than the Sandunovskye crowd. No one had Natasha the *banshitsa*'s verve, Gallia's candor ('Russian men are all pigs'), gold-capped teeth, or felt hats. Could a society really be this even-keeled, or did the Finns just internalize their dysfunction, while the Russians made no attempt to hide their madness?

That evening, fresh from my excursion to Lauttasaari, I went out for a drink and dinner, on the prowl for intriguing people watching and feeling surprisingly nostalgic for St Petersburg. I struck up a conversation with the waitress about the few remaining public saunas in Helsinki – they are almost extinct – and a few minutes later a man approached my table and said, 'I couldn't help but overhear you asking about saunas. May I offer you some advice?'

'Yes, please,' I said. 'Have a seat.'

Bjorn had the bearings and reserved charm of a spy, though he introduced himself as a caterer. He wore a thick navy turtleneck sweater that flattered his eyes and his torso.

'Have you heard about Sauna Island?' he asked.

'You're joking, right?' Finland was more saturated with saunas than I could ever have imagined, and the mention of a Sauna Island stretched my credulity almost to breaking point.

'No, I'm quite serious. It's a new development started by an acquaintance of mine, Rainer Hilihatti. In fact, at this moment he's putting the finishing touches on it, because in two weeks a huge group will be going out there for this ridiculous Sauna of the Month program.'

'You don't sound like a supporter.'

'Another stupid marketing ploy, just like this European City of Culture business. Anyway, here's Rainer's card. You should call him, I'm sure he'd give you a tour. What he's done is very impressive.'

'What has he done?'

'He managed to get a very cheap thirty-year lease on this island that the city of Helsinki has been trying to develop forever. He renamed it Sauna Island and started building all different kinds of saunas. I think he has five of them, one even floating on a boat.'

It was an odd encounter. After handing me the card, Bjorn returned to his table and companion on the other side of the dining room. I pondered the Finnish efficiency of carrying other people's cards in your wallet to hand out – this was the third time someone had, on the spur of the moment, pulled out a sauna-related card. Yesterday, through another random meeting, I'd learned about SaunaBar, a nightclub with a public sauna, and about Café Tin Tin Tango, a café, Laundromat, and sauna in one where you can wash your clothes and then your body.

The next morning, I called Rainer on his cell phone. As luck would have it, Rainer was near the harbor, the unpronounceable Eteläsatama, about to cast off and motor to Sauna Island to check construction progress, and taking me for a journalist – I didn't correct him – he invited me along. My hair still wet, I made a mad dash to the harbor.

Rainer was an ageing matinee idol: brushed-back brownish red hair, a tanned face with character-enhancing wrinkles, and quiet blue eyes. To smooth over my own jitters, and out of fear that he might realize I was not, in fact, a journalist, I immediately started plying him with questions in my aggressive American way; then I gave up and just enjoyed the private three-kilometer boat ride across the sun-kissed waves in the gulf, with the breeze lifting my hair. I wore sunglasses. I didn't need coffee to feel good. This was my wake-up call. In his small silver motorboat, we buzzed past the huge Silja and Viking ocean liners standing guard in the gulf. They were so massive with their fifteen floors of cabins, casinos, and bars that they dwarfed the city behind it, sending Helsinki into dollhouse relief.

Sauna Island took the Finnish Sauna Society fantasy one step further. In Finnish sauna hierarchy, the more remote the sauna the better, and Sauna Island's boat-only access elevated it to the height of sauna chic. As we neared the small dock, I heard the sound of chain saws and hammering. All I could see through the woods were several outcroppings of log cabins and a huge Japanese soaking tub right next to the waterline.

Four of the five saunas were completed and had already been used for parties and events. In fact, Sauna Island's main business would come from corporations and groups that came out here for retreats. The masterpiece, the forty-person savusauna with an octagonal stove, had yet to be finished.

'This savusauna had one hundred kilos of rocks – imagine! – and will seat forty,' Rainer said proudly, 'but we have to have it ready in two weeks. We already have over one hundred bookings for Sauna of the Month.' I am no expert in construction, but judging from the fact that the structure was still being erected, a ribbon cutting just two weeks away struck me as a tad optimistic.

Rainer showed me around the island. He had colonized a small nook of the island with his sauna village, and he was the reigning king, his daughter and son-in-law the administrators who kept the saunas warm. It was a little Club Med devoted to the sole activity of sauna. The view was of Helsinki, scarred by oil drums and a refinery that were supposed to disappear within the next ten years; hence the cheap rent.

'I'm looking forward to coming back for your grand opening,' I said. 'Do you really think the savusauna will be finished?'

'It has to be.'

★   ★   ★

I heard Reeta before I saw her. 'Axel, Anders, Axel, Anders,' then faster like the firing of artillery: 'Axel, Anders, Axel, Anders . . .' The staccato homing pattern of a mother goose. Axel and Anders were her six- and four-year-old sons, mischievous little rays of sunshine running around the ice-cream parlor.

I approached them. 'Reeta? Hello.'

'Oh, you found us,' she said, sounding surprised. I'd never met Reeta or even seen a picture of her. She was about thirty, with short bobbed blond hair, wide-set blue eyes, a small, freckled nose, and a clear, pink-cheeked complexion. Her clothes were tidy and practical. She was what the world expected of a Finnish woman.

'I followed the Axel, Anders refrain,' I joked, and hugged her in what seemed like excessive affection for Finland; but my parents were Axel's godparents, so it seemed to me an appropriate gesture. I was reminded of a cartoon that depicts a Finn in eight different emotional states from exhilaration to utter despair. The expression in all eight frames is identical. Reeta returned my hug awkwardly and then quickly suggested the most efficient way to get ice cream. 'You watch the boys at that table over there and I'll get the ice cream.'

Axel and Anders danced around the ice-cream shop, their blond hair flying, button noses upturned, making silly faces. I almost found myself saying, 'Axel, Anders, Axel, Anders,' in an attempt to control them. Their mother might have the one-note emotional range of a Finn, but their father, who was a close friend of my family's in Vermont, was an Italian American. Their dance around the ice-cream shop would have gone over better in Naples than in Helsinki. Reeta arrived carrying a tray of ice cream and two coffees. The Finns practically mainline coffee, drinking 9.2 cups a day on average.

'I invite you and your boyfriend out to the country with me and the boys,' she said, getting right to the point. Chitchat is not a Finnish art. 'My mother's house is in southern Karelia and you can experience a real Finnish country sauna. Would you like that?' I accepted her offer gratefully, and we set a date for next weekend, the day after Charles arrived from New York. Charles would enjoy a weekend in the country, I thought, and he could stare across the border into Russia. Reeta suggested that I come out to her house in Espoo – a separate municipality, but as far as I could tell, a suburb of Helsinki – to have a little dinner with her and the boys.

In her silver Volvo, during the twenty-minute drive to the wooded Arcadian Espoo, the rambunctious Axel and Anders were inspiring an endless battery of 'Axel, Anders, Axel, Anders.' I began to hallucinate about what a four-hour drive to southern Karelia with Charles and me scrunched between the car seats might feel and sound like. We arrived at Reeta's condo. The floor was littered with toys, mostly LEGO from a recent trip to LEGOLAND in Denmark. Reeta showed me around, including the upstairs bathroom, where instead of a pedestrian tub and shower there was a sauna unit with a shower inside. Through the glass door I could see the two tiny wood-slatted benches.

'Boys and I take a sauna here every other day,' Reeta informed me. 'They love it.'

Axel concurred by chanting, 'Sauna, sauna, sauna,' with an enthusiasm most children reserve for sugar and toy guns.

'I first took Axel in the sauna when he was six weeks old,' Reeta said. 'I covered him with a damp towel, and we stayed for just a few minutes.'

'It's so little. Can you get comfortable in there?' I asked.

Axel opened the door and perched on the bench, where he demonstrated 'sauna position': legs spread slightly, arms resting on thighs, head bowed in religious observance. In his five-year-old sauna reverence, he was suddenly more Finn than Italian.

Anders ran in. 'Sauna? Are we taking sauna?'

'Maybe later tonight. Right now we are showing Alexia what a little apartment sauna looks like. Do you want to show her how you sit in the sauna?'

Anders jumped up next to Axel, assumed sauna position, and they sat, hunched over and serene, like two little blond Buddhas. Anders grabbed the wooden bucket and ladle and demonstrated. 'It's my job to throw water on the rocks,' he said, ladling invisible water on the tiny electric heater topped with several layers of grayish black rocks, 'and steam goes *sssssssss* and makes the sauna soft.' Impressive, even a preschooler could articulate the sauna phenomenon.

I decided to take a bus back into Helsinki after dinner. The sun was still high in the sky at eight-thirty as I waited at a bus station that seemed buried in the middle of a forest. It was hard to believe that Espoo is the second largest city in Finland after Helsinki. A huge bus rolled by, filled with stacks of books. The lady next to me explained that it was a traveling library that delivered books to remote areas of Finland. 'This is why our taxes are so high,' she said dourly. Utopia doesn't come cheap.

Reeta issued our marching orders. Take the train from Helsinki to Imatra, where she and the boys would collect us for the rest of the eastward journey into the Karelian countryside, stopping just shy of the Russian border. Charles, newly arrived and sleep-deprived, dreamed of a relaxing weekend in the country punctuated by naps, a sauna, and an occasional walk. I planned to dip into the *Kalevala,* Finland's national epic, inhabited by heroes with names like Väinämöinen (Zeus' Finnish cousin) and Lemminkäinen, an Arctic Casanova. Reeta could spend time with her boys. We prided ourselves on being low-maintenance guests.

The verbal air-raid siren started before hello: 'Axel, Anders, Axel, Anders, make room for Charles and Alexia.' Charles smiled, eyes rolling back in his head from fatigue. 'Sauna is the best cure for jet lag,' Reeta informed him.

While the weekend wasn't as tightly scheduled as the first day of basic training, as guests of Reeta's we did have certain obligations to hop to whenever a new opportunity for Finnish cultural education presented itself:

11:40 – Grocery shopping in Imatra.
1:10 – 'Axel, Anders, Alexia, Charles, time to heat the sauna. Come on, everyone.'

Charles looked at me desperately and popped two Advil. We traipsed across the lawn to a log cabin, carrying kindling and firewood. Reeta explained in minute detail how the sauna worked. Charles slumped on a sauna bench, and I nodded enough for the both of us.

1:20 – The preparation of lunch.
2:15 – Sauna time.

We went in shifts, Charles and me, then Reeta and the boys. When we were finally alone in the soundproof sauna, Charles said, 'I feel like I'm at camp. I don't know how many more scheduled activities I can take.'

'She's trying to give us a flavor of Finland. We should be grateful,' I said.

'I'd prefer a gradual induction as opposed to total immersion. I think I heard her say something about going to a traditional dance tonight.'

'Very funny. I'm sure things will calm down tonight.'

4:40 – Reeta announced that her friend Mariella, who possessed a postcard beautiful lakeside sauna, had invited us over for an evening session. We threw together a picnic of beer and sausages, boarded the Volvo, and drove down narrow dirt roads deep into formerly Soviet territory. Mariella lived alone with her loom and her dogs in a treehouse perched high above the lake. The cabin didn't have running water or electricity. The outhouse was up by the dead-end road that was her driveway, and the sauna was down by Lake Saima. Mariella may not have had much in the way of earthly possessions, but she had a fine sauna.

4:50 – Reeta announced a vasta-making lesson. We all headed off, clippers in hand, to collect as many leafy birch twigs as possible. Charles returned with three, I had about ten, and Reeta an entire armload full. When we set about creating the birch whisks – following instructions to line up the tops of the branches and to make sure the leaves faced the same way – I told Reeta about the veyniks used inside the Russian banyas. *Banya* and *veynik* were new words to her. Reeta, like most Finns, had no concept that the Russians had a similar bathing tradition. Generations of internecine Karelian warfare and swaps of this territory has made the Finns much more eager to discuss their dissimilarities to the Russians than to recognize any kindred customs.

5:00–8:00 – Charles was won over by the country sauna spectacle. A merry-go-round of swimming, sauna, swimming, drinking beer. Shampooing our hair in the lake, beating each other with vastas, total tranquillity.

The next morning at 8:00, Axel and Anders jumped into bed with us. In her efficient Finnish way, Reeta threw together a traditional breakfast of gravlax, assorted whitefishes, piles of dill rye bread, and rivers of coffee. Charles said, 'Reeta, thank you for a most delightful day yesterday. We don't want to put you out at all, so really, don't worry about us today. We'll just read and maybe take a walk.'

'It's not an inconvenience for me at all. I love showing you Finnish culture. Today I thought you might like to see the cabin that my mother is building.'

'That sounds wonderful,' I said before Charles could get a word out.

Getting to the cabin required forty minutes of trekking through felled timber groves, swatting flies, and tripping over mushroom patches, with Reeta stopping us for mandatory berry tasting. 'That looks poisonous,' I said.

'It's not. I'm a Finn. I know berries. Eat it.'

When we finally reached the cabin, set back from a small lake in a young grove of spruce trees, Charles asked, 'And how does the refrigerator get here?' We New Yorkers, with narrow hallways and six-story walk-ups, are fixated on the installation of appliances.

'No refrigerator, no electricity, no running water. This is her *country* house,' Reeta explained.

Charles and I exchanged baffled glances. Most would consider the other house where we were spending the weekend to be a country house. But in Finland, the true ideal of a country house means no lights, no flushable toilets, and no phone lines. But invariably a sauna, and hopefully a savusauna.

The second day of our weekend in the country followed similarly frenetic lines, but by then we had adjusted to Reeta's frequency, though we still hadn't adjusted to the flurry of 'Axel, Anders, Axel, Anders, boys, where are you . . . boys, come here . . . boys, don't climb on Charles.' One thing Charles and I were in complete agreement about: We could not endure the four-hour drive back to Helsinki. An hour into the ride, Charles's near perfect temperament was showing the first signs of fracturing. His innate sense of fun displaced by a very practical request, he asked, 'Reeta, it's pretty tight back here. Maybe you could just drop us off at the train station.' We spent the next two days recovering.

Charles and I had seen a lot of saunas in the last two weeks. We'd been up to Kuopio and watched the sunset from inside the world's largest savusauna, men and women together wrapped in togas covered in the savusauna's telltale soot. We'd spent a morning with Hanu the sauna major, drinking coffee and throwing alder wood into the 700-degree-Fahrenheit fire. Charles had had his own experience out in Lautasaari with the men of the Finnish Sauna Society and reported it lovely but lonely. Everyone was very quiet,

drinking their beer, talking occasionally in Finnish. Charles remembered a joke he'd been told before coming to Finland: How do you
spot an extroverted Finn? When conversing with you, he's actually
looking at your feet instead of his own.

And now, two weeks after my excursion with Rainer Hilihatti, Sauna Island was about to make its Sauna of the Month
debut. As soon as we arrived at the harbor to catch a water taxi,
I recognized people from the society. I waved to Sinikka. This
was the sauna social event of the month. 'Charles, we're in with
the sauna cognoscenti,' I whispered. They all looked cheerful and
expectant.

'Sinikka, everyone looks so excited,' I said curiously.

'I know, we're all very excited to see Rainer's saunas. Also, no
one much liked last month's Sauna of the Month. The Suomenlinna
military sauna was too humid and soggy.' With all the excitement
and anticipation in the air, I felt like a wine connoisseur on the way
to taste the first Beaujolais nouveau. The only person not looking
happy and relaxed was Rainer, who was talking with the water taxi
captain and looking at his watch nervously.

The forty-person water taxi was filled to capacity, and twenty-
five people were still standing on the dock. I was witnessing the
Finns at their most aggressive. Rainer's eyes had retreated far into
their sockets. I walked over to him and asked, '*Hur mår du?*' He
looked over to see who was speaking Finnish so badly. 'Did you
finish the savusauna?' I asked.

'Yes.' He smiled, and I noticed beads of sweat across his hairline.
'We tested it for the first time last night at one A.M. My son-in-law is
sweeping the sawdust away right now.'

I congratulated him, delighted by the notion that finishing a sauna
on time could take on the urgency of a space race.

I sat back down next to Charles, and he took my hand. I adored
him, but it wasn't enough. My friend Julia had summed it up: 'How
did you manage to find a straight gay man?' He was the envy of all
my girlfriends. Charles was smart, attractive, organized, sensitive,

and charming, and he loved to shop more than any woman I knew. Truthfully, I couldn't imagine a better companion. Yet something elemental was missing – a lump in my throat, an occasional bout of the shivers. I kept thinking excitement would come later, the better we got to know each other. But familiarity steered us further and further from spontaneous tango music, and I wondered if this romantic inertia was mutual. He smiled at me and snapped a digital picture.

All forty of us, carrying bags filled with towels and vastas, filed off the water taxi and into the wilderness. We walked Indian file through the woods, silent save for the sound of snapping branches. At the smaller inlet, where the boat sauna was moored, everyone stood in silent awe as Rainer pointed out the many charms of his sauna colony – the pagoda sauna, the two large (one enormous) savusaunas, the Japanese soaking tub for ten. The landscaping, the birch trees and berry bushes, shielded one sauna area from the next, so that, Rainer explained, just last week the nurses association and the police association had separate sauna retreats and didn't even see each other. And in this country, generally ranked 'the least corrupt' in the *Economist*'s annual poll of ninety-one countries, there was little danger of a randy policeman trying to sneak a peek.

The women outnumbered the men, so we were awarded the inaugural use of the new, larger savusauna, Sauna Island's crown jewel. In über-democratic Finland, it was refreshing to see rule three turned on its head. For once, women were getting the choicer facilities. After depositing our clothes in a cushy pagoda changing room and dousing ourselves with warm water, we lined up to enter the smoke sauna's miniature door. We had to duck through the three-foot door (the smaller the door, the less hot air that escapes) to enter the large, double-platform structure, but that turned out to be a good thing. So hot was it inside the savusauna that bending over at the waist was the only way to avoid getting scorched by the upper echelon of air. If I had raised a wet finger to the sky, it would have sizzled.

I hobbled to the second level and spread my towel on a soot-covered bench. A few small windows lit the large, octagonal room in silhouettes. At least fifteen of us were inside, yet a reverential hush kept things quiet. The expression 'In the sauna you must behave as in a church' came back to me. I heard the sibilant sound of a deep inhalation through the mouth. Finns are fond of making a sucking-in sound through their mouths, especially when they are thinking about or savoring something delicate. Everyone was tasting the heat. It was as hot as the Sandunovskye, but the air was dryer and softer. I was waiting for the verdict.

And so was Rainer, who when I went out for a break was pacing by the buffet table. 'I think it's incredible,' I said. He smiled. I wasn't a Finn, so my opinion was close to irrelevant. What did I know about saunas? The more discerning connoisseurs came out later with blissed-out smiles.

I expected a day of sauna parties, some lighthearted reveries, storytelling in the soaking tub, dancing naked in the woods, any gregarious element of a Brueghel peasant painting. We were on an island with alcohol, after all. In Finland I didn't have to hanker after the glory days of the public bath. The Finnish love affair with the sauna continues full steam ahead. But it's an intimate love affair. I kept forgetting that the Finns don't go in for bacchanalias or free-spirited abandon. Excitement, if it existed for the Finn, was taking place on the inside. I found myself wishing that a pushy person would come over and lecture me on sauna posture or tell me that I was using my vasta incorrectly. I would have welcomed the witches from St Petersburg, Gallia muttering, 'This country has no future,' or Natasha not allowing me to leave the parilka midsession.

These two northern countries, Russia and Finland, belonged to the same school of bathing, the *shvitzers*, as I like to think of them. For purposes of categorization, the Turks are steamers and the Japanese soakers. But despite the fact that the Russians and Finns take joy in sweating in absurdly hot wooden rooms and then plunging into icy water, they know little about each other's traditions. The Russians and the Finns both regard their bathing traditions with a sense of nationalistic pride that precludes them from recognizing that their historic enemy has almost identical habits. Subtle differences have emerged. I'd learned that in a sauna there are no leaves strewn blizzardlike on the floor, no oils or eucalyptus unguents allowed to touch the sacred sauna rocks. The sauna is an upstanding citizen, a bath whose complexity lies in its guarded purity; the banya is an enfant terrible inhabited by witches and goblins and all manner of eccentric behavior.

I wondered if Charles was enjoying himself in the other savu-sauna. If anyone was good at bringing people out, it was Charles. His extroversion topped the charts, and the only people who weren't drawn into conversation with Charles generally couldn't speak English. Gregarious chitchat came as naturally as breathing to Charles. Maybe the party was happening on the men's side.

The group today seemed to be treating the sauna as an endurance sport, and I was reminded of Tahko Pihkala's dream that someday saunaing would become an Olympic event. Though this never happened, the sauna did make a profound international debut at the 1924 Paris Olympics, when the Finnish contingent had a model sauna built using special wood imported from Hyvinkää. Admitting to myself that I had been outsaunaed after two hours, I hit the buffet bar and found that Charles had thrown in his vasta a half hour earlier.

'So, did you make any friends?' I asked.

'No. These people don't talk,' he said, baffled. 'They'll talk about saunas until you drown them out by whipping yourself loudly with the vasta, but any efforts at real conversation failed utterly.'

I was relieved. If I'd found Charles joking around with his new circle of Finnish friends, I would have felt like a social failure. But the Finns were impenetrable for him, too.

Back in the States, Charles and I no longer had the adventure of travel to distract us. Charles's bag never came and, despite our dogged efforts, was never found. Inside were thousands of pictures capturing our time in Finland, idealized images to cast a halo over every rainy day, petty frustration, or stupid argument. The missing photos seemed ominous. All our happy memories were gone.

But, really, who were we kidding? We were no more a perfect couple than Finland was a perfect country. Everything perfect and harmonious on the outside, and underneath the calm veneer, well, who knew? Why scratch beneath a placid surface? Yet it's hard to live life commenting on how nice everything looks, how good everything tastes, how wonderful every experience is, and never get to the heart of the matter – even if I don't really know what the heart of the matter means. All I knew was that I ached for something more than what Charles and I had. We began to say our good-byes.

japan:
the story of yu

Cleanliness is one of the few original items of Japanese civilisation . . . the bathers stay in the water for a month on end, with a stone on their lap to prevent them from floating in their sleep.
– Basil Hall Chamberlain, *Things Japanese* (1890)

After four weeks in uninspiring Saunatopia, I still felt that my exploration was unfinished. I hadn't fulfilled the promise I'd made to myself the previous spring in Turkey – that I would visit all the great bathing cultures of the world. I had visited the steamers and the sweaters, and I had wandered through the ruins of the greatest bathing culture the world has ever known, but I hadn't visited the soakers.

Even my optimistic expectations did not prepare me for the bathing fervor that awaited. Japan, the land of the rising sun, is also the land of ten thousand hot springs. From what I'd heard, every square mile of Japan's volcanic archipelago offered up a hot spring resort more delightful than the last. A fanaticism and a huge industry surrounded these hot springs, called onsen. (If a bathing fanatic learns one Japanese word, it should be *onsen*.) And the Japanese, like the Romans, have two district bathing traditions – the city baths with normal tap water used to great effect, as well as the countryside curative baths.

Besides my curiosity, personal circumstances pushed me on. After two years, Charles and I called it quits. We had reached that point when you spend all your time talking about 'the relationship' and cease actually to have one. No matter how much we cared about each other, there was something missing that not even all the good will in the world could cover up. I wanted to muffle the sadness and patch over my loneliness in one final adventure.

Marina, who approved of all extravagant ventures related to world travel, registered one reservation. On a phone call from London she said, 'Alexia, remember we are opening a hamam. I'm worried that you're going to come back, your head filled with onsen, and want to start changing everything around. We're open-ing an alabaster hamam, got it?' she said with mock bossiness. 'Oh, and e-mail me if you spot any deals on Issey Miyake.'

'Issey who?'

'You know. The Japanese designer who makes clothes with tiny pleats.'

I chalked this up as another manifestation of Marina's textile obsession but added Issey Miyake to the growing list of things to check out in Japan. I packed a tiny suitcase just as Marina would have and left without looking over my shoulder at all the wreckage in my life.

I wasn't dreading the fifteen-hour nonstop plane ride so much as anticipating a catered study hall. In my yellow bag was a small library of books about Japanese bathing: a lavish coffee table book called *Furo,* a slim, information-packed paperback entitled *Japan: A View from the Bath*, and two guidebooks to the hot springs. By the time I got off the plane at Narita, I'd be a leading expert on Japanese bathing.

I chose an unassigned bulkhead seat. The blond man two seats away looked over and smiled, then went back to reading *Artforum.* I pulled out *Japan: A View from the Bath,* ready for a page turner. And it was. I started taking notes:

'Yu' is the kanji symbol (Kanji symbols are the ancient Chinese pictograms that the Japanese language borrowed) for hot water and all its attendant mysticism. Bathing was not a matter of sitting in a tub with water up to your chest. No, there were hundreds of permutations such as the steam bath (*mushiyu*), the sand bath (*sunayu*), the electric bath (*denkifuro*) and the natural outdoor soaking bath (*rotenburo*).

'Well, it looks like we made it,' whispered my seatmate conspiratorially across the two empty seats.

'What?' I looked up from my reading. I had just penciled a large question mark next to 'electric bath.'

'They've closed the doors. We get to keep our seats.'

'You weren't assigned here, either?'

'No, and I'm six-four, so the regular seats are *unbearable.*'

I recognized his accent immediately. It was Belgian, very much like a French accent, only harsher, with some added phlegm. He spoke and looked a lot like the only other Belgian person I knew.

'You're a French-speaking Belgian, right, a Walloon?'

'Very good, Henry Higgins.'

I returned to my book, embarrassed by my show-off remark and impressed that a Belgian knew *Pygmalion.*

To is another word for hot water and *Sen* means money. So it follows that a *sento* is a place where you pay money for hot water. Sentos, public baths with regular tap water, were popular in the cities. Sento culture was once as socially vibrant as the coffeehouses of Europe. In the 1975 there were 2,163 sentos in Tokyo; by 1996 that number had dropped to 1,341.

I looked up and noticed the handsome self-proclaimed giant was watching me curiously.

'What book has you so absorbed?' he asked.

There's an unwritten law of travel, according to a *New Yorker* article I once read, that if two people are seated next to each other, they will never speak, but if they are separated by an empty seat or two, they'll become the best of friends.

'It's a book on Japanese baths.'

'Yes, I have heard that Japanese people are very clean.' He smiled, exposing the mysteriously sexy bad teeth of a European. 'Forgive me for not introducing myself, my name is Philippe. And your name is?'

'Alexia.' Ahead of us, the stewardess was demonstrating how to use the flotation device. 'Are you traveling to Tokyo on business?' I asked.

'Yes. And you?' Philippe replied.

'Business. Sort of,' I said, echoing his vagueness.

'What kind of business?' Philippe probed.

'Business of the floating world,' I said, using the Japanese euphemism I'd just learned for the seamy underworld of sex shops, strip clubs, and baths that provide 'extra' services.

'Oh, very mysterious. Are you a . . . dancer . . . or a hostess?' Philippe teased.

This was fun. I think it's called flirting – lighthearted banter like an endless tennis volley that picks up speed. Maybe there would be life after Charles. But I felt terrible as soon as the thought crossed my mind. I should have been mourning the failure of a two-year relationship that was supposed to end in marriage. Instead I felt a sense of exhilaration and an appetite for adventure.

The fifteen-hour plane ride passed as quickly as a promising first date – minor revelations, arms that casually brushed up against each other, elliptical allusions to past and present relationships. Actually, it was like five dates strung together. We had the dinner date, then the movie date where we talked through the movie, a cocktails date, a chess-playing date, and a breakfast date.

Soon I had Philippe confessing all sorts of things: he was a modern art dealer in Manhattan, he hadn't finished reading a book in the last two years, he used to play professional tennis, he was thirty-two and had never had a serious relationship. He was, in a word, a temptation. I told him about my dream of opening a hamam in Manhattan with Marina and about how my roommate/boyfriend and I had just split up. He said, 'The problem with living with someone is that you don't have an opportunity to meet other people.' I was starting to understand why he'd never had a serious girlfriend.

As we neared Tokyo and everyone was filling out their entry forms, Philippe asked me where I was staying.

'I didn't book a room,' I said. 'I'll find something at the train station.' If I had learned nothing else while traveling, it was that things left to chance always turn out better than you ever could have planned.

Philippe seemed concerned by my apparent homelessness and said, 'A Japanese friend, Mizuo Miyake, is picking me up at the airport. Mizuo can give you a ride into Tokyo, and I'm sure he can help find you a hotel room.' Philippe didn't seem like a serial murderer; besides, we did yoga at the same studio in New York and even knew someone in common.

Reading nothing more into his offer than the kind of hospitality and generosity that overseas travel engenders, I accepted gratefully. Instead of popping another ENADAlert jet-lag relief pill (it's a good idea to stop at five), finding the train into Tokyo, and navigating linguistic hurdles to find a hotel, I got to take on the blissfully unencumbered role of passenger.

Since our friendship and strange attachment seemed incongruous for two people who had just met on the plane, Philippe introduced me to Mr Miyake as a 'friend from yoga who I ran into at the airport and I couldn't believe she was coming to Tokyo, too!'

'It's very nice to meet an old friend of Philippe's,' said Mr Miyake, who drove us via a Gerhard Richter exhibition into the center of

Tokyo. Tokyo's bay and massive bridges melded into a jet-lagged blur of cranes and early autumn sunshine.

Mr Miyake's tidy dollhouse apartment was so small that were one thing out of place, one sock on the floor, one chair overturned, the entire place would be a mess. Displayed on the living room wall were two curious red-and-white sand panel 'paintings' – I'm not sure what to call them. Side by side and connected by interlocking glass pipes, one was the Japanese flag, the other an American. The sand surface was crisscrossed with tens of tiny tunnels of sandblasted emptiness.

'Where did all those little tunnels come from?' I asked.

'Ants,' Mizuo explained.

'Right. Of course,' I said, feigning enough sophistication to make the leap from paintbrush to ant army.

Mizuo served us steaming cups of green tea from his alcove kitchen, and we sat around the small table.

'Mizuo, do you have a favorite onsen?' I asked.

'I think my favorite is Takaragawa, north of Tokyo in the Gumma mountains. It has the most exquisite stone-paved *rotenburo,* an outdoor bath, overlooking a river. Early in the morning the brown bears still bathe in the pools. You know, animals are responsible for teaching humans about onsen. Wandering monks would see wounded animals bathing and healing themselves in the onsen waters, and slowly they began to realize that the onsen had curative powers.'

'Have you visited Takaragawa many times?'

'Only once. It is special but very remote, so most often I go to Hakone. It's a one-hour train ride from Tokyo and near enough to Mt Fuji to see it on a clear day.'

Philippe looked up from his chocolate (he was already halfway through the box he'd brought as a present for Mizuo). 'Onsen, what are onsen?'

Mizuo explained, '*Onsen* literally is a special kind of curative hot water, the kind of hot water with healthful minerals for bathing or drinking, like your spas in Belgium and France. And this special, therapeutic hot water is everywhere in Japan, because the entire country is positioned on top of a volcanic archipelago.' He nabbed a chocolate from the near empty box and continued, 'But if I say *onsen* in conversation, then it means a place to go, like a resort, to take the onsen waters. Some onsen are large, glitzy resorts, some are *ryokan* – a traditional type of Japanese inn with special bathing facilities – and other onsen are very remote places that you must hike far to reach.'

Philippe eyed me. 'Maybe you and I should visit an onsen together?'

Mizuo, who I sensed knew Philippe and his predilections well, chimed in, 'Philippe, in Japan men and women do not bathe together.'

'Oh, well, forget it, then,' said Philippe, who winked at me and popped the last chocolate into his mouth. 'Don't worry, I have another box, Mizuo.'

'Mizuo, why do you visit onsen?' I asked. 'And do all Japanese people go?'

'Yes, almost all Japanese people visit onsen. It's an unusual concept for Westerners to understand, that we go on vacation with the express purpose of bathing. We will choose an onsen destination based on the beauty of the bath or the type of waters it has. My mom said she could not conceive until she visited the iron-rich waters of Ikaho, which cured her infertility.' He raised an eyebrow as if to suggest that he was not a total believer. 'Certainly there are health benefits, but not miracles. As for why we go, well, it's relaxing. Everyone, especially in Tokyo, is working so hard, so many long hours. When we go to onsen we do nothing except bathe, eat, drink, sleep, and bathe. There's even a person to scrub your back if you want. Japanese men like to revert to childhood sometimes.'

We both looked at Philippe, who had polished off twenty-four pieces of dark chocolate in the Belgian version of reverting to childhood. Mizuo started to work the telephones, and after an alarmingly long string of receptionists saying 'fully booked,' he found a room for me at the Asia Center, a 'business' hotel for people in less than lucrative businesses. At $40 a night, it was the bargain of downtown Tokyo. I was thrilled. I left Philippe and Mizuo to talk ant canvases and Warhol values. Philippe invited me to dinner the following night.

My digs at the Asia Center had a desk, a narrow cot, and a coin-operated television set. Down the hall was a communal bathroom with a shower stall that also doubled as a mop closet. Must find sento, I thought with a desperation compounded by jet lag. Sentos are city bathhouses – places for long, languid soaks with other neighborhood women. I assumed sentos would be so prevalent in Tokyo that I'd have literally a dozen to choose from on any given street. I found the receptionist downstairs and pointed to the sento listings in my guidebook. 'Please help me find sento?' I implored.

'Hmmm, I don't live around here,' the young man at the desk said apologetically. 'There are sentos everywhere. . . .' He scratched his cheek, looking toward the ceiling for divine inspiration. If you ask a Japanese person for directions, he or she will, as a cultural point of pride, try to help, until you realize that they are looking at the map upside down and, in fact, aren't even from the city you're lost in. You have to bow out, literally bend at the waist, and absolve them of responsibility before they'll leave you to fend for yourself on the convoluted, unmarked streets of Japan. But I waited out the confusion and got some inspired advice.

The receptionist said, 'Maybe good idea to go to Asakusa. Asakusa is still like an old Edo village with Shitamachi spirit.' I nodded in false comprehension. Edo, I remembered, was the old name for Tokyo when it was just a collection of small fishing villages clustered along Tokyo Bay. But I knew not of Shitamachi. It sounded like a fake Japanese word that Western kids might make up in the playground: 'You big Shitamachi, give me back my Pokémon card.'

Shitamachi, as it turns out, refers to the low-lying plain of Tokyo that was traditionally less affluent and more villagelike than the tonier area of Yamanote, the uptown. Artisans and craftspeople gravitated toward Shitamachi, and the communal, salt-of-the-earth ethos continues uninterrupted today. So pleasing was it phonetically that I started incorporating Shitamachi into as many conversations as I could, and indeed, it's one of those insider words that Japanese people are flattered and surprised you've learned. How does one get to Shitamachi? Well, you can take a train there.

Walking on the streets of a large Japanese city, like Tokyo or Kyoto, is a uniquely alienating experience. Street drama does not unfold with the same spontaneous electricity with which New York's soul bursts forth from every hot dog stand and overheard cell phone conversation. The Japanese scuffle along briskly, eyes to the pavement or glued to their DoCoMo phone interface (they read from their phones more than they speak into them), as they rush between work and home. The women totter along chicly in elevator heels (now illegal to drive in after a spate of fatal traffic accidents when a five-inch shoe sole prevented the driver from moving her foot from the gas to the brake in a timely fashion); the men clutch briefcases, looking weary and embattled; and the young kids, resembling junior naval officers in their school uniforms, move in amoebic hordes. Everywhere there are people, but there's no interaction. As one longtime expat described it to me: Japanese people operate on an AM frequency and Americans on FM. Different decibels of existence.

Don't these people talk and laugh and shout and get rowdy? It's so unlike the one thousand little dramas unfolding daily on the streets of any American city, where men and women jostle and bump up against one another, homeless people have tantrums, construction workers make lewd comments, and everyone is eyeing everyone else for better clothes and smaller cell phones. In Japan, the street dynamics operate on a barely audible frequency, and in a country where I don't speak the language this makes me feel invisible, alone, and, most of all, in need of a bath. Where else would one go to see the Japanese at their most animated?

Tokyo does not look the way it's supposed to. I expected small winding alleys of craftspeople making kimonos and tatami mats, brewers of saki, culturers of tofu. Where were the dark wooden buildings with lanterns out front? The rows of *machiyas,* elegant traditional town houses, with nearby teahouses and rock gardens? All the fairy-tale aspects of a traditional Japan were conspicuously absent. Tokyo today, with the exception of small Shitamachi pockets, is a blinking neon light illuminating high-rise office buildings in an endless sea of convenience stores. The ultramodernity is not so surprising when you consider that Tokyo's been leveled twice in the twentieth century: once by the great Kanto earthquake in 1923 and a second time by aerial bombing during World War II.

Ueno and Asakusa are the last two stops on the Ginza line, Tokyo's oldest subway line. On a crisp late September evening, I disembarked at Ueno, an eastern subcenter. The train station was in the middle of a huge shopping arcade, the funky, junk-filled Ameya-yokocho Arcade. There were stalls selling mysterious oils and unguents, a man hawking huge bins of socks, and vendors of dangerous-looking yakitori skewers. I stood in the middle of a sea of intersections – blinking lights and beeping crosswalks – with no clue in which direction to head. I popped another jet-lag relief pill.

I was looking for Rokuryu, a sento-style bath with onsen waters, a rarity in Tokyo. I didn't have the exact address, but my Japanese onsen bible suggested that Rokuryu was hard to miss: in back of the Ueno Zoo, left at a noodle shop, and down a small lane. Child's play. Unfortunately, I am cursed with no internal compass, and I would spend almost as much time in Japan searching for baths as I would spend in them.

It took only five minutes to find the enormous leafy park known as Ueno-Koen (Ueno Hill), filled with every distraction from teahouses to ice-cream stands to museums of modern art, eastern antiquities, and science. Two hours, three miles of walking, and eight direction givers later, I found the white-tiled façade and cloth banners, called *noren,* of Rokuryu.

Out front there were lockers shaped like shoeboxes. In Japan, shoes are a scourge, a vile contagion, lumped in the same category as hypodermic needles. I slipped my shoes in the box and shut it, and a clunky wooden chip with grooves popped out. My key. Nearby, in the digital enclave of Akihabara, where skyscraper after skyscraper is a megastore shrine to gadgets that store media in bytes and bits, this stone age key would be looked upon with derision.

There were two doors into the sento. One would lead to a room crowded with naked men scratching themselves (or so I imagined), the other to a more sisterly realm of bathing goddesses. I opened my onsen bible in an attempt to identify the hiragana characters for male and female. Before I had time to distinguish *otokoburo* (bath for men) from *onnaburo* (bath for women), a young woman pedaled up to Rokuryu with a bundled-up child on her backseat, removed their shoes (even though the child couldn't walk, good habits start early), and chose the door on the right. I followed.

Before entering a sento dressing room, there is always a *bandai-san* to contend with. Traditionally the *bandai-san,* who can be either a man or a woman, sits impassively on a raised platform overlooking both the men's and women's sides. The *bandai-san*'s job is to collect the small entry fee, usually $3 or $4, and to sell soaps, shampoos, and towels. For regulars, the *bandai-san* might tell them who's inside and fill them in on local gossip. Newer sentos often place the *bandai-san* in an outer lobby, like a hotel concierge. It seems customers, especially younger women, don't like *bandai-sans* of the opposite sex having a bird's-eye view into the dressing room. It's a eunuch's job.

I handed the *bandai-san* a 500-yen note (roughly $4) and pointed to one of the hand towels for sale, a *tenugui.* Sento regulars arrive with their own *furoshiki,* an all-purpose square cloth for carrying the necessary bath ointments, brushes, and loofahs. The *furoshiki* can also be used inside the bath for covering up if a *bandai-san*'s gaze turns lecherous.

'Onsen?' I asked.

'Hai, onsen,' replied the male *bandai-san*, followed by a long explanation of I don't know what: the mineral content of the baths, the hours of operation, how foreigners weren't allowed. Foreigners, or gaijin, as the Japanese refer to all non-Japanese, are still sometimes turned away from onsen in the northern province of Hokkaido, but in cosmopolitan Tokyo this kind of gaijin prejudice is no longer prevalent.

I stripped to nothing, even removing my earrings (onsen water can tarnish), and placed all my belongings into a straw bucket that slid neatly into a locker. The design utility of the Japanese was matched only by the Finns, I thought. I looked at all the naked Japanese women, both dressing and undressing around me, and in the presence of their flowerlike bodies I felt as three-dimensional and relentlessly curvy as a helium balloon figurine, like the pictures Picasso painted of rotund, billowy female figures overtaking the canvas. All the Japanese women had delicate frames, with breasts that swelled but weren't big enough to sag, narrow shoulders, and flat bottoms.

Japanese women are far too polite and discreet to stare at another person's physical differences, but my fleshiness and comparative corpulence would, I was sure, turn into an 'Amazon gaijin at the sento' story later that night. I tried to pretend I was still in a Finnish sauna surrounded by lumpy, pear-shaped bodies. A scenario where I was the relative flower. But I noticed one thing Finnish and Japanese women had in common: the unruliness of their pubic hair. It was only the Slavs who waged a war of hot wax on their hair follicles.

I slid back the water-streaked glass door and tiptoed barefoot into the hot and steamy sento room. It was a high-ceilinged, light-flooded room with blue metal rafters and a twenty-foot partition separating the men's and women's sides. I didn't hear much noise coming from the men's side. From the women's side there was a cacophony of babies gurgling, women laughing, and, predominantly, water flowing.

All the women in the bathing room stopped what they were doing to look at me. What was a gaijin doing at their local sento? The innocent question etched across their quizzical, knitted eyebrows. A couple of them smiled and nodded at me in welcoming recognition, and then they went back to scrubbing and soaking. This was pretense, though. Really they were watching my every move to make sure that I cleaned myself properly.

A tub in Japan is not where you clean yourself, it is where you go after you are thoroughly cleaned, sterilized, a germ-neutral expanse of epidermis. I wanted to impress my fellow bathers with my mastery of this concept. I wanted to give them a story of the gaijin with scrupulous hygiene so that night over their dinner of shabu-shabu they could say, 'Americans are much cleaner than we thought. Today I saw a giant American girl clean herself for fifteen minutes before getting into the water.'

Along both walls were rows of showers. Unlike showers in the West – the high-water-pressure nozzles that you stand underneath as hot water cascades down your shoulders and washes the shampoo from your hair – Japanese showers jut out of the wall at hip level, reminding me of so-called hip baths of the ancient Greek gymnasia.

I scanned the humid, soap-scented room for instruction and inspiration. The idea, it seemed, was to pull a stool up to the nozzle and scrub yourself silly. Some of the older women forwent the stools and sat on their haunches directly on the floor, just as I'd seen in eighteenth-century Japanese woodblocks. I watched the woman and child who had come in before me head over to an empty stool, pour soap on the stool, scrub for ten seconds, and then wash it off with cold water. Now it was clean enough to sit on. She followed the same procedure with one of the small pink buckets, washing it and then using it to douse herself with water. I was teaching myself the ritual.

I chose the vacant shower stool next to her. There was a mirror directly in front of me, and I examined my face, colorless and waxy, and my body, jet-lagged and bloated. I pictured Charles moving out of our New York apartment. I couldn't imagine life without him, my best friend. Making hot chocolate thick as soufflé on winter nights, lazy Sundays leafing through photo books, our constant comforting phone calls. I felt very alone imagining a life without these shared joys. Yet as much as we would miss each other, we both knew that a life together would be based on tacit disappointment. Then, inexplicably, I wondered what Philippe was doing across town. Was there anything wrong with accepting his invitation for dinner? Shouldn't I be contemplating my solo life, getting to know myself again, reading self-help books and following twelve steps to something? I turned on the handheld shower and set to work cleaning myself in an ablution of guilt.

I noticed that the older ladies didn't use the shower head (too modern!) and instead just filled and refilled their small buckets, pouring a constant stream of water over themselves. The lady next to me had taken a cloth and begun what was to be a fifteen-minute process of soaping herself from head to toe, in between every fold of skin. I mimed her exactly. She rubbed in circles at the nape of her neck, and so did I. Underneath the armpits, down the torso, inside the belly button, a thorough attack on the groin, a careful tiptoe across the shanks and calves, and in between every toe. Then she bucketed off all the soap, and I watched it flow down the drain in foamy snakes. I repeated this elaborate process while she was washing her child, who had turned a shade of pink in the heat of the room. I looked around, hoping to collect impressed, approving nods. I was the cleanest gaijin in Tokyo. That I was certain of.

Now I just had to choose a tub to soak in. I was overwhelmed the same way I was at the Finnish Sauna Society. There were two tiled tubs of hot water in the middle of the room that looked enticing. More intriguing, however, were the two larger tubs in the back of the room, filled with mysterious black water.

I chose the onsen water, the color of grape soda. It was hot, about 105 degrees Fahrenheit. I know water temperatures like a wine connoisseur knows grape varietals. This water was almost first-degree-burn hot. All around me sat Japanese women with expressions of utter contentment and contemplation. How did they summon such serenity inside a lobster pot? Didn't they know we would die if we stayed in too long? I wanted to warn them, but I didn't know how. Then I remembered an expression from the onsen bible: *'Atsui desu.'* (It's hot!)

'Hai, hai, hai,' said an older woman next to me, laughing.

A woman closer to my age, sitting in the adjacent tub, whispered, 'It is a little cooler in this tub.' I crossed the divide. I wouldn't exactly say it was a relief, but the water was slightly more tolerable.

'Arigato gozaimasu,' I said, a polite form of 'thank you' in Japanese.

'You like onsen?' she asked in a soft, willowy voice. Her accent sounded almost British.

'You speak English?'

'Yes, I spent many years abroad with my husband. He works for a plastics company and we lived in London. Is this the first onsen you visit?'

'Yes, my very first. I thought onsen were for long soaks. Are all onsen this hot?' Next to me I noticed a woman in her seventies, hair wrapped carefully in layers of diaphanous hairnets, easing into the hotter tub and placing a small sand dial next to her. She was going to measure her soak in grains of sand.

'This onsen is special for Eddoko. In this part of Tokyo, Shita-machi, we take bath extra hot. Oh, forgive my rudeness, my name is Ayako. What is yours?'

'Alexia. It's very nice to meet you. I've only been in Tokyo for two days, but I am realizing how rare it is to meet someone who speaks fluent English.'

'Yes, it's a problem. We learn it in school so everyone can read English, but the schools don't teach how to speak it, and of course Japanese people are very shy to do anything that they cannot do perfectly.' That explained a lot. Meanwhile I watched incredulously as the woman I'd come in with dunked her one-year-old baby. I expected cries, but instead he cooed in delight and splashed around in the black water.

'Ayako, why is this water the color of grape soda?'

'Yes, it is unusual. This used to be just a normal city sento, or so the story goes, but the water bills were making the owner poor, so he began to drill for natural onsen water. Everyone thought it was silly, especially in Tokyo, since there is not much onsen water here, but at five hundred meters he hit this black water. At first he thought it was useless because it's not the normal color for onsen water. But then he had it analyzed and found that it has thirteen different minerals and cures everything from rheumatism to heat rash to obesity. Now he is a very rich man.'

'So hitting onsen water is like striking oil.'

'Maybe,' she said, contemplating my sensationalist analogy.

Ayako and I were both feeling light-headed and drugged. We wandered over to the showers to cool off.

'Are you a regular here?' I asked as we both threw buckets of cold water over our shoulders.

'I live uptown, but my mother lives in Asakusa, so when I visit her I sometimes stop here to enjoy the water. It gives me energy.'

'Are there many wonderful sentos to visit in Tokyo?'

'The old neighborhoods still have traditional sentos, though many have closed down or modernized, adding a gym facility or a karaoke room. If you want to visit a place where sentos are still a big part of life, you must go to Kyoto. Kyoto is a more traditional, spiritual city.'

'How so?'

'We have a popular joke that shows the difference,' she began. 'Imagine a huge temple made of solid gold. It is a beautiful place, and there are many tourists inside. The tourist from Tokyo wonders how the temple was constructed, who designed it, and when it was built. The tourist from Osaka tries to calculate how much money the gold is worth . . .' She paused for effect. 'And the tourist from Kyoto just worships.'

We sat in worshipful silence for a few minutes. I noticed an official notarized document framed on the wall. The Onsen Association, which categorizes all the types of thermal waters in Japan, had classified Rokuryu as 'sodium hydrogen-carbonate' water. Onsen authentication is serious business. Onsen owners must disclose the exact temperature of the water when it comes out of the ground, how much it is heated, and whether or not they add any minerals to the *yu* (hot water). Some sentos, in order to market themselves, boast 'onsen' baths where they add special mineral salts to the bath. Indeed, these kinds of bath salts are popular all over Japan, Ayako explained as we slipped into another, smaller tub with cooler, clear water.

'At night I will ask my husband if he wants Beppu, Atami, or Nagano bath,' she said, naming three of the premier onsen destinations.

'Oh, so you have bath salts from each of those places?'

'Yes, you can buy these salts in Tokyo or when you visit onsen in other cities.'

'So after this bath you will go home and fix your husband a bath?'

'Yes,' she answered shyly.

'Japanese women prepare baths for their husbands?' I asked, struggling with this concept.

'Yes, every night. He's out working, and I'm a lazy housewife.' She laughed innocently.

'Do you want to work?'

'Not really. You see, I am of a strange, in-between generation. My younger sister works, and she lives at home. She doesn't really want to get married and take care of a man.'

I had read about this phenomenon of young Japanese women who live at home well into their twenties and thirties. The Japanese even coined a special name for this large demographic group, which translates as 'parasite singles.' Because they live at home, housed and fed by their parents, virtually all their income is disposable, and they almost single-handedly keep Louis Vuitton and Michael Kors in business. This generation of women consciously resists marriage and all its inherent sacrifices and caretaking responsibilities in Japanese society.

Ayako continued, 'But I was never raised to work. I was raised to get married. When I was twenty-two the matchmaker began to set up meetings for me and my husband. He was my second meeting, but he had met over seventy girls before me. When I was your age it was considered very bad if you weren't married by twenty-five. An unmarried woman over twenty-five was called "Christmas cake the day after Christmas." '

I leaned my head back in the tub and wondered if there were Japanese translations of Gloria Steinem. I tried to imagine Marina or myself as dutiful wives drawing baths for our husbands. No, we'd have a hamam to wash strangers, but our husbands would be on their own.

'Ayako, do you have a favorite onsen?' I asked, changing the subject.

After some deliberation, she revealed: 'It is a place high in the Gumma mountains, very remote, very obscure, called Takaragawa.'

'Takaragawa! That is Mr Miyake's favorite onsen also.'

'Mr. Miyake?'

'The only other Japanese person I know.'

That reminded me: they were picking me up for dinner in an hour and a half, and a confusing subway ride still lay between me and the Asia Center. So after soaking for an hour with Ayako, we exchanged phone numbers, agreeing to visit another Tokyo sento together and maybe do some shopping in Ginza. She was delightful, and her fluent English was a gift from the gods.

At 8:00 on the dot, a minivan of art dealers came to collect me at the Asia Center. It was a veritable UN of aesthetes – a Japanese, a South American, a Frenchman, and a Belgian; I was the token American and girl. Most of us were too jet-lagged to have a conversation any more sophisticated than an ongoing stream of Belgian jokes. Max, an Argentinean, and Philippe's best friend, began with, 'Let me present the attributes of a modern European. He combines the moral courage of the French, the fighting spirit of the Italians, the work ethic of the British, and the sense of humor of the Germans. In short, a Belgian.' Philippe rolled his eyes and put his arm around me.

We arrived in good spirits at Fuku-sushi, a fashionable Rappongi sushi restaurant with gleaming navy tables and lavender accent lights. As we entered the dining room, we were greeted by a deafening chorus of *'Irashaimase!'* from the five sushi chefs behind the long counter. *Irashaimase* means roughly 'Welcome,' and the louder it is said, the greater the sign of respect. Since Mizuo was a regular at Fuku-sushi, we got the high-decibel Broadway version. A lacquered tray of sushi arrived: an enormous assortment of buttery pieces of fish, teriyaki eel, heaps of salty red caviar, and foamy sea urchin atop small lumps of lightly vinegared rice. No California rolls or crabstick rolls – in fact, no rolls at all. Just huge pieces of the freshest catch from Tsukiji, the world's largest fish market.

With his round, dimpled face and gentle, questioning blue eyes, Max looked like a Buddhist monk in an Italian suit. Max had lived and worked in Tokyo for eight years and had become as assimilated as a foreigner in Japan is allowed. As Donald Richie, the foremost writer on postwar Japan, pointed out, 'Shortly, however, the visitor discovered that Japan insisted that he keep his distance . . . though he desired intimacy, Japan was gently teaching him to keep his distance.' This ultimately was Max's experience. Though he spoke nearly flawless Japanese, understood and abided by all Japanese proclivities, and had visited the sento every evening when he lived in a six-tatami room in Tokyo, he would always be a gaijin.

'I had a tiny apartment, and if I took a bath at home, I'd have to sit like this,' he explained, pulling his legs tightly to his chest in demonstration. 'So every night I went to the sento with friends, and of course I made sento friends as well. At the sento you can see all the *yakuzi,* the Mafia guys, who are covered from head to toe in the most insane tattoos.'

'The Japanese are very romantic about baths,' I mused.

'Yes, very much so. The Japanese still romanticize the *furo* of old, the tub made out of *hinoki* wood, a fragrant wood considered sacred. I guess it's cedar in English. And of course the Japanese never varnish everything. Don't mess with nature. So the tubs become silky to touch when the wood ages.'

'And what's this thing called skinship?' I asked.

'Ahh.' Max smiled and took another sip of sake. 'That's a more metaphorical romanticism about the baths. There's an expression, *Hadaka no tsukiai,* which means "Companions in nudity" or "Naked association." The idea is that by sharing the same bath and bathwater, you do away with all the normal social barriers in life and can forge closer bonds. Occasionally I also hear the expression "Bath friends are best friends," and it's true that the atmosphere of the bath makes possible a closeness rarely experienced otherwise in Japanese life.'

As it turned out, locating old, traditional sentos involved hours of sleuthing – looking for clues like tall, slender chimneys, asking for directions, and waiting for twenty minutes while an old woman with no vocal cords lovingly drew a detailed map of Kita-ku, a rough Tokyo suburb. Sentos, I was discovering, are the poor cousins of onsen, using normal tap water instead of mineral-infused curative water, serving city dwellers in need of a bath instead of vacationers in search of a soak. The sento, once a vital urban institution, today fumbles for respectability and survival, but still I searched daily for still-functioning reincarnations of the rowdy Edo period sentos.

I quickly found that the sentos in Tokyo's outer suburbs were best, but Kyoto was continually invoked as the place to experience old-fashioned sento life. Kyoto apartments and *machiyas* were still small and cramped and lacked adequate plumbing such that many Kyotoites visited the sento for their nightly bath.

So I made a plan. Rather than risk disappointment at another

Tokyo sento with recently installed karaoke bar or gym wing (blasphemy!), I decided to cut my losses, activate my J&R rail pass, and check out Hakone before setting off for Kyoto.

Only one hundred kilometers away, Hakone is Tokyo's not-so-secret garden and most convenient onsen getaway. Mt Fuji, or Fuji-san, as the Japanese affectionately refer to their highest peak, is visible on a clear day, furthering Hakone's appeal. Despite the crowds that Hakone draws, it was a huge relief to let down my city guard, to smell the azaleas, see mountainsides of trees, and adopt a more provincial pace.

I expected a single Hakone train stop, with a *Hobbit*-style signpost directing bath-seeking Bilbos to one of the town's spectacular onsen – a straightforward system with painted wood postings that read, 'Backaches this way,' 'Depression and anemia that way.' But Hakone was a sprawling destination, dotting several mountain ridges and running for several train stops. I got off at Hakone-Yumoto, the most popular stop, and walked two miles up the side of a mountain to the Tenzan onsen.

The Tenzan-noten-buro is the bath junkie's ultimate pleasure complex, surrounded by bamboo groves and pine trees. Inside the dark-wooded tatami wonderland, I unlaced my shoes for the eight hundredth time, cursing myself for not bringing slip-ons to Japan. The bath fee, even at a place as remote and upscale as this onsen, was still under $8. I wanted to wander around, exploring the tatami recesses of the long passages and hidden alcoves, but the Japanese are helpful to a fault, and I was whisked straight back to the women's onsen area, bypassing the massage area, cafés, a mysterious room of sleeping bodies, and what I like to imagine was an opium den but was probably just a VIP lounge for tea ceremonies.

Again I found myself in a changing room, taking off my clothes in front of strangers, wondering how this mountainside onsen would compare to the Tokyo sentos. The shower room, a wooden, steamy-windowed cube, had not one synthetic object. The stools, the shelves, and the buckets for washing were all constructed of light, fragrant cedar. The foggy windows peered out onto the most enchanting and aesthetically perfect bath scene I'd encountered. The Japanese, I was realizing, possessed the rare ability to improve on nature. The outdoor pavilion of four hot pools was fenced off from the men's side by a thick grove of six-foot green bamboo stalks. The rock-hewn pools, shaped like amorphously floating continents, boasted sodium chloride thermal water, which is said to cure every conceivable malady. This water inspired sixteenth-century Edo dwellers to walk for three days straight, over fifty miles along the Tokaido Road, to soak in Hakone's pools. Even early visitors from France, where water has never been trusted, got over their fears in the late nineteenth century and discovered the pleasures of onsen bathing in Hakone-Yumoto.

I stood on the slated walkway, cataloging all the pools, one with a straw pagoda, another that recessed into a cave, a third with a small Buddha shrine at the far end. The women looked young, beautiful, and immortally vital with their flushed onsen complexions. Many carried young children. Everyone looked grateful to be here in this bathing garden, far from Tokyo, if only mentally. I chose the pool with the Buddha statue, and immediately a group of teenage girls started to chat me up. They began with a school-scripted dialogue that, after a week in Japan, I'd performed at least twenty times.

'Where . . . are . . . you . . . from?' they summoned slowly.

'New York City,' I replied, and enjoyed the usual ohhs and ahhs that pronouncing New York City your hometown garners abroad. It's an instant passport to rock star status.

One of the girls told me, 'This water is the most original in this pool,' which I took to mean was most direct from the subterranean source. They splashed the water onto their faces, and I followed. Their serene happiness was infectious, and the thought that hot spring bathing constituted a major girls outing thrilled me.

After my delightfully natural Hakone bathing experience, I set out for what I knew would be a ghastly curiosity. I walked another three miles along a highway in search of Yunessun, a newly opened theme park devoted to bathing. I was simultaneously sickened and awed by this uniquely Japanese brand of genius kitsch – the synthetic, Formica version of the Turkish hamam and the prefab, 'decaying' Ionic columns and urns surrounding the Roman bath. If four thousand people a day traipsed through this tacky Epcot Center of bathing cultures, then surely Marina and I would attract a stampede of visitors to our impeccably tasteful establishment.

While I did this, Philippe did whatever art dealers do – inspect paintings, seduce prospective buyers, drink Champagne. Despite Philippe's lack of depth and genuine understanding, his sense of humor and playfulness made him compelling. He was the perfect antidote to heartbreak, if a slightly guilty one. When he suggested that we visit Takaragawa together, the onsen that Mizuo and Ayako had both mentioned, I balked at first. Of course, nothing sounded more enjoyable than to soak with an attractive man in a mountain-side *rotenburo*. But nice people don't run off with Belgian art dealers days after a breakup.

Throughout our two-day excursion, Philippe and I made enough gaijin gaffes to keep area sushi bar conversations humming for weeks. Philippe had told me on the plane that he was 'proficient in Japanese.' To me, 'proficient' means you can decode directions and engage in cursory chitchat, but you can't tell a joke or discuss literature. Proficient obviously meant something else entirely to Philippe. When left to our own devices, without Max or Mizuo to translate, Philippe could barely ask for a glass of water.

It took us over an hour of involved pantomime and phrase book pointing to check into the Takaragawa *ryokan,* a traditional Japanese inn deep in the Gumma mountains, where the jagged peaks were shaped like Egyptian pyramids. Upon arrival, we had been shoved into the gaijin hotel. Whereas hundreds of Japanese people were at the inn down the road, wearing enviable rough cotton brown robes, we were the only guests at our hotel and stuck with prissy blue silk robes to boot.

Mikono Ono, the proprietor with four missing front teeth, did the *ryokan* song and dance, explaining the many features of the room, except perhaps the most important one – that inside the quaint-looking bathroom was a toilet capable of physical assault. Innocently, you might press a button hoping to flush the toilet, and the next second a stealthy projectile instrument emerges from the back of the bowl and with dead-on accuracy sprays warm water up your bottom. We would learn that later; now we learned about the exhausting choreography of slipper changing. Here's a summary:

When you arrive at the *ryokan,* leave your contaminated street shoes at the front door and put on special corridor-roaming slippers. At the entrance of your bedroom, remove dirty corridor-roaming slippers. Walk on the tatami-matted floor with stockinged feet (bare feet only if you must). If you go to the bathroom, make sure to put on the special bathroom slippers, marked 'toilet' on the toe and found by the bathroom door. After you flush – with a possible hose-down by the electronic proctologist – make sure to remove the bathroom slippers. Walking around in slippers marked 'toilet' is the ultimate gaijin faux pas. If you decide to stroll in the garden, you must again don dirty corridor-roaming slippers; by the door of the garden, you'll see a supply of dirtier, nastier garden slippers. A good rule of thumb: If you haven't changed footwear in over fifteen paces, you've done something horribly wrong.

We dressed carefully. I introduced Philippe to the essential leisurewear of any onsen stay. The yukata is a loose-fitting, wide-sleeved cotton robe. *Kata* means garment and *yu* hot water; thus yukata is the garment designed for strolling to and from the baths. More problematic are the geta, wooden clogs commonly worn at hot spring towns that force all wearers, from children to sumo wrestlers, to shuffle along like delicate geisha.

We stumbled through an outdoor bamboo tunnel lit by kerosene and filled with stalls selling a bizarre bric-a-brac of Buddhist statues, plastic action figures, stuffed animals, and incense sticks. After the wares, we passed a temple precinct, an alcove for *zazen,* silent meditation. We peered into the cages of brown bears and finally emerged into the open autumn air, the fiery-leafed maples bending toward the rocky valley of *rotenburo,* as if to listen to the water. The crisp October wind rustled the leaves and shook the branches, muting the sound of the water. A fifty-foot bamboo pipe stretched from the mountainside where we stood down into the bath, delivering hot water.

This incredible natural beauty is considered sacred in Japan's Shinto culture. I knew the onsen had religious origins; almost all of Japan's hot springs were originally founded by Buddhist monks wandering through the wilderness on forty-day fasts. During the Tumulus period, many Shinto shrines were built next to hot springs. Takaragawa looked like one of those shrines, the straw-thatched pagoda covering part of the enormous, amoeba-shaped pool, the stone lanterns, so common at shrines, set up like an altar at one corner of the pool, a stone-sculpted Buddha presiding over another corner. It was a glorious scene. I admired the baths, registered the many people soaking in the pool, but in my eagerness to get out of the cool air and into the hot water, I didn't observe as much as I should have.

Philippe and I each disappeared into our separate changing rooms, agreeing to meet naked outside in a moment. Bath nudity never causes as much anxiety as bedroom nudity, at least not for me. This main *rotenburo* at Takaragawa was reputed to be one of the few mixed-gender baths in the country, and Mikono Ono had vouched for that, too. All Japanese baths used to be mixed gender until Commodore Perry arrived in 1853 and was so scandalized by the sight of men and women bathing together that he forced the new Meiji government to segregate the baths according to Western Victorian standards of morality. (This is the story, but the actual history is more complicated.)

Because I thought myself to be at a mixed bath, I left the dressing room carrying only the *furoshiki,* the small square cloth ten inches by ten inches. I stood at the steps of the red-stone *rotenburo,* surveying the

other bathers. Everyone was studiously not looking at me. Not only
was I the only gaijin woman, which would have been distinction
enough, but I realized in a sudden, horrifying flash that I was the only
naked woman. All the Japanese women had wrapped huge beach
towels around their bodies, hiding everything in between their
shoulders and midthighs. Philippe came out of his dressing room
and stood next to me. It took him a moment to register that one of
these things was not like the other. He could easily do what all the
Japanese men did – delicately place the washcloth over his groin. For
me, however, there was no hope. What should I even try to cover
with the tiny cloth? Summoning inner reserves of poise – and there
wasn't much to draw from – I quickly and deliberately descended the
steps into the bath. One hundred pairs of eyes pretended not to watch
me. Philippe was in hysterics.

In my moment of supreme embarrassment, I tried to focus again
on the religious origins of these baths. I remembered a passage from
Furo that explained: 'Bathing in Japan is best when communal.
Never inhibited by Judeo-Christian embarrassment about the human body or taboos on public nudity, the Japanese have always
bathed in groups. Until quite recently, men and women soaked
together in public bathhouses as well as hot springs.' Those days
were sadly over. 'Judeo-Christian embarrassment' had firmly taken
root, but no one had told me. I alone was enjoying the innocence of
the Garden of Eden, while the rest of the bathers were decked out in
fig leaves.

I recovered my composure after several dunks in hot, clear water.
At least my clumsy naked entrance hadn't been caught on film.
Philippe and I, now guarded by a mist rising off the hot water, made
our way over to the bamboo pipe resting on a rocky ledge. The
water, straight from the deep, underground source – I imagined
raging geothermal fires presided over by the Shinto fire god – was
hotter than the water in the pool, and we took turns arching our
heads under the spout. The flow was gentle, and as the water
massaged my head I looked toward the sky. Brilliant red and orange

leaves flapped in the wind, barely tethered to the trees, while some leaves danced in the air and fell toward the pool. Other bathers, lying on their backs, floated around the pool, also staring at the sky. Were we tricking nature by not braving the elements, but instead contemplating nature from inside the heat of this red-stoned pool? Luckily nature gave us this pool, making this a religious pleasure, not a hedonistic one. Not that I needed to justify pleasure anymore.

We stayed in the pool for hours. When the heat started to make us dizzy, we'd sit on a rock ledge in the 40-degree-Fahrenheit air, our bodies coughing steam and feeling not the faintest nip in the air. Then we'd play a game to see who could stand the cold the longest and who first took refuge in the pool. Philippe would always get cold first (Vermonters are heartier than Belgians), but he's more competitive, so I lost every time.

Philippe and I had nothing in common, but when he left for New York, I missed him for the first few days. Between Hakone and Takaragawa, I had caught the onsen bug and wanted to focus my search on more remote onsen. But first, I had to see how they bathed in Japan's most compelling and cultured city, Kyoto.

One need only open a guidebook to learn that Kyoto is a city of 1.4 million people. But somehow this fact completely escaped me, and I arrived expecting an intimate jewel box of a city. First I figured the high-gloss, futuristic train station was an exception, the bleak avenues and ugly skyscrapers other aberrations. Finally I realized that the Kyoto of Western imagination is hidden in small pockets around the city. It takes a diligent and persistent traveler to find the intimate sake bars, the raked gardens, and the geisha-inhabited lanes. I cursed Pico Iyer, one of my favorite writers, for misleading me in *The Lady and the Monk,* his book about Kyoto that conveniently skims over any urban blight and concentrates on footbridges, changing leaves, and his growing obsession with a Japanese housewife.

Kyoto's most interesting accommodations include a dozen or so Buddhist monasteries that offer room and board. The sentos were, as promised, everywhere. Moreover, they were still vital without needing to curry contemporary favor with slapdash exercise and karaoke wings. I quickly fell into a pattern of nightly visits to the Santo-Yu Sento (translation: Good Health and Hot Water Bath). Not only was it three 90-degree turns away from my monastery, it had an intriguing *denkifuro* that I liked to flirt with.

The *denkifuro* is a uniquely Japanese invention: a bath with electric current running through it. What sicko thought of this? I wondered. The Japanese believe that the light electric current stimulates the circulation. Game for any bath, no matter how freakish, I dipped my leg in and my body seized in horror. It felt like hundreds of crickets were trying to jump out of my calf. A woman sitting in the six-foot-square pool smiled encouragingly at me. I added my second leg and began to lower myself into the bath. The current felt anything but light. A rash of pins and needles stabbed my lower body, and I began to wonder how beneficial to my health submerging my body into electrified water actually was. Add to that a concern that I might never have children if I dipped my body any lower. Embarrassed, I bowed to the other bather, a strangely formal thing to do at a sento, and retreated upstairs to the sento's large sauna with a glassed-in television. Ten women were sitting on pink plastic foam cushions, passively watching the Osaka-Tokyo baseball game.

Overall, the Kyoto sentos were bigger than Tokyo's and more crowded as well. In a city of tiny apartments, the sentos' wide tubs and water largesse – in fact, the Japanese love to watch the expensive hot water splash decadently over the tub's side – made an otherwise cramped life tolerable. Also, many of the sentos had outdoor decks to showcase fabricated *rotenburos,* so bathers could enjoy the pinch of cold air from the safety of warm water. For a real *rotenburo* experience, Kyoto had one lovely outdoor onsen on its outskirts, Kurama Onsen. Kurama was simplicity itself. From the confines of a twelve-foot rectangular wooden box, bathers would sit shoulder deep in 101 degrees Fahrenheit and contemplate the opposing hilltop of swaying pines.

The Geishas of Kii-Katsuura

The onsen ideal involves hiking ten kilometers into the wilderness and finding rock-sculpted hot springs next to a riverbed – or better yet, sculpting your own tub out of rocks the way they do along some riverbeds. Realizing that this ideal required more rugged individualism and camping equipment than I could muster on this trip, I compromised by taking a train to a remote fishing village in the Wakayama prefecture. Though many onsen have colorful stories of discovery and awesome perches, this description held special allure:

> The special bath, called Bokido, is situated in a natural cave . . . Bokido means 'Forget-to-Go-Home-Bath,' named after what a nobleman of the Edo period did, so infatuated was he with this area. The water is sulfate and was once used by wounded warriors of the Taira clan after skirmishes with the Minamoto clan in the 12th century. It's still good for any battle injuries you might have . . .

The dramatic seaside setting and the evocative name and history immediately seduced me. I'd also seen a picture in another book of two Japanese girls relaxing in a 'jungle bath' at Kii-Katsuura. So the bonanza prospect of both a jungle bath and a Forget-to-Go-Home-Bath kept me anchored to my seat as the train emptied out in the popular resort town of Shirahama. Yes, I was becoming Japanese in my pursuit of as many different bathing experiences as possible. I settled in, the only passenger in the car, for another three-hour chug to Kii-Katsuura.

The coastline came in and out of view. Crags cropped out of the water, overshadowed by cypresses and birches blazing yellow and orange like bonfires falling into the sea. It was thrilling to see the Pacific Ocean, to be out of the mechanized chaos of Tokyo and

Kyoto. On this train to nowhere, I felt as though I were getting closer and closer to *satori,* the elusive Zen Buddhist enlightenment brought about through *zazen.* My preferred setting for mediation, of course, was chest deep in hot water.

The JR train had petered out to an exhausted chug as it scaled the mountainous coastline. Finally we stopped at the square of a little town and I recognized Kii-Katsuura, not from any landmark, but more from a feeling. The town was tiny and charmingly provincial, comprising two intersecting thoroughfares with festive banners overhead that seemed left over from a long-forgotten parade. The avenues were lined with shoe shops, women's clothing stores, fishmongers, sushi stalls, and coffee bars. In the West, we hear so much about Japanese tea ceremonies, but it's the coffeehouses that are ubiquitous, and coffee seems to be the preferred vehicle for caffeine. Despite the assurances of the banners, it was eerily empty and quiet in Kii-Katsuura. With my small wheeled suitcase in tow, I was the only person walking down the long wide street toward the ocean.

For a moment, I had an unsettling flashback to the deserted entrance of the Tchaykovsky banya in St Petersburg. I took heart at the sight of three women approaching me on the dusty street. They were my age, maybe younger, and two appeared to be Japanese, while the third was a tall, slender Caucasian girl with a shock of bleached blond hair. She was dressed in a white tank top, her bra straps sticking out, blue Adidas sweat pants, and a pair of rubber flip-flops. She carried a plastic bag filled with hot dog buns. As she passed, she nodded to me in acknowledgment, as Caucasians in remote parts of Japan are wont to do. Perhaps she was an exchange student from Düsseldorf, but she was most certainly not a tourist. Tourists generally don't walk around with hot dog buns.

Before I could even think about finding the Forget-to-Go-Home-Bath or a place to stay, I had to find lunch. All I'd eaten the entire six-hour ride from Kyoto were two packets of Pocky, a popular Japanese snack food of pretzel sticks dipped in chocolate. I passed a dimly lit coffeehouse with a large group of women chatting and laughing. My entrance was welcomed with a warm chorus of *'Irashaimase,'* and I took a seat at the bar. A moment later, the trio I'd seen on the street walked in and sat at a table behind me. I ordered yakisoba, noodles and cabbage fried up in soy sauce, and an iced coffee, which the Japanese make deliciously strong. The blond girl also ordered an iced coffee and then joined me at the bar.

'Are you a tourist?' she asked shyly.

'Yes, are you?'

'No, I work here.' She pulled a box of cigarettes out of her pocket and offered me one.

'Do you work in one of the hotels?' I asked hopefully.

'No,' she said, examining her fingernails. She looked up at me. Her brown eyes were tough and sweet, and she had a don't-mess-with-me vulnerability that was instantly endearing. Finally she said in a pout, 'I don't like it here. Tokyo I like. But here so boring.'

'Where are you from?'

'Romania.' She took such a deep drag on her cigarette, I thought it would disappear into her mouth. 'My name is Kristy,' she said on the exhale.

Her cheeks were somewhat hollow underneath her high, chiseled cheekbones. Her skin was porcelain white and flawless. She was, I guessed, every Japanese man's fantasy woman.

'And this is Mama,' she said, introducing a preppie sixty-year-old Japanese lady who wore a yellow Izod shirt and a windbreaker outfit. 'She takes care of me and the other girls,' she said, pointing to her two friends. 'They're from the Philippines.'

'So you used to live in Tokyo?' I asked, her line of work slowly dawning on me.

'Oh yes,' she said dreamily, 'I spent six months in Rappongi, and it was so wonderful. So much money, so much fun. Here so boring.'

Rappongi, I remembered from a night out with Philippe and his entourage, was the red-light district of Tokyo, tightly packed with strip bars featuring women of every nationality.

'Here I work at a club called Sweet Spot. Every night I have to be there from seven until three in the morning. And only two days off per month.'

'Is the money good, at least?' I asked.

'No, it's terrible. One hundred dollars on a good night. They lure us here with a contract telling us "so much yen, so much yen," so I come from Tokyo and there's nothing here. Just a few fishermen and whalers.'

'Can't you go back to Tokyo?' I asked.

'No. If I break my contract here, I have to go home to Romania, where I can only earn fifty dollars a month. Japanese men, I don't like Japanese men. They are always trying to grab me when they get drunk.'

'So you don't do lap dances?'

'No lap dances. Just dancing and talking.'

'You speak Japanese?'

'*Hai. Nihon-go wa wakarimasu ka?*' she said with a proud smile.

'*Wakarimasen,*' I responded. It was one of my few Japanese expressions, and it meant 'I don't understand.' 'How did you manage to learn Japanese?'

'We have no choice. How else we get tips? Why are you in Japan?'

'Umm, to see the baths, you know the famous onsen of Japan,' I said, slightly embarrassed at the frivolity of my pursuit in comparison with her life of survival.

'I have heard good things from my customers about these baths, but I have never been.' Then Mama, who didn't speak English, said something to Kristy in Japanese, who explained, 'Mama is wondering about where you are going to stay tonight.'

'I have the name of two hotels in this book – Urashima and Nakanoshima. I'll be fine.'

'Are you lonely?' Kristy asked.

'Do you mean traveling alone?'

'Yes, yes, traveling by yourself, lonely. It harder to find a room for one at a *ryokan*. Mama said she will help you.'

After we'd each had three iced coffees and filled an ashtray, we set off, with Mama in the lead, for the quay. The quay is the real town square of Kii-Katsuura. Small chug boats designed to look like sharks and cartoon characters shuttle guests back and forth from the mainland to the two floating island hotels.

Mama and Kristy negotiated on my behalf at the hotel booking office. It seems 'lonely' travelers get penalized. *Ryokan* prices generally include a lavish dinner and breakfast and as many baths as you can handle. A price of $90 was agreed upon after an initial insistence of $200.

Kristy repeated, 'So expensive, so expensive. You lonely, so they charge you more.'

'Yes, it's very expensive to be lonely,' I said, thinking more of her customers than myself. 'Kristy, do you want to come to the hotel with me and we can visit the onsen before you have to go to work?'

She looked at her watch. It was nearing 5:00, and she had to shower and be in full makeup by 7:00. 'Maybe tomorrow,' she said, utterly without enthusiasm.

'Can I come see you dance tonight?' I asked. There were only so many baths I could take, and Kristy was sweet and her life a mystery.

'You want to see me dance?' she said, simultaneously aghast and flattered.

'Yes, if you don't mind.'

She didn't say yes or no. She and Mama walked onto the dock with me, and I hopped on a chug boat designed to look like Casper the Friendly Ghost. I thanked them profusely and bowed deeply to Mama. She was beaming. I was another saved street urchin. I took a seat on the boat and looked back to the dock, expecting to see them retreating up the gangplank. But they stood just outside my window, watching the boat. Suddenly Kristy jumped on the boat, rushed over to me, and said, 'You understand yen, right? Don't pay more than ten thousand yen. You understand?' And then she rejoined Mama on the quay.

As the boat zoomed away, I watched Kristy put her arm through

Mama's and head back into town to put on eye shadow and a bra-and-panty set, her workplace attire, for a night of dancing for groping fishermen. I wanted to see her again, to show her the onsen, expose her to the pure side of Japan. And I wanted to thank her for helping me find a home for the night.

Casper the Friendly Ghost spat me and ten Japanese couples out onto the dock of the Urashima Hotel, a lush fantasy island of six separate onsen areas, dining rooms, *pachinko* parlors, souvenir stalls, and karaoke bars. Hiruko, the only English speaker on staff, met me at the first reception desk. His proficiency in English was slight, but we pantomimed dinnertime and onsen locations.

I had shin splints by the time we reached my room. It was a good half-mile walk through endless white corridors crammed with video games and small walled-in cubicles for one-on-one romantic kar-aoke sessions. My room, on the seventh floor of a tower building facing the Pacific, was really a suite, a trio of six-tatami rooms. In a country where space is measured in two-by-four-foot tatami mats, and where Max spent seven years living in a single six–tatami mat room, I was living large at the Urashima.

The main room had a knee-high lacquered table with two *zabuton* pillow chairs and an alcove for the traditional calligraphy scroll and flower arrangement. A thermos of green tea and yunohana buns were laid out in customary *ryokan* fashion. At night, the table and chairs were exchanged for a futon and bedding. Behind a shoji screen was a sitting room overlooking the rocky Pacific coastline. Having explained all the usual features of a *ryokan* room, with special emphasis on the need to change from 'tatami' slippers into 'bath-room' slippers before using the facilities, Hiruko left me in peace to contemplate the stresses of slipper etiquette.

I replaced my clothes and shoes with yukata and geta and set off for Bokido, about a quarter mile away, through a cavernous tunnel that rounded the hotel by the ocean. At the end of the tunnel, the walls gave way to gray, exposed rock faces. I was inside a grotto.

It was pure madness inside. Every newly arrived female guest was trying to squeeze in a predinner bath. I showered in front of exposed rock, walked on slate. Not a synthetic material in sight. A series of three tubs moved toward the Pacific, pulling the bather's eyes toward a hole, like the eye of a needle, that opened out on the wide expanse of cresting waves. Curious to investigate, I made my way by wading through different pools toward the pear-shaped hole. I looked over the edge to the waves crashing on the rocks below, dark blue swells cresting into foam. A few hundred feet beyond my safe perch in the cave, other large rocks jutted up from the ocean, looking monolithic and sacred, like the second coming of Stonehenge emerging from the ocean's floor.

Satisfied by my exploration, I returned to the first large pool, with a fountain in the middle bubbling over with yellowish green water. The deep smell of sulfur went straight to my head, a smell I was growing very fond of and that I equated now with health and good skin instead of rotten eggs. The water at the fountain was the purest, and I watched the women eagerly approach the fountain and splash the hot, sulfuric water on their faces. Nature's Clearasil. I got in line. I splashed my face and licked my upper lip. The water tasted like sulfur salts mixed with cayenne pepper. It had a nice kick. I could feel my pores tighten after the jolt of sulfur. This was the good stuff.

I soaked with the other women. We smiled at one another as we listened to the waves crashing just beyond us. We sat there in skinship, joined by the act of sharing water, an act of trust and of affection. Everyone was alone with her thoughts. As I entered the cold pool, goose bumps spread across my skin. I looked down at my body. No, I could never be an exotic dancer.

At dinner that night, still stumbling around in my yukata and geta, I was seated alone in a large, glitzy dining room crowded with people wearing identical kimono-style cotton robes and struggling not to dip their wide sleeves into the soy sauce. I was plied with course after course of sushi, tempura, shabu-shabu, and strange slimy morsels in pretty bowls. I quietly read my book of essays on Japanese life.

Trying to pull all the pieces together, I realized that Japan's diversity is manifested through its fetishes, from its high-art fetishes such as tea ceremonies, flower arranging, sumo wrestling, and compulsive bowing; to its bizarre and flashy fetishes – mandatory Louis Vuitton handbags, baseball, French pastries, Pokémon, germ paranoia, and kabuki theater – to its base and, quite frankly, perverse fetishes, among them schoolgirl porn, the brisk market for used underwear, blowfish roulette at the dinner table, and motel love affairs. And to wash away the guilt, stress, absurdity, and defilement of all the fetishes: the bathing obsession.

After a glorious bath and gluttonous dinner, I felt so contented being out of a city, so relaxed from all the pampering – having learned firsthand about the typical Japanese vacation of total sensory gratification – I couldn't help but wonder about Kristy's very different evening back on the mainland. She didn't seem overly enthusiastic about my visiting her at Sweet Spot, but she was so kind, staying on the quay, worrying about me getting ripped off. So I speculated that between her concern and her hesitation to see me go, she might not be altogether upset if I showed up to watch her dance.

I went back to my room and took off my yukata, dressed in a knee-length black skirt and purple shirt, and left looking rather smart. I caught the Scooby-Doo water bus back to the mainland, through the bay of rocks like ossified pterodactyls, and found my way to Sweet Spot. The small, dark club was completely empty at 9:00, save for the bartender, manager, and the ten bored dancers. A disco ball hung over the black vinyl booths, and pink lights bathed the long stage. Kristy teetered over in four-inch white heels, flushed and excited to see me. She had traded her tank top and sweats for a lacy turquoise bustier and a micromini black-and-white-checkered skirt. Her eyes were shadowed in blue, and her lips were lined in red but not filled in. She welcomed me like a hostess at a fancy dinner party.

'You are a bombshell,' I said.

'A bombshell?' she questioned, looking alarmed at the mention of bombs.

'A knockout. You look gorgeous, like Marlene Dietrich,' I said, momentarily forgetting that Dietrich was German, not Romanian.

'Oh, thank you very much,' she said, looking pleased. 'Come, I want to introduce you to my friend.' It turned out Kristy had a Romanian friend, Ava, who was also living and dancing in Kii-Katsuura. The three of us sat down. I was shocked when the manager, a pathetic twenty-two-year-old sociopath, wanted to charge me the normal 6,000-yen entrance fee. Kristy, the fast talker, ironed that over: it was decided that I just had to pay for what I drank and not the exorbitant entrance and hourly fee.

For the first hour they had no customers, so we drank Sapporo and discussed the bleakness of their lives in this tiny fishing and onsen outpost. Kristy and Ava complained that everyone wanted the Filipino girls because they look like Japanese girls and were therefore less intimidating. Ava, the softer, more melancholy of the two, confided, 'Every time I go out there, I am nervous and shy. I will never get used to it. This is not a good life.' Later we talked about their life in Romania – about Kristy's five-year-old daughter, Ava's boyfriend, and her career as an aerobics teacher in Bucharest.

Suddenly I heard a little electronic ditty. All the girls jumped, and thirty seconds later a group of customers walked through the door. Girl time was over. The manager asked the new arrivals, 'Philippine, Russian, or Romanian?' A smorgasbord of imported international beauties – though none of the girls, with the exception of Kristy and Ava, were beautiful at all.

Two more entourages of testosterone arrived, and the chosen girls delivered drinks and joked around in Japanese. The most amazing thing to me about this whole bizarre scene was the fluency these women had in Japanese after just a couple of months. Then, suddenly, it was showtime. The lights dimmed and the disco ball began spinning in the blue haze of the smoke-filled club. I sat back, ready for anything. First, one of the Filipino girls emerged from behind the curtain and performed a karaoke version of 'The Greatest Love of All.' She walked around the room in a black ball gown, staring into different customers' eyes, even mine, during her solo. I felt as if I were watching *Star Search* and hoping the judges would vote for her. Things heated up slightly when the four Russian girls came out – two in shiny red vinyl bondage suits and the other two in black gimp suits.

After the Russian S&M romp, the Philippine Quintet sauntered out in pink baby doll outfits and did a cutesy – I'd go so far as to say innocent – dance to an instrumental version of 'Mambo #5,' another song best forgotten. I sat in the back, watching the bartender holding the spotlight in her hands, and thought, This is pretty tame.

Finally, Kristy and Ava strutted out in denim shorts and tight denim jackets. After a couple of exotic pirouettes, they pressed up against the back wall and ripped off the jackets and shorts. They were naked except for pink g-strings. A huge applause rose from the audience. They gripped the silver pole in the middle of the stage while enacting male fantasies of lesbian sex. Kristy groped Ava's breasts while Ava did her best to appear turned-on. I thought back to our earlier conversation when I'd stupidly asked where they had learned to dance and Ava had rolled her eyes and said, 'It comes from within.' After their dance, they shimmied around the room collecting 1,000-yen notes in their g-strings. Any protectiveness I had felt disappeared when I saw how much loot they were collecting. This must have been be why the Russian girls hated them.

The audience was pretty worked up after Kristy and Ava's lesbian tryst. For a finale, all the girls, the whole United Nations of exotic dancers, convened onstage for a good-bye dance and bows. Then they headed off to individual tables for more personalized entertainment. It was late, and the last water bus was about to leave for Urashima. Kristy ran over to say good-bye. I handed back the picture of her daughter dressed as a cat and reminded her that we'd meet at 1:00 in front of my hotel for a trip to the hot springs. 'You will be my guests.'

'Yes, yes, we look forward to it,' she said, rushing back to her guests.

They didn't come on the 1:00 boat, nor did they come on the 1:30 boat. I was sad that they had stood me up and also surprised that in what sounded like a routine life, with not even a movie theater for distraction, they didn't want to see the Urashima. Feeling rejected by my new friends, I hopped on an escalator to explore new parts of the onsen island. One escalator turned into six escalators, until I realized I was ascending the side of a mountain, at least a thousand feet straight up through a corridor of mirrors and chintzy casino décor. At the top, instead of the aesthetically anticipated roulette tables and slot machines, a glass door led outside to a Shinto temple precinct. The long, narrow precipice gazed down upon the placid bay of Kii-Katsuura on one side and the crashing waves of the Pacific on the other. Orange torii gates announced several open-air dark-wooded shrines and, on the left, on the Kii-Katsuura side, a greenhouse.

A greenhouse? Could this be the famed jungle bath? Not speaking or reading Japanese, I tended to miss a lot. Whatever it was, it seemed out of place amid the temple architecture. I slid open the glass screen door and walked into the steamed-up greenhouse. To my right was a door leading outside to two small pools, rectangular boxes of cypress overlooking the bay. They were delightfully situated, but nothing I hadn't seen before. I was becoming an onsen snob.

Inside, though, I hardly knew where to look through the mass of foliage. The high-beamed structure was a labyrinth of ferns and flowers, palms and hydrangeas. The leaves were changing outside, but in here it was a beautiful day in Tahiti. Then I noticed that this wasn't just a greenhouse, but that slate-carved soaking pools were hidden in every leafy nook of this overgrown jungle. Small groups of women went from pool to pool, each hidden in an alcove of foliage and blossoms, extolling and comparing the virtues of each.

This must have been why the temple precinct was deserted. Everyone was bathing.

Just as I was removing my yukata, I heard my name being paged. 'Miss Alexia. Miss Alexia. Please come reception.' A phone call? Unlikely. Was the karaoke master demanding an encore of my rendition of 'It's Still Rock and Roll to Me'? Very unlikely. Or had Kristy and Ava shown up? I raced down the escalators to reception. And there they were, with thinly veiled scowls, dressed for a day at the beach. Kristy wore a neon green swimsuit with white drawstring pants. Ava was more tasteful in a tank top and khaki shorts. They had been waiting for over an hour.

'Oh, I'm so sorry. When you weren't here by one-thirty I figured you weren't coming.'

'We get to bed late, so we sleep until one.'

Everything would be fine as soon as they were relaxing in the baths. 'I can't wait to show you this place. I just peeked into the jungle bath. It looks divine, so let's save it for last. First let's go to the *genfuro,* a bath inside a grotto.'

'Okay,' they said blankly. They looked hungover.

'Late night?'

'Yes, one group stayed until three and we had to drink so much beer with them. We are gaining weight,' Ava said sadly.

'Well, you looked great onstage. Your routine was miles better than the other girls,' I said like a supportive stage mom. 'And the onsen water purges your body of all the toxins from alcohol and cigarettes. Some people think it even helps you lose weight.'

This was the first thing I said that aroused their interest. On the way to the *genfuro,* a small jewelry store selling gold bracelets caught their eye and they wanted to browse.

'What do you do with all the money you've made?' I asked. 'Send it home or put it in the bank?'

'I either lock it in my room or keep it with me,' said Kristy. That didn't sound like the most secure arrangement, considering there was an icy détente between the Russian and Romanian girls after frequent fights over shower privileges.

When we entered the grotto I couldn't stop myself from shouting, 'Isn't this insane! The Forget-to-Go-Home-Bath; a shogun was so entranced with this cave bath that he forgot to return to battle.' I flailed around like a delirious tour guide, and they looked through the glass wall into the natural cave grotto with mild interest. I began to take off my yukata.

Kristy asked, 'You go in the pool *naked*?'

'Yes, of course. The men are on the other side. First you take a shower along that wall, then you soak in the baths. And the water, it's very good for your skin and your joints, and it will make you lose weight,' I added, again holding out the carrot.

'Pew. It stinks in here,' Kristy said, and scrunched up her nose.

'It's the sulfur. You get used to it after a while.'

While I was busy washing, Kristy and Ava tentatively stripped to their bathing suits and joined me in the cave. They washed with their swimsuits still on. In a minute, they would see that all the other women were naked and that it was perfectly normal to soak without a suit.

I set the example and got into the big pool.

'Will I smell like rotten eggs if I get in?' asked Kristy.

'Of course not,' I answered. 'Well, not for long.'

Ava, the more intrepid one, the one who actually ate Japanese food whereas Kristy subsisted on frozen chicken nuggets and fries, joined me in the pool, albeit with her orange neon swimsuit still on. Kristy pouted by the steps of the pool.

At this point, I realized that Kristy and Ava had no intention of taking off their swimsuits. It would be a triumph if I managed to get Kristy in the water at all. They had no problem strutting around in g-strings, rubbing their crotches against silver poles, or squeezing each other's breasts onstage, but soaking in a pool of naked women was more than they could handle.

Kristy went back to the dressing room, weighed herself, and

informed us that she had risen to sixty kilograms. 'Really, Kristy, the minerals in the water break down the fat.' Whatever it took, I was determined that she try the bath. Ava reassured her that the water wasn't toxic, and finally Kristy descended into the pool, giving us a wan smile. We applauded.

They didn't want to stay in the water for long. I didn't lecture them on skinship or try to convince them to ascend with me to the botanic jungle bath. Maybe in retrospect Kristy and Ava will remember the experience fondly, maybe even as they wait their turn to dance they'll think back to our bath today and wish they'd taken off their swimsuits.

After seeing them off, I stepped straight onto the jungle bath– bound escalator. I reentered the greenhouse and removed my yukata and geta, my *ryokan* outfit that I now wore as comfortably as sweats. The only sound of water, the gush and bubble of a modest waterfall, came from the back of the greenhouse where the water poured down from stone-hewn shower spigots. I walked past the other bathers to examine this strangely monolithic structure. Huge square blocks of stone stuck out of the wall at six feet, and a steady stream of warm water flowed out of the stones and into the long rectangular tub below.

After a thorough scrub, I began to bounce from pool to pool. In the long rectangular pool I lay down, positioning myself under the spigots so that water bounced on my feet, back, and head at the same time. Free reflexology. I don't know how long I stayed like this. Idly, I cupped some water in my palms. The water had tiny particles of black, organic minerals. I remembered what Ayako had said back in Tokyo about how you could see organic matter in the best onsen water.

I felt better than I had at any point along the trip. Everything was coming together – the perfect setting, a clear state of mind, a readiness to drink in my surroundings. My mind was quiet: no interior criticism, no nagging guilt, nothing but the pure physical sensations of this place. Every sense had been elevated to an almost surreal heightened awareness. I could smell the chlorophyll in the leaves, the iron reddening the water, I could even smell the rocks, as if they were freshly quarried. The sound of the bouncing water and the low reverberation of voices echoing off the rafters sounded pleasantly tinny.

I was alone, and so happily alone. I promised myself that my days of guilt seeking were over. I would trade in guilt seeking for thrill seeking; I would stockpile rosebuds instead of apologies. Life would be different.

east 10th revisited

Back at my empty New York apartment, home did not feel like home anymore. After six months of travel, I had the new, invigorating sense that home could be anywhere. All I needed were the essentials of a well-packed bag. This kind of liberation was disorienting.

I called Marina for counsel. She was having her own issues in London. Her problems with Colin had gone way beyond his unwillingness to speak Russian, and her job was a tedious intermission between vacations.

'Marina, we both need to make a change,' I advised by phone. 'Come visit. Any bank holidays coming up?'

'Actually,' said Marina, sounding chipper, 'the Queen Mum's birthday is just next week and we have a long weekend. Let me see if I can get a good fare.'

I trusted Marina to get a good fare, and a week later there she was, yelling up to my fourth-floor walk-up, and wearing pink silk trousers and an embroidered pink sweater and carrying a tiny bag.

'Did you just bring shoes?' I asked.

'Your apartment looks like a photographer's studio,' Marina said. Since Charles had moved out, the place looked empty and the bare white walls and hardwood floors made my small loft look more like a white seamless backdrop than a place for cozy dinners.

'I'll take your head shot later,' I said. 'I know you just got here, but I think a field trip to East Tenth is in order.'

'Oh God, no, not that place.'

'Why? You've never actually been inside.'

'Isn't that the place Natalia and I wouldn't set foot in last year? And you stood on the stoop for fifteen minutes trying to convince us it was safe?'

'Exactly. You said it was "too close to the earth."' That was Marina's euphemism for skeevy. I continued, 'Trust me, I spent many cold nights there before I left for Istanbul. Yeah, it's a little grimy, but it has a soulful quality, and it will purge the toxins from your system.'

If nothing else, I knew my audience. Marina was a sucker for detoxification, adhering religiously to a quarterly detoxification that involved prolonged dietary and alcoholic sacrifice.

'Oh, all right, but I'm bringing my own towel.'

'Marina, we've visited some very *close to the earth* places together in Istanbul and Moscow. East Tenth is no worse.'

'It's all relative. In Russia the bar is considerably lowered, and in Turkey at least water is constantly flowing.'

On East 10th Street, between First and A, hangs a white sign that says, 'Russian Turkish Bath,' a replica of the original from when it first opened in 1892. In 1900, New York City contained forty-two commercial bathhouses, largely owned by Jews and called *shvitzes,* just like this one. Izzie Sirota, my great-grandfather, frequented these types of sweating establishments, where he'd rub shoulders with his favorite actors of Yiddish theater – Boris Thomashefsky and Maurice Moscovitch. Now East 10th and a few holdouts in Brooklyn are the only *shvitzes* to survive the encroachment of gyms, spas, and lavish home bathrooms. With five thousand members and a tightly knit group of regulars, East 10th still offers the camaraderie, gritty intimacy, and heat-induced relaxation of the old New York steam baths.

The faint scent of eucalyptus hit us when we walked in, a reassuring smell in the face of a grungy reception room and changing area. A television blared the evening news in the café. Several customers wearing navy bath coats sat on brown plastic chairs, eating cold, mayonnaise-drenched salads. Marina and I left our watches and wallets at the check-in, bought two bottles of cold water, and put on bathing suits. I wore a blue sports suit and Marina a black leotard. Not once on my trip had I needed a bathing suit. Marina clutched a thick hunter green cotton towel, and I grabbed a handful of the threadbare brown towels no bigger than dishrags. We descended the steep, slippery steps to the basement steam compound. Within roughly 1,200 square feet, they managed to fit a ten-yard blue-tiled plunge pool and four rooms of different heat.

Marina inspected the plunge pool by sticking her head toward the water and inhaling deeply, and rather loudly, through her nose. Some of the old guys, the regulars, squinted their eyes at her, wondering if this uppity visitor might be from the board of health. 'It reeks of chlorine, and the water isn't flowing. This is not good,' she declared. I understood her alarm. East 10th can come across as a run-down, poorly funded YMCA if you don't have a special place in your heart for its history and soulfulness.

After a quick shower, we headed straight to the Russian room, which at 215 degrees Fahrenheit is also called 'the Oven.' On this Tuesday evening there were a few other women, mostly dancers, but the average client was a man over fifty, generally named Abe, Morty, or Saul, with a hairy watermelon-size gut and a Brooklyn accent. We sat on the second tier of pebbled concrete benches. Marina decorously placed the towel, folded up like a cushion, on the concrete. The only light source – an exposed light bulb – cast the room in shadows.

'This place is growing on me,' admitted Marina. 'Look at those guys over there. They look like *Gorky Park* extras.'

'I think I recognize that guy,' I said, pointing to a hulk of a man, tall and wide as a walrus. We could overhear his conversation with two other Central Casting mobsters; in fact, East 10th would be the perfect place to cast a Russian-themed *Sopranos*. They were standing next to the furnace, each wearing long, baggy swimming trunks with brown towels thrown over their shoulders. They were comparing linoleum costs and quality. Marina drank some water, and I rubbed peach enzyme peel on my face. A few minutes later, the walrus man approached us and asked if either of us wanted a platza, the same veynik body-thwacking treatment Natasha had taught me in Moscow. He was a hobbyist, he said, and would be glad to provide us with a free service. Giving platza is a nice 'hobby' for an old man because it requires a topless suppliant. We demurred, but I was sure I recognized him from previous visits.

'I've seen you here before, right?' I asked.

'I'm here almost every night,' he said. 'The name's Morty Hirsh.'

The legendary Morty Hirsh! A construction contractor, former owner of the famed Luxor Baths in Midtown, and the great *shvitzing* aficionado of New York City. Whenever someone at the bath had a *shvitz*-related question, someone always piped in, 'Morty will know.' And here he was, in the flesh – in a lot of flesh. I seized the opportunity to ask him about the history of this place. I'd always been mystified by East 10th's lack of upkeep, and Morty seemed eager to chat.

'Oh, where to begin. Let's see, in the 1940s, this place was owned by a guy by the name of Jumbo, a big fat guy.' Morty cleared his throat. 'He sold it to a guy who worked in Brooklyn at Silver's, another popular bath, and his name was Fat Al.'

'Fat Al?' Marina asked doubtfully. This was not her scene.

'Yeah, Fat Al. He was about three hundred pounds. His family was in the notions business on Thirty-eighth Street, buttons, zippers, that sort of thing. Then Fat Al died giving a platza treatment, he had a heart condition. Fat Al had loved the *shvitz,* but his family just wanted to sell the place, so they sold it to three partners – that would be David, Boris, and a third guy who got out early. Then the feud started in the early 1980s.'

'What was the origin of the feud?' asked Marina, suddenly intrigued.

Morty lowered his voice. 'These are just rumors, but what I've always heard is that David and Boris accused each other of not turning over the common receipts, something like that. Then a friend of mine, a lawyer, he's known as Fat Ralph, another big guy, came in to arbitrate. He set up the alternate week program, whereby David and Boris take turns running the bath and share the common charges. That's been the arrangement for almost fifteen years now.'

Marina and I looked at each other apprehensively, apparently thinking the same thing: 'I hope that doesn't happen to us,' joked Marina.

'Marina, unless you abscond with our start-up capital to buy Caucasian rugs, I think we'll get along famously as business partners.'

'The rugs will be for our collection at the bath,' she said, and already I could see she was calculating the potential to write off antique kilims and carpets. Collectors, I am convinced, are as compulsive as gamblers.

'Marina, are we bathers or businesswomen? Do we love baths too much to open one? A brick-and-mortar establishment might fall short of our vision of the perfect bath.'

Morty, who was sitting close by, piped up, 'I bought the Luxor because I loved baths so much I had to own one.'

Both Marina and I dared not ask him how it panned out.

epilogue

So where does this leave me? Marina and I are no closer to opening our bath. My bath odyssey, instead of answering all my questions, left me with an entirely new and much longer set of questions. As I tried to make sense of where home was and what I wanted to do for the next fifty years, I kept remembering the last chapter of a book my father had force-fed me at fifteen. When most other parents were passing along old J. D. Salinger paperbacks, my father thought nothing could shape an adolescent mind so well as Samuel Johnson's hit from 1759 – *Rasselas, Prince of Abyssinia,* about a young prince who wanted to leave the 'happy valley,' his utopian home, in search of wisdom. The final chapter began with the all-time perfect chapter title: 'The Conclusion, in Which Nothing Is Concluded.'

A sense of closure, completion, tidily closing the lid on any search, is as sweetly naïve as buying into happily ever after. Rasselas searched for happiness and wisdom, I searched for the perfect bath – OK so I wasn't exactly his second coming, but still I related to the intrepid prince's curiosity. Curiosity follows a compounding principle, end-ing only in further questions. What you learn is never what you set out to learn, such that now, after visiting places I thought I would see only on a map or the travel channel, I had an entirely new set of dreams. Marina and I didn't have a business plan or a deep-pocketed partner (we'd hoped to meet a generous Turkish philanthropist with fond hamam memories from childhood). Instead I'd achieved a lasting, richer satisfaction – that of doing something for myself in the present moment, as opposed to constantly postponing for fear of cutting comforting safety nets.

The trip became about the baths themselves, not about the business of baths; and 'my bath' became a jigsaw puzzle of all I saw that was great. Despite my initial handicap as a pragmatic American, I soon realized that I was approaching the baths just like many modern spa-goers approach spas. I was too focused on results. Many American spas place too much emphasis on the one-on-one treatments, the guru, and quick fixes. Baths also offer specific treatments, but mostly the treatments are general, aimed at overall well-being. Baths were places for relaxation, regeneration, occasional childhood regression, socializing, whimsical debauchery, and most of all, just free-spirited fun. Relaxation is not something you can study, nor is quiet reflection quantifiable. And these were the kinds of moments I found and savored inside the baths, not imagining blueprints or calculating profit margins on products and treatments.

Yes, somewhere in Russia I abandoned my pragmatism. Where better to leave practicality behind than amid unfightable chaos? And though I felt as if I were a living cliché of the newly enlightened American abroad, I started to get off on simple joys like nibbling salty volba in between dehydrating banya sessions. I even stopped asking people what they did for a living – a sure conversation stopper, especially in Turkey and Russia. Who cares where your money comes from? It's not nearly as important a question as 'How do you make baklava?' or 'Where is your favorite banya?' These are the questions that animate people, make them talk fast and gesticulate wildly.

I expected to learn concrete things during my tour: optimum ceiling heights and floor plans, loofah suppliers, Turkish marble dealers, and recipes for modern elixirs of nectar and ambrosia. I did learn where to buy the softest *peştamals* in the Covered Bazaar and how to use a veynik from Natasha, the Martha Graham of birch bough choreography, but what I'll remember in five years' time goes much deeper than practical knowledge.

Hanging out with crazed Russians, quiet Finns, and solemn Japanese in baths where people shared sensations – through nods, smiles, maybe a couple of words – was the ultimate satisfaction, a rare community of kindred spirits. Savoring apple tea, obsessing over the demise of the Roman baths, inhaling lavender stewing in hot water, and contemplating quivering pines from the warmth of an outdoor onsen were all pleasures I had never experienced in America. And maybe – and here was the rub – they were pleasures I never could have enjoyed in America, so obsessed was I with tomorrow and getting there faster.

At most of my stops along the way, people went to the baths simply because it was part of their identity, part of what made them Finnish, Japanese, or Russian. The sauna, onsen, and banya are simply an unquestioned part of how they relax and relate to friends and family.

I no longer feel that I need to open a hamam to justify this trip or my existence. Marina is Eastern and never felt a need to justify anything. I suppose I am catching on. For me now, it is about the baths and not about re-creating the baths for New Yorkers, much though I loved and still love the idea. Maybe we'll still do it, open a Turkish-Japanese bath, but it really doesn't matter.

The same way some people traipse through flea markets collecting ceramics or textiles as a lifelong hobby, I will always visit public baths. The baths I have already experienced became like familiar friends whom I'll continually revisit until I'm a wrinkly old lady. A long list of novel curiosities remains – the ultimate old-school hamam in Aleppo, Syria; maybe the Italians were still bathing in high Roman style at Montecatini; I had never gotten to visit an Aalto sauna or dance naked at midnight around a Russian banya. Luckily, I have my whole life to collect baths. And I know Marina will be there, too.

resource guide

So many baths, so little time. This public-bath guide is culled from my travels and from the travels of other bath enthusiasts. No matter where in the world you find yourself – Milan or Moscow, Tokyo or Turkey – chances are there's a good local establishment for a soak, a shvitz, or a steam. Hot-springs enthusiasts take note: I mention several that have public bathing facilities, but given that there are thousands of hot springs, and public baths for that matter, I urge you to explore for yourself once you've exhausted this primer.

Keep in mind that many baths alternate between mixed-gender, women-only, and men-only sessions. Admission fees and opening hours frequently change, so call ahead for this kind of information. Baths as a rule are inexpensive and the ones listed here range from ten cents to twenty dollars.

Canada

While Canada has fantastic hot springs, there aren't many public bathing establishments. This one gets a lot of press.

Miraj Hammam Spa, 1495 West 6th Avenue (at Granville), Vancouver, British Columbia, V6H 4G1. Tel: 604.733.5151.
www.mirajhammam.com.
One of the few proper hamams in North America, the Miraj offers Middle Eastern treatments and 'opulent sweating.'

England

In the late nineteenth century, the English had a love affair with what today is termed the 'Victorian-Turkish bath.' Beautiful bathing establishments were built throughout the British Isles. If you are keen to explore Turkish baths in England and Scotland, I urge you to visit Malcolm Shifrin's superb Web site, a loving tribute to and celebration of Turkish baths. You can find it online at www.victorianturkishbath.org.

Thermae Spa Bath. Hetling Pump Room, Hot Bath Street, Bath, BA1 1SJ. General: 44.1225.33.5678. Reservations: 44.1225.33.1234.
www.thermaebathspa.com.
After a twenty-five-year hiatus, visitors to Bath can once again soak, scrub, and steam in its legendary waters. This £25 million project contains five bathing buildings, including the four-story New Royal Bath, which has a rooftop pool with bubbling airbeds, glass steam pods infused with essential oils, and treatment rooms offering a variety of international spa services.

The Porchester Centre. Queensway, London W2 5HS.
Tel: 44.20.7.792.2919.
The ground level of this slightly tattered but good-spirited bath looks like an art deco train station where people in bathrobes and towels sip tea and lounge on plastic recliners. The basement level offers a variety of saunas and steam rooms at different temperatures, as well as a very chilly cold plunge.

Ironmonger Row Baths. Ironmonger Row, London EC1V 3QN.
Tel: 44.20.7.253.4011.
The close-quartered baths in this community center boast a crowd of
longtime regulars, including many artists and writers who have immortalized the place. A laid-back vibe and very comfy relaxation area
makes this a popular spot, even if it doesn't have as many steam rooms
and saunas as the Porchester Centre.

Finland

Finland is the home of the sauna (pronounced SOW-na in its native
land), and you can experience all manner of sauna novelties from the
world's largest smoke sauna to a nightclub sauna.

Café Tin Tin Tango. Töölöntorinkatu 7, Helsinki. Tel: 358.9.2709.0972.
A Helsinki entrepreneur thought to combine a café, art gallery, coin-
operated laundry, and sauna rental in this quirky and popular destination.

Finnish Sauna Society. Vaskiniementie 10, FIN–00200 Helsinki. Tel:
358.9.6860.560. www.sauna.fi. Take bus number 20 from Erottaja
(Helsinki's central Esplanade Park). The journey takes approximately
fifteen minutes.
There's no better place to learn about the sauna than at the Finnish Sauna
Society, which has several thousand members. Try all five saunas – the
two savusaunas (traditional smoke sauna), the two wood-burning saunas,
and the space-age electric one at their compound on the Gulf of Finland.
In between sweating sessions, dash down a long jetty and hurl yourself
into the water.

Jätkänkämpällä Smoke Sauna. Katiskaniementie 8, FI–70700 Kuopio. Tel:
358.17.473.473. www.rauhalahti.com.
Jätkänkämpällä is reputed to be the world's largest savusauna (smoke
sauna), seating up to sixty. It takes a full twenty-four hours to fire up the
sauna for the Tuesday and Friday sessions, which are open from 2 P.M. to
8 P.M. year-round. In the summer guests can enjoy the outdoor music,
restaurant, and swims in the lake. Togalike wraps are provided.

Kotiharju Sauna. Harjutorinkatu 1, Helsinki. Tel: 358.9.753.1535.
The last fully wood-fired public sauna in Helsinki. A washerwoman is
available for a pre-sauna scrub with pine soap, massages can be booked in
advance, and there's a terrace for cooling off outdoors in between sessions.

Palace Hotel. Eteläranta 10, Helsinki 00130. Tel: 358.9.1345.6656.
www.palacehotel.fi.
Helsinki's power brokers meet on the eleventh floor of the Palace Hotel
for the ultimate in the swish sauna experience. Choose between the
wood-fired or electric sauna areas, both of which offer an outdoor
terrace with breathtaking panoramic views of the South Harbor. This
sauna must be booked ahead of time and is ideal for small groups who
want a customized, catered sauna experience with refreshments and the
attentions of a sauna attendant.

Saunabar. Eerikinkatu 27, Helsinki. Tel: 358.9.586.5550.
www.saunabar.net.
Book your sauna in advance at this underground bar cum sauna. Groups
of friends gather to detox before or after drinking and dancing at the bar.

Saunasaari (a.k.a. 'Sauna Island'). Helsingin Saunasaari Oy, PL 105, 00160
Helsinki. Tel: 358.50.525.0393. www.saunasaari.fi. Waterbus m/s Leila
departs from the Market Square twice daily.
A whole island devoted to the sauna? Yes, saunas and a few rustic
country homes. Sauna Island is a ten-minute boat ride from downtown
Helsinki and caters mostly to large groups. The various saunas and
soaking tubs are in an idyllic, beautifully landscaped setting. On the
island you can also enjoy grilled salmon, dark bread, sausage, and drinks.

Yrjönkatu. Yrjönkatu 21-b, Helsinki. Tel: 358.9.3108.7401.
First built in 1928, this mosaic-covered swimming hall in the middle of
Helsinki possesses the grandeur of a Roman bath, but is strictly single
sex. On three levels, there are two swimming pools and four saunas.
Washerwomen and masseurs are available for pre- and post-sauna
treatments.

Villa Hvittrask, Hvitträskintie 166, 02440 Luomo Bobäck.
Tel: 358.9.297.6033. www.hvittrask.com.
Finnish design aficionados and sauna-revelers alike will love this secluded
spot about forty-five minutes from Helsinki. Designed and built by
Herman Gesellius, Armas Lindgren, and Eliel Saarinen, Villa Hvittrask
now has a museum, restaurant, and lakeside sauna available for private sauna
parties. You must call several days ahead of time to book the sauna and
gather lots of friends, because at roughly $300 for three hours, plus $10 for
each bather, it's not cheap. The sauna can hold up to fifteen people, and
food and drink from the restaurant can be served in the sauna building.

France

Paris is known for its many hamams or 'hammams,' as the word is often spelled in Europe. Here are three of the most popular.

Les Bains du Marais. 31–33, rue des Blancs Manteaux, 75004, Paris. Tel: 33.1.44.61.02.02. www.lesbainsdumarais.com.
I had my first public-bath experience at Les Bains du Marais, so it will always be close to my heart. This small, serene spot in the middle of the Marais boasts an excellent Middle Eastern café and terrific gommage treatments in a room just off of the central steam room. The peaceful *salle de repos*, with cushy divans and plentiful mint tea, completes the experience.

La Mosquée. 39, rue Geoffroy-Saint-Hilaire, Paris. Tel: 33.1.4331.3820.
This hamam is part of a larger complex that the French government built for the Arab community in 1922 to thank them for their help in World World I. The hamam has a wonderful Felliniesque central room where bathers repose on cushions and massage tables line the walkway. Inside there are myriad steam chambers for those who like it hot and very hot.

Hammam Pacha. 147, rue Gabriel Péri, 93200 Saint-Denis. Tel: 33.1.48.29.19.66. www.hammampacha.com.
A popular spot, this hamam on the outskirts of Paris has a eucalyptus-scented steam room and a variety of other rooms for both steaming and relaxing.

Georgia

This former Soviet republic has a long tradition of banya and miner-water bathing.

Tbilisis's Sulfur Baths. A handful of eighteenth-century bathhouses line a square in the Old Town. These naturally fed sulfur baths are a Tbilisi institution that inspired Alexandre Dumas to comment after a visit in 1858, "A great sense of freedom and well-being permeated me. All my tiredness had gone and I felt strong enough to lift a mountain." Favorites include the King Irakli Baths and the Blue Baths.

Germany

Germany has a vibrant *badkultur* with everything from 'liquid sound' bath experiences to traditional hamams to the gracious continuation of nineteenth-century spa culture. These are some of Germany's best-known baths.

Caracalla Therme. Römerplatz 1, Baden-Baden. Tel: 49.7221.275940. www.carasana.de.
The atmosphere at this large complex is more water park than intimate public bath, but it's a great option if you want to bathe as a family or if you want to keep your swimsuit on. With opportunities to swim indoors or outdoors, Caracalla also offers lots of water stations, grottos, underwater jets, and a variety of saunas and steam rooms.

Friedrichsbad. Römerplatz 1, 76530 Baden-Baden. Tel: 49.7221.275920. www.carasana.de.
This 'Roman-Irish' bath just next door to Caracalla was built in 1875 and inspired Mark Twain to say, 'Here at Baden-Baden's Friedrichsbad you lose track of time in 10 minutes and track of the world in 20.' The Germanic approach to bathing divides the experience into sixteen carefully regimented stations. After steaming, sweating, and getting scrubbed for a prescribed number of minutes, male and female patrons are merged in the Romanesque pools. This being Germany and the home of Free Body Culture, *herren* and *frauen* bathe together *au naturel*.

Toskana Therme. Bad Sulza. D–99518 Bad Sulza, Wunderwaldstraße 2a. Tel: 49.36461.91080. www.toskana-therme.de.
'Bathe in sound, colour and light' at Toskana Therme, where there are seven cascading saline pools, four whirlpools, myriad saunas and steam rooms, and a variety of spa treatments.

Thermen am Europa-Center. Nürnberger Str. 7, Berlin. Tel: 49.40.25760. www.thermen–aktuell.de.
This rooftop complex has five Finnish saunas, three steam rooms a swimming pool, outdoor sunbathing terrace and restaurant. Aside from the restaurant, in which one must wear a robe, this is an FKK (free body culture) bath, so no need to pack a swimsuit, and remember, it's also mixed gender.

Sultan Hamam. Bülowstr. 57, 10783 Tempelhof-Schöneberg, Berlin. Tel: 49.30.2175.3375.
This mixed-gender bath is Germany's largest Turkish bath, with over 10,000 square feet of marbled interiors. In addition to the steam rooms, there are also eight pools and traditional Turkish massagte and exfoliation treatments.

Hungary

Bathing has been a popular pastime in Budapest ever since the Romans arrived in 100 A.D. and christened the area Aquincum, from the Latin *aqua quinque*, or 'five waters.' The Turks arrived in the sixteenth century and built domed hamam-style buildings for palatial soaking. Hungarians today continue to take advantage of the city's abundant thermal waters at the beautiful, if slightly run-down, Ottoman and art nouveau bathing establishments.

The Gellért Baths. 2–4 Kelenhegyi ut, District XI, Budapest. Tel: 36.1.466.6166.
The most famous and spectacular of Budapest's many baths, the Gellért opened in 1918 as part of the Hotel Gellért. Swimming pools, including the one featured on the cover of this book, are mixed gender, while the thermal pools are separate. With a wave pool and sundecks outside, as well as mosaic thermal baths and hearty mineral oil massages available inside, you can easily make a day of it at the Gellért.

Király Baths. 82–84 Fö utca, District II, Budapest. Tel: 36.1.202.3688.
Built by the Turks in the sixteenth century, Király is arguably Budapest's most architecturally important bath.

Rudas Baths. 9 Döbrentei tér, District 1, Budapest. Tel: 36.1.358.1322.
This bathhouse dates back to the Turkish occupation in the sixteenth century. The thermal baths are for men only, but the lovely neoclassical pool is mixed gender and in recent years has hosted some legendary Cinetrip parties where silent cinema, music, dancing, and splashing around meet poolside at these all-night parties.

Széchenyi Baths. 11 Állatkerti körút, District XIV, Budapest. Tel: 36.1.321.0310.
Second only to the Gellért in popularity, the Széchenyi Baths in Budapest's City Park are simply massive. The huge outdoor bathing complex, where

old men concentrate on chess and young families whiz around a pool with centrifugal force, recalls Roman times in its size and grandeur. Inside there are separate-gender Turkish-style steam facilities and thermal pools.

Iceland

Iceland, with its volcanic landscape offering an abundance of thermal water, is a bather's Elysian Fields, albeit in lava. Between the Blue Lagoon and Reykavik's hot pots, there's enough to keep a soaking aficionado occupied for weeks. Also, in the summertime, you can take excursions further afield to Mytvan and other more remote pools in the northern countryside.

Arbaejarlaug. Fylkisvegur 110, Reykjavik. Tel: 354.567.3933.
www.spacity.is.
The newest of Reykjavik's thermal complexes, the spic and span Arbaejarlaug has a long row of outdoor hot pots, big indoor and outdoor pools, and enough water amusements to make kids feel like they are at an Icelandic Six Flags. Other facilities include a thermal steam bath, sauna, and sun lamps.

The Blue Lagoon. 240 Grindavik, Reykjavik. Tel: 354.420.8800.
www.bluelagoon.is.
The waters of the Blue Lagoon have been curing psoriasis and eczema patients for generations. Since the early 1990s the Blue Lagoon has become a full-fledged tourist destination, with large changing quarters, a café, spa boutique, etc. Despite its popularity, the Blue Lagoon remains an eerie, mystical destination. The lagoon is a massive amoebic pool and gusts of steam envelop bathers. The mushy clay bottom and the surrounding black lava fields all add to the surreal bathing experience.

Breidholtslaug at Austurberg, Reykjavik. Tel. 354.557.5547.
www.spacity.is.
If you want an unpretentious place to soak with the locals, Breidholt-slaung is a good bet. With an outdoor and indoor pool, thermal steam bath, sauna, and 'muscle-tenderizing' pot, this pool complex is popular with local people and offers excellent walking and jogging routes nearby.

Grafarvogslaug at Dalshús, Reykjavik. Tel: 354.510.4600. www.spacity.is.
Near the coastline, this thermal establishment offers hot pots, thermal

steam bath, and Jacuzzi. Also, with walking routes, a golf course, trout fishing, and horse rental nearby, this area is a veritable country club.

Laugardalslaug. Sundlaugarvegur 105, Reykjavik. Tel: 354.553.4039. www.spacity.is.
Reykjavik's largest thermal establishment is about ten minutes from downtown. Laugardalslaug offers prime soaking for young families and twenty-something couples. In addition to the usual array of hot pots, a thermal steam room and sauna are on offer. Laugardalslaug also is the only one of Reykjavik's thermal establishments to offer massage.

Sundhöllinn at Barónstígur, Reykjavik. Tel: 354.551.4059. www.spacity.is.
This art deco pool complex is in the heart of downtown, such that after window-shopping the length of Laugavegur, you could pop in for a swim, soak, and steam at Sundhöllinn's indoor pool, outdoor Jacuzzi, and hot pots overlooking the downtown area.

Italy

Italy has over 150 spas, or *terme,* supervised by doctors; these aren't public baths but rather medicinal treatment centers with a pleasurable component.

Hammam Della Rosa. Viale Abruzzi, 15, 20131 Milan. Tel: 39.02.2941.1653. www.hammamdellarosa.com.
A women-only hamam on the outskirts of Milan. The rooms – tepidarium, caldarium, frigidarium – follow the Roman model, but the interiors are Turkish inspired.

Montecatini Terme. Viale Verdi, 41, 51016 Montecatini Terme, Pistoia. Tel: 39.0572.7781. www.termemontecatini.it.
One of the most famous bathing locales in Italy, today Montecatini is a genteel resort town where people still occasionally take the waters. There are eight terme, or spa centers, where you can take a medically supervised bath.

Terme di Saturnia. Hotel Terme di Saturnia, 58050 Saturnia (Grosseto). Tel: 39.0564.600.800. www.termedisaturnia.it.
Whether you take the waters in one of the seven thermal pools at the Hotel Terme di Saturnia or head to the all-natural pools in the nearby

countryside, the sulfurous, alkaline waters that gush out of the earth at a constant 98.6 degrees are sure to invigorate.

Japan

Japan has 2,500 hot spring resorts called *onsen*, as well as thousands of *sento*, city bathhouses. If you want to do some serious onsen–hopping, there are two excellent guidebooks to this country's amazing baths:

A Guide to Japanese Hot Springs, by Anne Hotta with Yoko Ishiguro. Kodansha International, 1986.

Japan's Hidden Hot Springs, by Robert Neff. Charles E. Tuttle Co, 1995.

Tokyo

Azabu-Jūban Onsen & Koshi-No-Yu Sento. 1–5 Azabu Juban. Tel.: 81.3.3404.2610.
In the heart of Tokyo, this unusual onsen and sento complex has baths with tea–colored onsen waters upstairs and a less expensive sento facility down-stairs.

Asakusa Kannon Onsen. 2–7–26 Asakusa.
Next door to Senso-ji, one of old Edo's biggest attractions. A convenient and traditional first sento experience (whether or not the waters qualify as an onsen is up for debate) with a few soaking tubs in a pleasant, light-filled room.

Daikoku-yu. 32–6, Senju-kotobukicho, Adachi-ku. Tel: 81.3.3881.3001
The temple-like structure is a big draw, as are the landscapes painted on the ceilings.

Green Plaza Ladies Sauna. 1–29–3 Kabuki-cho. Tel: 81.3.3207.4921.
This women's bathhouse is open twenty-four hours a day. In addition to tubs for soaking, there is massage offered at all hours, a café, and a large room with reclining chairs where legions of women sleep before catching early-morning trains at the nearby Shinjuku station.

Finlando Sauna. In the basement of the Joypak Building, Kabuki-cho Koma-mae. Tel: 81.3.3232.8310.
This twenty-four-hour bath is the men's version of the Green Plaza Ladies Sauna and is also located in the bustling Shinjuku neighborhood.

Nijuseiki Yokujo. 1–34–1, Nohonzutsumi, Taitou-ku. Tel: 81.3.3873.8409.
This sento, built in 1926, still relies on firewood to heat the water. It's known for its Taisho-Showa architecture and stunning painting of Mt Fuji.

Rokuryu Sento & Onsen. 3–4–20 Ikenohata. Tel: 81.3.3821.3826.
In northern Tokyo, just a few minutes' walk from Ueno station. A traditional sento that is very popular with locals and that offers purplish onsen waters said to help skin conditions.

Kyoto

Shomen-yu. South of Gojō–dōri and east of Kamo-gawa.
Shomen-yu is a huge three-story sento compound with an elevator to shuttle bathers naked from washing room to rooftop outdoor bath. The sauna has a glassed-in television where the women like watching baseball games.

Funaoka Onsen. Kuramaguchi-dōri. Tel: 81.75.441.3735. Head west from the Kuramaguchi/Horiikawa intersection; Funaoka Onsen is on the left shortly past the Lawson convenience store and is marked by large rocks at the entrance.
Many believe this large indoor and outdoor bath is the finest in Kyoto, which says a lot for a city that's retained its vibrant bathing culture. Funaoka Onsen has cypress tubs, a sauna, an herbal bath, and an electric bath.

Kurama Onsen. Take the subway from Kyoto to Kurama station (about twenty minutes) and then walk up the main road for ten minutes.
The only serene countryside onsen within easy reach of Kyoto. You can soak in a large rectangular cypress pool while meditating on the tree-covered mountainside in front of you.

Countryside

Tenzan Onsen. Yumoto Chaya 208, Hakone. Tel: 81.0460.6.4126.
A short shuttle bus ride away from the Hakone-Yumoto train station, this is where stressed-out Tokyoites come for a quick dose of rest and

relaxation. Since Hakone is just an hour by train from Tokyo, many come for the day to enjoy the restaurants, gardens, tatami relaxation room, massages, and of course the stunning outdoor baths and sauna. Tenzan Onsen has been in operation since the seventeenth century.

Takaragawa. Located in the northern Gumma Prefecture; it takes approximately two and a half hours to get here from Tokyo. From Ueno station in Tokyo, take a train to Jomo Kogen station and then find a bus to Takaragawa.

The most photogenic of all of Japan's onsen, this onsen has appeared on the cover of numerous books and magazines. Breathtaking in any season – cherry blossoms to winter snow – it has four pools; two mixed gender, one men only, and a very large and lovely women's–only pool. Two *ryokans* (traditional Japanese inns), including Osenkaku Ryokan, are a short walk away.

Kii-Katsuura. On the eastern coast of the Kii peninsula in the Wakayama Prefecture.

Take the JR train to Kii-Katsuura and then go to the quay, Kanko Sanbashi, to catch a water ferry to one of the two island hotels: the Urashima Hotel or the Hotel Nakanoshima. Both hotels have superb and diverse bathing facilities from grottos overlooking the Pacific Ocean to mountaintop 'jungle baths.'

Kazakhstan

As an Islamic country, Kazakhstan has a bathing tradition that is a local variation on the hamam, though many of the older baths are no longer functioning.

Arasan Baths. 78 Tulebaeva St., corner Aiteke Bi, Almaty. Tel: 7.3272.692598

This Soviet-era bath is Almaty's most popular. Built in the late 1970s, the five-story complex has three self-contained areas – a Turkish steam bath, a Russian banya, and a Finnish sauna each requiring its own ticket for entry and each with its own tea room and relaxation area.

Korea

Similar to the sentos of Japan, South Korean *moyoktang* are public baths where people congregate after work to relax in the steam and warm water. Korea also has hot springs resorts similar in style to Japan's onsen.

Choksan Hot Springs. Tel: 82.392.636.4000.
A popular resort for middle-class Koreans that offers fantastic hot springs at low prices.

The Osaek Green Yard Hotel. Tel: 82.392.636.7540.
In the same national park as Choksan, this hotel is a sprawling resort complex tucked into the mountains near Osaek Hot Springs. There are a variety of accommodations available in the main building and the Green Yard's bath complex is larger and more luxurious than the Choksan's, with a wonderfully hot sauna scented with fragrant wild mountain herbs.

Russia

For the uninitiated, the banya is like a wayward sauna – the air is more humid, making the heat feel more extreme, leaves and branches from a veynik cover the floor, and there's often vodka involved. The banya has been a Russian institution for almost a thousand years and people still make weekly trips to the local banya for both health and beauty.

St Petersburg

Banya #17 (a.k.a. Tchayskovsky banii). Ulitsa Tchayskovsky. Tel: 7.812.272.0911. Near the Bolshoy dom, off Liteyniy prospect.
A vibrant neighborhood banya located on the top floor of a large municipal-style building. Once you find it, you'll be rewarded with locals who share their *veyniks* and banya advice.

Banya #50. Ulitsa Malaya Posadskaya 28 (Metro Gorkovskaya). Tel: 7.812.233.5092.
A basic banya that is simple, pleasant, and clean.

Banya #57. Gavanskaya ulitsa 5. Tel: 7.812.356.6300.
Like many banyas, Banya #57 has both a regular section and a deluxe section. There is also the option of renting out part of the banya for your own private party.

Mytninskie Banii. Ulitsa Mytninskaya 17/19 (trolleybus 10). Tel: 271.71.19.
One of the few city banyas still heated with wood.

Yamskie Banii. Ulitsa Dostoevkovo 9 (Metro Vladimirskaya). Tel: 7.812.312.5836.
A favorite among local banya-goers, Yamskie is well maintained and the heat is addictive.

Kruglye Banii. Ulitsa Karbysheva 29A (Metro Ploshchad). Tel: 7.812.550.0985.
Supposedly this banya used to be a favorite among KGB workers, since their headquarters were nearby. There is a very nice deluxe section available for private rentals.

Moscow

Bani Na Presnye. Stolyarny Pereulok 7 (Metro Ulitsa 1905 Goda). Tel: 7.95.255.0115.
This modern banya is for serious heat lovers willing to heed the instructions of an exacting Mistress of Steam who likes her *parilka* hot and steamy.

Sandunovskye Banii. Ulitsa Neglinnaya 14 (Metro Kuznetsky Most). Tel: 7.95.925.4631.
The Sandunovskye has it all – history, great architecture, popularity, and fame. It even had a cameo in the movie *Gorky Park*. This is Moscow's fanciest banya (you'll see black SUVs and snoozing drivers lining the street out front) and its most expensive. If you're going to try one banya in Moscow, it should be the one-hundred-year-old Sandunovskye.

Seleznovskye Bani. Ulitsa Selznovskaya 15 (Metro Seleznovskaya Ulitsa). Tel: 7.95.978.8491.
For the hard-core banya lover, the *parilka* is always extra hot and the cold pool freezing cold.

Krasnopresnensky. Stolyarny pereulok 7 (Metro Ulitsa 1905 Goda). Tel: 7.95.253.8690.
A good representation of a Soviet-style banya, the facilities, which include a gym, pool, and solarium, are still in good shape.

Sweden

Sweden shares a love of the sauna and bathing with Finland, which you'll see reflected in these baths.

Centralbadet. Drottninggatan 88, Norrmalm. Tel: 46.8.242.402. www.centralbadet.se.
This earthy, friendly bath was designed in 1904 and is set back from the street with a pleasant garden. Customers are attracted by the art nouveau interiors, the reasonably priced café, and, of course, the pool, Jacuzzi, multiple saunas, and Swedish massage.

Hasseludden Yasuragi. Hamndalsvägen 6, Saltsjö-Boo. Tel: 46.8.747.6100. www.hasseludden.com.
This is a Japanese spa hotel with a pool, outdoor hot bath, sauna, and restaurant. Beauty treatments are available. It's located in the Stockholm archipelago and serves as a recuperative day trip.

Sturebadet. Sturegallerian, Stureplan, Östermalm. Tel: 46.8.5450.1510. www.sturebadet.se.
This place is a hoity-toity members-only club that also offers day memberships. Opened in 1885, it's where Stockholm's beautiful people work out and steam. The bath offerings include a Turkish bath for twenty and an art nouveau pool.

Switzerland

Switzerland has many famous spa resorts, such as Bad Ragaz and Interlaken, where the infirm come to take the waters, but very few would qualify as public baths. Therme Vals is a stunning exception.

Therme Vals. 7132 Vals/GR. Tel: 41.81.926.8080. www.therme-vals.ch.
If you've ever wondered how Augustus or Claudius felt at the Roman baths, head to Therme Vals in Switzerland's easternmost canton. Therme Vals is more than a bath, it's a protected architectural monument designed by minimalist master Peter Zumthor. Cavernous, labyrinthine chambers carved out of the local silver-gray quartzite contain hot pools, frosty plunges, flower petal pools, echo chamber pools, and an outdoor pool staring into a solid Swiss mountain face.

Syria

Syria, like many Middle Eastern countries, has its own style of hamam that reflects the architecture of the region.

Hamam Yalbougha an-Nasry. Aleppo. Tel: 963.21.362.3154.
Wedged between the busy souk and the touristy citadel, this exquisite ablaq-tiled hamam is surprisingly uncrowded. Communal yet private, with sofas arranged in individual compartments in the resting lounge, the hamam offers a genuine community and wonderful scrubbing treatments.

Turkey

Turkey is home to thousands of hamams. While hamams were once a cherished weekly ritual where people cleansed themselves and socialized, hamams today are more relics of the past, at least in the cities. This is slowly changing as a new generation of Turks rediscovers the appeal of this ancient tradition.

Most hamams use steam and running water because the Koran prohibits soaking in still water for health reasons. In areas with abundant thermal waters, such as Bursa and Bodrum, pools are allowed because the mineral-rich water is constantly replenishing itself.

Bodrum

Bodrum Hamami. Cevat Şakir Cad., Fabrika Sokak (Garaj Karşısı) Bodrum – Muğla. Tel: 90.252.313.4129. www.bodrumhamami.com.tr.
The Bodrum outpost of Istanbul's Çemberlitaş, this hamam boasts Bodrum's thermal waters and separate men's and women's areas.

Bursa

Yeni Kaplica (New Spring), Yeni Kaplica Cad. 6, Çekirge. Tel: 90.0224.236.6968.
Built by Suleyman the Magnificent's Grand Vizier in 1552, the men's

side still possesses its original grandeur while the women's side is smaller and more intimate.

Kervansary Hotel's 700-year hamam. Çekirge Meydani, 16080 Çekirge. Tel: 90.0224.233.9300.
Although this hamam is attached to a modern hotel, it is Bursa's oldest hamam, built in 1389 by Sultan Murat I on top of the original Byzantine baths. The old masonry and soaring domes, especially in the central relaxation room, make this the prime place to bathe in Bursa.

Kara Mustafa Pasa Thermal Bath. Mudanya Cad. 10. Tel: 90.0224.236.6956.
This Byzantine bath includes one section with all the expected hamam facilities, as well as a second section where you can ease yourself into a tub of hot mud.

Çelik Palas Hotel thermal pool. Çekirge Cad. 79, 16070 Çekirge/Bursa. Tel: 90.0224.233.3800.
This hotel hamam is clean and modern and has the amenities you'd expect in a Western hotel. This is a good alternative if you're put off by the grittier local hamams.

Istanbul

Çemberlitaş. Vezirhan Cad. 8, Çemberlitaş-Eminönü. Tel: 90.212.520.1850. www.cemberlitashamami.com.tr.
Owner Rusen Baltaci lovingly maintains his hamam, carrying on the tradition and culture with integrity. Built in 1584, this hamam has both a men's and a women's section and traditional Ottoman architecture. It's easy for tourists because much of the staff speaks English, they accept credit cards, and discounts are available for people with International Student IDs.

Cağaloğlu. Prof. Kazım İsmail Gürkan Cad. 34, Çemberlitaş-Eminönü. Tel: 90.212.522.2424. www.cagalogluhamami.com.tr.
Like Çemberlitaş, this is another historic Sultanahmet hamam. Built in 1741, it was the last big bath to be built in Istanbul displaying all the flourishes of bath architecture. It is not maintained as well as Çemberlitaş, and the women's facilities are not nearly as nice as the men's.

Örücüler Hamam. Kapalıçarşi Örücüler Kapısı Sok. 32, Beyazıt-Eminönü. Tel: 90.212.527.9263.
This men-only bath was built sometime prior to 1489 and can be found

next to the Oruculer or 'Weavers' Gate to the Covered Bazaar. It's popular with tourists because it's clean and well run.

Çinili Hamam. İtfaiye Cad. 46, Zeyrek-Fatih. Tel: 90.212.631.8883.
Çinili means 'tiled' and many hamams bear this name, so take special care in finding the right one, which is located in a traditional, religious section of Istanbul. Built by Mimar Sinan (Turkey's most famous architect) in 1546, it is a prime example of the accomplishments of hamam architecture.

Süleymaniye Hamam. Mimar Sinan Cad. 20, Beyazıt-Eminönü. Tel: 90.212.520.3410. www.suleymaniyehamami.com.
Built in 1557 by Mimar Sinan, this bath is renowned for its grandeur and beauty. Available for men or mixed tourist groups if they call ahead and book, the hamam has many historic relics from Sinan's time.

Ağa Hamam. Turnacıbaşı Sok. 60, Beyoğlu. Tel: 90.212.249.5027.
In the newly chic neighborhood of Cucurcuma, the Ağa Hamam has been in operation since 1562. Open twenty-four hours a day for alternating single-gender sessions, this hamam epitomizes the warm neighborhood vibe of the best hamams. After two visits the *tellaks* will recognize you and give you 'the usual' – a *kese*, soaping, and massage.

United States

Many immigrants, in particular Russians, have set up versions of their native baths in America. This is a sampling of some historic and well-known bathhouses, as well as some therapeutic spas known for their bathhouse vibe.

New York

The Russian Turkish Baths. 268 East Tenth Street, New York, NY 10009. Tel: 212.473.8806.
Known by admirers as East Tenth Street, this old shvitz has been in business since 1896. The basement steam complex, especially the Russian Room (a.k.a. The Oven), certainly exudes soul that people with a fondness for hard-core heat and Lower East Side history will appreciate, but everyone wishes the owners would make a bit more of an effort to keep the place up. New towels please!

Spa 88. 88 Fulton Street, New York, NY 10038. Tel: 212.766.8600. www.spa88.com.
A cleaner alternative to East Tenth Street, Spa 88 is popular with young expat Russians because the upstairs restaurant serves Manhattan's best *pelmeni* and the banya master has a way with the *veynik*. There's also a pool and Jacuzzi on the second floor, but most bathers divide their time between the hot rooms and cold plunge downstairs.

Mermaid Club. 3701 Mermaid Avenue, Brooklyn, NY. Tel: 718.265.5188.
This Brighton Beach banya was recently remodeled. You won't hear much English, and it's a good approximation of the real Russian banyas except that men and women, in bathing suits, are shvitzing together.

Bania. 602 Coney Island Avenue, Brooklyn, NY 11218. Tel: 718.853.2525.
A traditional banya favored by Russians living in Brooklyn.

Juvenex. 25 West Thirty-second Street, 5th Floor. Tel: 646–733–1330. www.juvenexspa.com.
The intricately tiled 5,000-square-foot bath has curved showers, three soaking tubs (hot, cold, and different infusions), a diamond-shaped steam room, and two saunas constructed out of eighteen tons of jade blocks. The effect is beautiful in a jewel-box sort of way, but it's overpriced.

California

Glen Ivy Hot Springs Spa. 25000 Glen Ivy Road, Glen Ivy, CA 92883. Tel: 1.888.CLUB.MUD. www.glenivy.com.
The daily admission includes all aspects of the Club Mud experience – seventeen pools, steam rooms, Roman baths, a covered saltwater spa, the red clay mud bath, towels, etc. A resort since the 1890s and revered by the Native Americans for thousands of years, today Glen Ivy Hot Springs is a rollicking, all-day retreat for bath and spa lovers.

Two Bunch Palms. 67–425 Two Bunch Palms Trail, Desert Hot Springs, CA 92240. Tel: 760.329.8791. www.twobunchpalms.com.
Made famous as the place Tim Robbins went on the lam in *The Player*, Two Bunch Palms has long been a favorite hangout and hideout for Hollywood's big names. The green clay mud treatments and therapeutic crystalline waters make it more than just a legendary lair.

The Kabuki Springs & Spa. 1750 Geary Blvd, San Francisco, CA 94115, in the Kinokuniya Building directly behind the AMC Kabuki Theater. Tel: 405.922.6000. www.kabukisprings.com.
The Kabuki Springs & Spa offers traditional Japanese bathing facilities as

well as a variety of spa services. The communal baths, with a full-time attendant, have a hot pool, cold plunge, dry sauna, and steam room. There are also a variety of complimentary bath products, sea salts, chilled cucumber face cloths, and teas.

Osento. 955 Valencia Street (between 20th and 21st Streets), San Francisco, CA 94110. Tel. 415.282.6333. www.osento.com.
This women-only bath was opened by two friends who were inspired by bathing traditions in Japan, Finland, and other bath-friendly countries. The facilities include three showers (outdoor, Japanese stool style, and Western style), a hot tub, a cold tub, a dry sauna, a wet sauna, and a deck for sunning, socializing, and reading. Massage is also available.

City Spa (formerly Pico-Burnside Baths). 5325 West Pico Boulevard (between Fairfax and La Brea Ave.), Los Angeles, CA. Tel: 323.938.4800 or 877.CITYSPA.
This Russian bathhouse opened in 1954, which means it's 'old school' by L.A. standards. Regulars love that the bath has lots of opportunities for cooling off, including a cold plunge and a cold swimming pool.

Beverly Hot Springs. 308 N. Oxford Avenue, Los Angeles, CA 90004. Tel: 323.734.7000. www.beverlyhotsprings.com.
A low-key place where bathers can congregate in a paparazzi-free environment to soak in the alkaline waters that gurgle forth from 2,000 feet beneath the bathhouse. The facilities, which include hot and cold pools and steam and dry herbal saunas, are spotless. After a long soak there's a spa area for a variety of Eastern treatments including acupressure, shiatsu, and various body wraps.

Florida

The Russian and Turkish Baths. Castillo Del Mar at The Castle, 5445 Collins Avenue, Miami Beach, FL 33140. Tel: 305.867.8316.
www.florida.com/russianandturkishbath.
The slightly more spic-and-span cousin of the New York original is essential bathing for the shvitzing aficionado. Regulars rave about the intensity of the heat and the hard-core platza.

Nirvana Spa. 8701 Collins Avenue (in the Dezerland Hotel), Miami Beach, FL 33154. Tel: 305.867.4850. www.nirvanaspamiamibeach.com.
This Russian bathhouse has four different steam rooms, including an all-cedar Russian steam room, a Turkish-style steam room, plus an aromatherapy steam room and Finnish sauna.

The Hotel Victor Spa. 1126–1144 Ocean Drive, Miami Beach, FL 33139. Paris-based decorator Jacques Garcia unveils his first American hotel, which includes a Turkish hamam as the spa concept. The bath-friendly spa, which along with the hotel opens in May 2004, has an ornate mixed-gender steam room with curved ceilings and intricate pillars as its focal point. Turkish-style massages take place on marble slabs and cold showers and chilled towels keep patrons cool.

The Standard Spa. 40 Island Avenue, Miami Beach, FL 33139. Tel: 305.673.1717. www.standardhotel.com.
Health meets hedonism at the Standard Spa, where innovative hotelier Andre Balazs has applied his quirky, stylish take to the bath and spa experience. The whimsical baths on Biscayne Bay are full of surprises, as are the similarly inventive spa treatments.

Colorado

Izba Spa. 1441 York Street, Denver, Colorado 80206. Tel: 303.321.1239. 17908 B Cottonwood Drive, Parker, Colorado 80134. Tel: 303.400.1001. www.izbaspa.com.
Both Izba Spa locations serve up the intense heat of a Russian banya as well as accompanying spa services and food. Although the owners pair the bath component with spa treatments, in many ways the experience is faithful to a true Russian banya.

The Lake Street Baths. 3540 W. Colfax Avenue, Denver, CO 80204. Tel: 303.825.2995. www.lakesteambaths.com.
Opened in 1927 by the Hyman family, the Lake Street Baths have been family operated ever since. With alternating single-gender days, this bathhouse has the friendly atmosphere and easy camaraderie of the best bathhouses. It offers a dry steam room, hot rock sauna (with ice water buckets), and Jacuzzi.

Illinois

Division Street Russian Bath. 1916 West Division Street (between Damen and Ashland Ave.), Chicago. Tel: 773.384.9643 (men's side), 773.394.0500 (women's side).
Opened in 1906 and immortalized in Saul Bellow's *Humboldt's Gift*. Famous for its icy cold plunge and Augie the platza-master.

New Mexico

Ten Thousand Waves. 3451 Hyde Park Road, Santa Fe, NM 87501. Tel: 505.992.5025. www.tenthousandwaves.com.

A sign on the property reads 'TOKYO 10,070 KM.' Think Japanese hot spring resort meets Southwestern adobe and you've got Ten Thousand Waves, 'the closest thing to an onsen outside of Japan.' With a choice of communal tubs and private tubs on the serene grounds, as well a variety of Eastern massage techniques, Santa Fe locals and further-flung furoholics flock here. Limited lodging is available.

acknowledgments

This book would not have happened without the inspiration and encouragement of Karina Duebner. I thank her for teaching me how to dream, and I can't imagine a better friend or partner in crime. Books always take longer to come together than anyone would imagine, and my family was there with kind words, great advice, and delicious meals every step of the way. To Nord, Suzanne, Erik, and Marget, my deepest thanks.

Friends to whom I owe a huge debt of gratitude for their encouraging words and insightful comments include Jennifer Humphries, Liz Weiner, Natalia Williams, Bird Goldstein, Julia Cumes, Brett Fadem, Paola Fantini, Nicole LaPorte, Ayesha Pande, Tom Cheung, Brian Donovan, Zeynep Guven, Josh Levine, Joseph Bowman, and bath studies goddess Judy Mabro.

I am enormously grateful to both my agent and publisher for believing in this book. Sterling Lord, my agent, helped me to shape the book and always had the perfect inspiring story for any quandary. The entire team at Bloomsbury made every step of the publishing process a joy. Special thanks to Karen Rinaldi, whom I admire for so many reasons. From proposal to finished book, she was a brilliant, insightful, funny, and unfailingly energetic editor. And to Panagiotis Gianopoulos, whose Herculean patience and instructive editing were an enormous gift for this first book. Thanks also to Alan Wherry, Greg Villepique, Lara Carrigan, Andrea Lynch, Alona Fryman, Sandee Yuen, Sara Mercurio, and, in England, fellow bathophile Rosemary Davidson. And thanks to Lynda McIntyre for her lyrical drawings that enhanced the pages of this book.

Finally, thank you to all the anonymous people who opened their homes and hearts to me while I was traveling. I hope to repay the favor.

a note on the author

Alexia Brue has written for *The New York Times Magazine*, *Vogue*, and *Spa Finder*. She has a B.A. in Classics from Grinnell College. She lives in New York City. This is her first book.

a note on the type

The text of this book is set in Bembo. This type was first used in 1495 by the Venetian printer Aldus Manutius for Cardinal Bembo's *De Aetna,* and was cut for Manutius by Francesco Griffo. It was one of the types used by Claude Garamond (1480–1561) as a model for his Romain de L'Université, and so it was the forerunner of what became standard European type for the following two centuries. Its modern form follows the original types and was designed for Monotype in 1929.